ALTERNATE ASSESSMENT

ALTERNATE ASSESSMENT
MEASURING OUTCOMES AND SUPPORTS FOR STUDENTS WITH DISABILITIES

by

Harold L. Kleinert, Ed.D.

and

Jacqui Farmer Kearns, Ed.D.

Interdisciplinary Human Development Institute
University of Kentucky

with invited contributors

·P A U L·H·
BROOKES
PUBLISHING Co

Baltimore • London • Toronto • Sydney

Paul H. Brookes Publishing Co.
Post Office Box 10624
Baltimore, Maryland 21285-0624

www.brookespublishing.com

Copyright © 2001 by Paul H. Brookes Publishing Co., Inc.
All rights reserved.

Typeset by PRO-IMAGE Corporation, York, Pennsylvania.
Manufactured in the United States of America by
Sheridan Books, Fredericksburg, Virginia.

The alternate assessment methods described in this book are not
necessarily correct under the mandates of specific states.

Cover photograph of Ryan Bracke is courtesy of the Bracke family.

The cases described in this book, with the exception of Ryan
Bracke and Martha and Christie, who appear in Chapter 8, and
LeAnn and James and his mother Terri, who appear in Chapter 9,
are composites based on the authors' actual experiences. Individuals' names have been changed, and identifying details have been
altered to protect their confidentiality.

Library of Congress Cataloging-in-Publication Data
Kleinert, Harold L.
    Alternate assessment: measuring outcomes and supports for
students with disabilities/by Harold L. Kleinert and Jacqui
Farmer Kearns.
    p.   cm.
    Includes bibliographical references and index.
    ISBN 1-55766-496-X
    1. Handicapped children—Rating of.   2. Educational tests and
measurements.   I. Kearns, Jacqui Farmer.   II. Title.
LC4019 .K543 2001
371.9'043—dc21
                                      00-069657
                                           CIP

British Library Cataloguing in Publication data are available from
the British Library.

CONTENTS

About the Authors viii
Contributors ix
Foreword   *Kenneth R. Warlick* xi
Acknowledgments xiii
Introduction xvii

Chapter 1: An Introduction to Alternate Assessment
Harold L. Kleinert and Martha L. Thurlow 1

The Historical Context for Inclusive, Large-Scale Assessments 2
The New Requirements of IDEA '97 in Curriculum and Assessment 3
The Relationship Between Curriculum and Assessment 5
Making the Process Work 6
The Parameters of Alternate Assessments: The Who, What,
    Why, and How 8
What Do We Believe? Principles of Alternate Assessments 12

**Chapter 2: Creating Standards-Based
Individualized Education Programs**
Jennifer Grisham-Brown and Jacqui Farmer Kearns 17

The Relationship Between Standards and the
    Individualized Education Program 18
Developing the IEP 18
Putting It All Together 24
Summary 28

**Chapter 3: Helping Students with Significant Disabilities
Gain Access to General Curriculum Standards**
Jacqui Farmer Kearns 29

So, What Is a Standard, Anyway? 30
Applying Curriculum Standards in Everyday Life 33
Using Standards to Guide Curriculum 36
Keeping the End in Mind: Culminating Performances 43
Merging Instruction and Assessment 46
Summary 47

**Chapter 4: Integrating Alternate Assessment
in the General Curriculum**
*Mike Burdge, Vanessa Burke Groneck, Harold L. Kleinert, Amy Wildman
Longwill, Jean Clayton, Anne Denham, and Jacqui Farmer Kearns* 49

Relating Student Objectives to General Education Units and
    Standards-Based Assessments 50
Summary 74

Chapter 5: Integrating Alternate Assessment with Ongoing Instruction
Jean Clayton, Mike Burdge, and Harold L. Kleinert 77

Six Steps to Embedding Alternate Assessment into Daily Instruction
from Day One: A Teacher's Experience 78
Developing Adaptations to Include Students with Significant
Disabilities in General Education 83
Embedding Alternate Assessment Activities into the Context of
Daily Instruction 87
Summary 87

Chapter 6: Systematically Teaching the Components of Self-Determination
Harold L. Kleinert, Anne Denham, Vanessa Burke Groneck, Jean Clayton,
Mike Burdge, Jacqui Farmer Kearns, and Meada Hall 93

Self-Determination: An Important Outcome for Students with
Significant Disabilities 93
Planning, Monitoring, and Self-Evaluation as Part of
Performance-Based Assessment 95
Making Choices During Normal Routines: Another Key to
Self-Determination 107
Documenting Student Choice Making: An Integral Aspect of
Performance Assessment 114
Teaching Students to Manage Their Own Daily Schedules 115
Summary 133

Chapter 7: Implementing Technology to Demonstrate Higher Levels of Learning
Anne Denham, Deborah E. Bennett, Dave L. Edyburn, Elizabeth A. Lahm,
and Harold L. Kleinert 135

How Assistive Technology Can Help Students with Significant
Cognitive Disabilities Plan, Monitor, and Evaluate Their
Own Performance 136
Electronic Portfolios: Tools to Organize and Evaluate Student
Performance 148
A Statewide Electronic Portfolio Assessment: The Indiana
Assessment System of Educational Proficiencies 154
Summary 164

Chapter 8: The Role of Social Relationships in Alternate Assessment
Harold L. Kleinert, Anne Denham, Colleen Bracke, Anthony Bracke,
Mary Reeves Calie, Mike Burdge, and Vanessa Burke Groneck 167

Friendships as an Educational Outcome 169
The Art of Making Friends: A Matter of Opportunity 170
A Week in the Life of Alternate Assessment 174
"All of This Sounds Wonderful, But My School System Is a
Long Way from What You Describe" 176
More Tips from the Field 180

Chapter 9: Demonstrating Performance Across Multiple Environments

Harold L. Kleinert, Mark D. Hurte, Vanessa Burke Groneck, Janet M. Fay, Michele Roszmann-Millican, Meada Hall, Jean Clayton, and Janet M. Lester

. 185

The Value of Inclusive Environments 186
Practicing Individualized Student Objectives Through Community
    Activities 186
Person-Centered Planning: Incorporating Activities Most Important
    to the Student 194
Opportunities for Self-Advocacy and Lifelong Learning in
    Postsecondary Educational Programs 198
Working with Families to Demonstrate a Student's Performance at
    School and at Home 207
Summary 210

Chapter 10: Research on the Impact of Alternate Assessment

Harold L. Kleinert, Jacqui Farmer Kearns, Kimberly Ann Costello, Karen Nowak-Drabik, Michelle Marilyn Garrett, Leah S. Horvath, Stephanie H. Kampfer, and Matthew D. Turner

. . . . 213

Findings from Research 213
Implications for Teachers 219
Summary 225

Appendix: Photocopiable Forms 229

Index 245

ABOUT THE AUTHORS

Harold L. Kleinert, Ed.D., is Executive Director of the Interdisciplinary Human Development Institute, University of Kentucky, and Associate Adjunct Professor in the Department of Special Education and Rehabilitation Counseling at the University of Kentucky in Lexington. Previously, Dr. Kleinert served as Director of Training for the Interdisciplinary Human Development Institute. A veteran educator, Dr. Kleinert taught special education at the classroom level for 14 years before directing a wide range of federal and state projects, including the Kentucky Alternate Portfolio Study, aimed at improving services for students with significant disabilities.

Jacqui Farmer Kearns, Ed.D., is Associate Director of the Inclusive Large-Scale Standards and Assessment Group (ILSSA) at the Interdisciplinary Human Development Institute (IHDI) at the University of Kentucky in Lexington. Among her many accomplishments at the IHDI, Dr. Kearns has served as the principal investigator on two groundbreaking initiatives for students with disabilities: the Kentucky Statewide Alternate Portfolio Project and the Including Students with Deaf Blindness in Large-Scale Educational Assessments Project. Dr. Kearns previously directed the Kentucky Statewide Systems Change Project for Students with Severe Disabilities and has extensive experience as a classroom teacher for students with moderate and severe disabilities.

CONTRIBUTORS

Deborah E. Bennett, Ph.D.
Assistant Professor of Educational
  Psychology
5122 LAEB
Purdue University
West Lafayette, Indiana 47907

Anthony Bracke, J.D.
15024 Decoursey Pike
Morning View, Kentucky 41063

Colleen Bracke
15024 Decoursey Pike
Morning View, Kentucky 41063

Mike Burdge, M.A.
Kentucky State Coordinator
  of Alternate Assessment
Interdisciplinary Human
  Development Institute
University of Kentucky
320 Mineral Industries Building
Lexington, Kentucky 40506

Mary Reeves Calie, M.S.
130 Redbud Drive
Berea, Kentucky 40403

Jean Clayton, M.A.
Teacher
Kenton County Schools
668 Bracht-Piner Road
Crittenden, Kentucky 41030

Kimberly Ann Costello, M.S.
School Psychologist Intern
Certified Special Education Teacher
University of Kentucky
Jefferson Parish Public Schools
6564 Fleur de Lis Road
Apartment #2
New Orleans, Louisiana 70124

Anne Denham, Ed.S.
Teacher
Earl D. Jones Elementary School
1112 Forest Avenue
Maysville, Kentucky 41056

Dave L. Edyburn, Ph.D.
Professor
Department of Exceptional
  Education
University of Wisconsin–Milwaukee
Post Office Box 413
Milwaukee, Wisconsin 53201

Janet M. Fay, M.Ed.
Special Education Teacher
White's Tower Elementary School
2977 Harris Pike
Independence, Kentucky 41051

Michelle Marilyn Garrett, M.S.
Attorney and School Psychologist
Interdisciplinary Human
  Development Institute
University of Kentucky
1500 Springfield Drive
Lexington, Kentucky 40515

**Jennifer Grisham-Brown,
  Ed.D.**
Assistant Professor
Department of Family Studies
University of Kentucky
315 Funkhouser Building
Lexington, Kentucky 40506

**Vanessa Burke Groneck,
  M.Ed.**
Special Education Teacher
Bellevue Independent Schools
201 Center Street
Bellevue, Kentucky 41073

Meada Hall, M.S.
Project Director
Training Rural Educators in
    Kentucky Through Collaborative
    Relationships (TREK-CR)
Department of Special Education and
    Rehabilitation Counseling
University of Kentucky
229 Taylor Education Building
Lexington, Kentucky 40506

Leah S. Horvath, M.S.
Research Assistant
Graduate Student
Interdisciplinary Human
    Development Institute
University of Kentucky
126 Mineral Industries Building
Lexington, Kentucky 40506

Mark D. Hurte, B.A.
Teacher of Exceptional Children
Lincoln County Middle School
285 Education Way
Stanford, Kentucky 40484

Stephanie H. Kampfer, M.S.
Research Assistant
Graduate Student
Interdisciplinary Human
    Development Institute
University of Kentucky
126 Mineral Industries Building
Lexington, Kentucky 40506

Elizabeth A. Lahm, Ph.D.
Assistant Professor
Department of Special Education and
    Rehabilitation Counseling
University of Kentucky
229 Taylor Education Building
Lexington, Kentucky 40506

Janet M. Lester, M.A.
Teacher
Campbell County High School
25 West Lickert Road
Alexandria, Kentucky 41001

Amy Wildman Longwill, B.A.
Special Education Teacher
Teacher Community Leader
East Jessamine High School
815 Sulphur Well Road
Nicholasville, Kentucky 40356

Karen Nowak-Drabik, M.S.
Research Assistant
Doctoral Student
Educational and Counseling
    Psychology
University of Kentucky
245 Dickey Hall
Lexington, Kentucky 40506

**Michele Roszmann-Millican,
    Ed.D.**
Assistant Professor
Special Education and
    Early Childhood Special Education
School of Education
Northern Kentucky University
Nunn Drive
Highland Heights, Kentucky 41099

Martha L. Thurlow, Ph.D.
Director, Senior Research Associate
National Center on Educational
    Outcomes
University of Minnesota
350 Elliott Hall
75 East River Road
Minneapolis, Minnesota 55455

Matthew D. Turner, M.S.
Doctoral Student
Educational and Counseling
    Psychology
University of Kentucky
1559 Chase Arbor Common
Virginia Beach, Virginia 23462

FOREWORD

With the passage of the Individuals with Disabilities Education Act (IDEA) Amendments of 1997 (PL 105-17), the practice of including students with disabilities in state- and districtwide assessments has irrevocably changed the dialogue surrounding assessments across the United States of America and has even begun to enter the international education assessment picture.

The simple fact that states are reexamining their overall assessment systems is a positive trend. People increasingly are aware of the implications for universal design to ensure access not only to instruction but also to assessments. In particular, the development of guidelines and designs for alternate assessments has turned educators' and state lawmakers' attention to the inadequacies of the accommodations and modifications available in many large-scale assessment systems. Inclusive assessments also have prompted states to re-examine their learning standards through a different lens. They now look beyond whether the standards are *challenging* to require that they be both *reasonable* and *accessible* to all students.

Including students with disabilities in assessment and accountability systems is important to everyone involved in schools. For students with disabilities, advantages include higher expectations for their performance, access to the same rich curriculum as their peers without disabilities, and enhanced educational opportunities. Educators and families benefit as well, as these more inclusive assessments provide valuable information to help educators and the public evaluate how students are progressing in school and how programs and services are serving all students. This initiative to include all students in assessment does not view participation for the sake of participation. Instead, participation in assessments goes hand in hand with access to the general curriculum and should result in improved teaching and learning.

Everyone who has followed the evolution of inclusive assessments in the United States of America is aware of the federal requirement that states were to begin implementing alternate assessments by July 1, 2000. The larger issue remains that many question how to effectively and efficiently implement alternate assessments. Therefore, it is with great enthusiasm that I endorse this publication by Harold L. Kleinert and Jacqui Farmer Kearns. These individuals are the trailblazers and pioneers of alternate assessment, particularly the alternate portfolio assessment prototype developed in Kentucky and later adopted with modifications in several states. This book is an excellent resource not only for those directly involved with alternate assessment issues but also for those concerned more broadly with high-quality delivery of instruction for students with disabilities. It is important for educators to understand the links among standards, curriculum, assessment, instruction (including accommodations, environments, and supports), and targeted individualized education program (IEP) goals. These issues cannot be approached separately. This book is a virtual "how to" guide for making such linkages.

Of particular interest to classroom teachers are sections on writing standards-based IEPs, integrating alternate assessment with ongoing instruction, and using technology as a tool in authentic assessment. Most important, the authors have demonstrated that a key to reducing teacher burden in portfolio management is teaching students self-determination through the process of alternate assessments. The skills reinforced through this approach, particularly when applied across multiple environments, are essential to helping students develop into independent adults.

This work should prove enlightening to policy makers, instructional supervisors, classroom teachers, and all members of IEP teams. As educators apply the principles and the recommendations contained in this book, these strategies and concepts should promote higher expectations for students with disabilities; enhance access to the general curriculum; and lead to improved benefits and results for students, educators, parents, employers, and all those who care about educational excellence.

Kenneth R. Warlick, Ph.D.
Former Director of the
Office of Special Education Programs (1999–2001)
U.S. Department of Education

ACKNOWLEDGMENTS

As with any large undertaking, there are many people who have provided invaluable assistance in the writing of this book. We would like first to thank the policy makers, teacher trainers, researchers, classroom teachers, family members of students with significant disabilities, and of course, the students themselves who contributed so much to this book. These individuals have provided their own perspectives on what is both a very exciting opportunity and a fundamental challenge in our field—the meaningful inclusion of all students in state and district educational assessments.

Specifically, we are indebted to Foreword author Dr. Kenneth R. Warlick, former Director of the U.S. Office of Special Education Programs, and all of our outstanding contributors: Dr. Martha L. Thurlow, Director of the National Center on Educational Outcomes, University of Minnesota, and the co-editor of *Exceptional Children*; Dr. Dave L. Edyburn, Professor, University of Wisconsin–Milwaukee, and the editor of *Teaching Exceptional Children*; Dr. Deborah E. Bennett, Assistant Professor of Educational Psychology, Purdue University; Dr. Elizabeth A. Lahm, Assistant Professor, Department of Special Education and Rehabilitation Counseling, University of Kentucky; Dr. Jennifer Grisham-Brown, Assistant Professor, Department of Family Studies, University of Kentucky; and Dr. Michele Roszmann-Millican, Assistant Professor of Special Education and Early Childhood Special Education, Northern Kentucky University.

Classroom teachers Anne Denham, Jean Clayton, and Vanessa Burke Groneck, whose ideas and examples permeate this book, contributed greatly to the book's hands-on approach. Their strategies for how to include alternate assessment as a part of ongoing, daily instruction; apply assistive technology to enhance student performance; and provide students with significant disabilities full access to the richness of the general curriculum, give this book its connection to the real world. We also owe a tremendous debt to Mike Burdge, who, before assuming the position of Kentucky State Coordinator of Alternate Assessment, taught students with significant disabilities for 25 years and was recognized as Kentucky Special Education Teacher of the Year in 1996 by the state Department of Education. This book would not have been possible without the insights of other classroom teachers as well, including Mark D. Hurte, Amy Wildman Longwill, Janet M. Fay, and Janet M. Lester. The work of former teacher Meada Hall, Project Director of the Training Rural Educators in Kentucky through Collaborative Relationships (TREK-CR) at the University of Kentucky and the recipient of the 2000 Alice H. Hayden Award by TASH, is illustrated through her classroom examples as well.

The voices of parents and family members also are included throughout this text. We would especially like to thank Colleen and Anthony Bracke for their introductory vignette to Chapter 8 and for allowing their son Ryan to appear on our cover. Our thanks also goes to Ryan for giving us *his* permission. We would like to thank Mary Reeves Calie for her wonderful story of her daughter Martha's sixth-grade science fair project, which provided us a wealth of ideas, and to parent Missy Phillips for her quote about the essence of parenthood. We would like to acknowledge the contributions of her daughter Christie, who passed away at the age of 13 but whose short life touched the lives of many. The importance of friendships in the lives of all children is vividly portrayed in a brief glimpse of Christie's friendships, as described in Chapter 8. We would like to thank Terri Turner for allowing us to include her son's story in Chapter 9 as a wonderful way to portray the partnership of school and home in promoting important outcomes for students with significant disabilities. We also acknowledge the contributions of LeAnn Raleigh, who allowed us to publish the journal excerpts chronicling her experiences as a student at Northern Kentucky University.

To our research assistants who provided much of the people power in conducting our research on the impact and instructional consequences of alternate assessment, we owe an equal debt of gratitude. Matthew D. Turner, Leigh Sanders Baldwin, Kimberly Ann Costello, Michelle Marilyn Garrett, Karen Nowak-Drabik, Leah S. Horvath, Stephanie H. Kampfer, Elizabeth Towles, and Christina Waddle all contributed, especially to the findings we report in the last chapter. We would also like to thank Mr. Brent Garrett, project coordinator for our two ongoing federally funded research projects on alternate assessment, for providing us with the most up-to-date data analyses of some very important questions.

This book would not have been possible without the generous support of the U.S. Office of Special Education Programs for funding two projects that generated the research reported in this text, as well as the ongoing support of our project officer, Dave Malouf. These projects, the Kentucky Alternate Portfolio Study (Grant No. H023F7004) and the Including Students with Deaf Blindness in Large-Scale Educational Assessments Project (Grant No. H324D990044), also served as the vehicles that enabled us to explore the relationship between assessment and instruction. Of course, the opinions we express in *Alternate Assessment* do not necessarily reflect the position or policy of the U.S. Department of Education, and no official endorsements should be inferred.

This book was made significantly better by the contributions of the two editors with whom we worked most closely at Paul H. Brookes Publishing Co. We thank Acquisitions Editor Lisa Benson, who initially urged the idea of alternate assessment as an important topic for a new book and who encouraged and guided us through the prospectus, development, and writing phases. Book Production Editor Leslie Eckard contributed greatly to the readability and format of the final text. Without their invaluable assistance, there would not have been a book!

Finally, we would like to thank our families for allowing us the time to write this book. ("Are you working on that book AGAIN?") Their support and love made all the difference!

To my wife Jane and my children,
Matt, Coady, and Lauren
—HLK

To my husband Kerry and my parents,
Mike and Ann Farmer
—JFK

INTRODUCTION

This book is intended as a useful guide for practitioners. Although Chapter 1 does discuss the broad historical development of alternate assessments and the "essential questions" that are guiding the development of alternate assessments, policy applications and research results are not the major focus of this text. Rather, we have tried to consider what alternate assessment means from the perspective of teachers and for the students and families with whom they work. We are aware that alternate assessments under the Individuals with Disabilities Education Act (IDEA) Amendments of 1997 (PL 105-17) cannot be confined to specific categories of students; we also know that the large majority of children currently identified as needing alternate assessments are students with significant disabilities, especially those with significant cognitive disabilities. It is largely with the educational needs of these students in mind that we have written this book.

This focus on alternate assessment from a teaching perspective is emphasized throughout the text. Thus, Chapter 2 describes a process for designing individualized education programs linked to state learning standards for all students; these same standards must also form the basis for each state's alternate assessment (U.S. Office of Special Education Programs, 2000). Chapter 3 extends that discussion to describe how state standards can be used to guide the curriculum process and, in turn, how that process can result in rich and inclusive instructional activities. Specific examples of how those activities are "built from the ground up" are provided to illustrate learning opportunities for students with significant disabilities.

Chapter 4 provides a series of examples across elementary, middle, and high school levels of how students with significant disabilities can participate in rich instructional activities that address individualized objectives and, at the same time, provide student performance data essential to alternate assessments. Strategies for integrating alternate assessment into both individual student planning and ongoing instruction from the start of the school year are explored in Chapter 5.

Chapter 6 provides a conceptual framework for how the process of alternate assessment can be used to teach students the component skills of self-determination. These component skills include learning to plan, monitor, and evaluate one's own work; to make choices that have a positive impact on learning; and to use individualized schedules to learn self-management skills. Educators may use the tangible products from all of these component skills, such as schedules and planning, monitoring, and self-evaluation forms, as evidence in the alternate assessment as well. This chapter ends with a process developed by a teacher for blending all of this into a coherent program for each student.

Chapter 7 illustrates the power of technology in both enhancing student learning and building the capacity of alternate assessments to fully capture that learning. A teacher and a university professor draw from their own experience to show how assistive technology can provide the basis for students with significant disabilities to attain literacy skills and how that learning is documented in the alternate assessment. The chapter also examines the potential of electronic portfolios to document and organize a broad range of student performances. Chapter 7 closes with a description of the *Indiana Assessment System of Educational Proficiencies*, a statewide alternate assessment that is fully electronic and computer-based.

The voices of teachers and families are featured throughout Chapters 8 and 9. Chapter 8 presents the concept that social relationships and friendships are instrumental educational outcomes whose importance should not be divorced from alternate educational assessments. For teachers who may still be "stuck" in more segregated programs, strategies are provided to help them to expand friendship opportunities for their students and to move toward more inclusive practices. Chapter 9 centers on the documentation of student performance across valued environments—including general classes, school projects, community education opportunities, and opportunities at home. All of these can provide important evidence for alternate assessments.

Chapter 10, which we have written in collaboration with our research assistants, presents our research findings in the context of important questions for practitioners. In this final chapter we discuss our research on a core set of criteria that should be used to score or evaluate alternate assessments, teachers' perceptions of how they are including alternate assessments into their daily routines, and what we know thus far of the impact of alternate assessments.

There are, however, important topics on alternate assessment that we have *not* addressed. These topical areas are mainly policy-based and include 1) how alternate assessments will be used (e.g., whether they will be tied to high stakes for schools and/or high stakes for kids), 2) whether it is "psychometrically appropriate" to combine alternate assessment and regular assessment scores into a single measure of school effectiveness, and 3) how to address the assessment needs of students in the so-called "gray area," who may not appear to fit into either the alternate or regular assessment but who may need something "in between." Although we recognize the importance of these questions, we have not considered them in the context of this text because these issues are very much a "moving target," that is, policy issues are ongoing and emergent, and the answers to each of these questions will prove, we believe, very state-specific.

As this book went to press, two policy issues related to alternate assessment were emerging on the national level:

- *Can alternate assessments be used in high-stakes environments for students?* More and more, schools are relying on assessment to demonstrate that students have met high standards and have acquired the knowledge they will need to succeed today. In fact, a number of states are linking such high-stakes goals as graduation and the attainment of a general high school diploma to exit exams of student performance on statewide assessments. In those states in which this is the case, it would seem reasonable that alternate assessment scores could be indexed to serve a similar function so that students taking the alternate assessment would have a similar opportunity to demonstrate mastery or to earn a diploma. We certainly are not recommending that states set high-stakes accountability environments for students, however, either in the general or alternate assessments!

- *Are alternate assessments appropriate for students with less significant disabilities who are achieving at typical rates academically but whose performance cannot be evaluated fairly on the general assessment, even with appropriate accommodations and modifications?* In Oregon, a blue-ribbon panel was appointed to examine this question. In the report *Do No Harm* (Disability Rights Advocates, 2001), the panel made recommendations about including students with learning disabilities in Oregon's high-stakes-for-students testing program, which sets minimum scores for a Certificate of Initial Mastery and for a general diploma. The panel's recommendations included the development of a *separate* alternate assessment, different from and in addition to the alternate assessment that Oregon had developed and piloted primarily for students with moderate and severe cognitive disabilities, so that students with learning disabilities could still demonstrate a level of academic achievement commensurate with the state's Certificate of Initial Mastery. Our position, which is similar to the participation guidelines of a number of states in this respect, is that students with learning disabilities usually are most appropriately assessed through accommodations in assessment rather than through an alternate assessment. This question depends greatly, however, on the range of assessment accommodations and modifications permitted or approved within a state, as well as the nature of the state or district assessment itself.

Although we recognize the importance of these issues, as well as the ongoing evolution of policy and practice in this area, these questions lie outside the scope of this text. Like the rest of our field, we will watch these developments with great interest.

For the most recent *national* policy statements by the U.S. Department of Education, we refer the reader to the U.S. Office of Special Education web site, http://www.ed.gov/offices/OSERS/OSEP/, and to its guidance documents on alternate assessment. The National Center on Educational Outcomes web site, http://www.coled.umn.edu/nceo/, also is an excellent resource in this area.

REFERENCES

Disability Rights Advocates. (2001). *Do no harm*. Oakland, CA: Author. (Available on-line at http://www.dralegal.org).

U.S. Office of Special Education Programs. (2000). *OSEP memorandum to state directors of special education (OSEP 00-24)*. Washington, DC: Author.

chapter 1

*Why include all
students in assessment?*

AN INTRODUCTION TO
ALTERNATE ASSESSMENT

Harold L. Kleinert and Martha L. Thurlow

This chapter, divided into five parts, discusses the historical context for the move to include all students in large-scale educational assessments and introduces the major themes of the book. These themes include

1. A brief review of recent educational reform in this country, including *standards-based* reform and the historical context for the new requirements of the Individuals with Disabilities Education Act (IDEA) Amendments of 1997 (PL 105-17) for the inclusion of all students with disabilities in large-scale educational assessments

2. A discussion of the IDEA '97 requirements for the participation of students with disabilities in large-scale assessments, including the use of alternate assessments and the parallel requirements for the inclusion of all students in the general curriculum

3. The relationship (or link) between the general curriculum requirements for all students and alternate assessments for students with significant disabilities, as well as broad conceptual strategies for including students with significant disabilities in the general curriculum

4. The parameters of alternate assessments under IDEA '97: The "who," "what," "why," and "how" of alternate assessment

5. The principles of alternate assessment on which we have based our own work and research

THE HISTORICAL CONTEXT FOR
INCLUSIVE, LARGE-SCALE ASSESSMENTS

Tremendous changes occurred in education in the United States during the 1980s and 1990s. Wave upon wave of reform movements have topped news media and various political agendas. Much of the push for reform started in the early 1980s, when the National Commission on Education's (1983) report, *A Nation at Risk: The Imperative for Educational Reform*, spoke of the alarmingly poor performance of students in the United States, and of the threat to our national security created by a nation where education was not meeting the needs of an internationally competitive society. This cry for renewed attention to the education of children in the United States has been repeated several times since *A Nation at Risk* hit the newsstands.

Three Waves of Education Reform

When referring to the umbrella of education reform begun in the 1980s, generally, three waves are identified. The first, initiated by the National Commission on Education, focused on higher educational standards for students, which were to be achieved by more courses, more homework, longer school days, longer school years, and more responsibility at the state and local levels. A second wave of reform, usually recognized as occurring about the time of the publication of the National Governors' Association (1986) report, *Time for Results*, called for greater federal and state support for a wide range of education initiatives (e.g., early childhood education, educational technology, parent involvement), with the caveat that this support would be given in return for concrete evidence that students' educational results (e.g., performance, graduation rates) were improving as a result of the support. Near the end of the 1980s, a third wave was already bursting forth, calling for common goals, the need to address students at risk, and public documentation of how students were performing and the progress they were making (Carnegie Council on Adolescent Development, 1989; Smith, 1988; William T. Grant Foundation, 1988).

In 1989, a watershed education reform effort occurred that was intended to promote a steady course of educational progress to usher in the new century. From an initiative led by President George H.W. Bush, governors from all of the states met in Charlottesville, Virginia, to work on a set of national education goals, which eventually resulted in the Goals 2000: Educate America Act of 1994 (PL 103-227). When Arkansas governor Bill Clinton, who was the designated leader of the education summit, later became president, he was able to push forward a reform effort that continues today, albeit in somewhat modified form. One of the key ideas behind Goals 2000 was the notion of national education standards. High, rigorous standards for all students, and ways to measure progress toward meeting those standards, are keystones of the third wave of reform that has carried through into the 21st century.

National content standards were defined in the early 1990s to clarify what students needed to know and be able to do. States soon were identifying learning standards for students in their educational systems. At the same time, states and districts realized the importance of finding their own ways to measure student knowledge and skills so that student progress could be publicly reported. These converging forces soon ran up against a systemic problem—the failure to include all students in these assessments. Early in the 1990s, it became evident that large-scale assessment programs were excluding students with disabilities, often to the detriment of those students (McGrew, Thurlow, & Spiegel, 1993). Unintended consequences for the system as a whole resulted from these exclusionary practices, including increased rates of referral to special education and increased retention in grade of non–special education students (Allington & McGill-Franzen, 1992), and incomparability of performance results from one place to the next (Zlatos, 1994). Consequently, the importance of including all students in assessment and accountability systems became evident.

The Focus Shifts to Including All Students

A major outcome of this revelation, then, was an end to the widespread exclusion of students with disabilities from large-scale assessments. First, educators and lawmakers focused on having students participate in the general curriculum, including students with milder intellectual, learning, and physical disabilities. Adding these students into the assessment picture, however, did not yet account for *all* students served in education. Slowly, there was a realization that higher standards could benefit all students. All that was needed was a clear delineation of appropriate educational standards and ways to measure the extent to which students were meeting those standards. As parents, educators, and policy makers alike realized the potential for dramatic changes in the lives of many students, there was a growing recognition that special education could no longer focus only on access to and compliance with the educational process, but rather it had to shift to looking at outcomes for students. This laid the foundation for dramatic changes in federal special education law, IDEA '97, and the inclusion of all students in large-scale educational assessments.

THE NEW REQUIREMENTS OF IDEA '97 IN CURRICULUM AND ASSESSMENT

IDEA '97 has created significant change in how we conceptualize educational programs for students with disabilities, including students with significant disabilities. Although some would argue that these changes have been implicit in previous formulations of IDEA, there can be no doubt that two of the most explicit and fundamental changes of IDEA '97 are the requirements that individualized education program (IEP) teams address 1) how students with disabilities will participate and progress in the general curriculum (i.e., the curriculum based on the learning standards identified for all students) and 2) how the learning of students with disabilities will be measured and reported in state- and district-level assessments for all students. This book reviews each of these new requirements in detail.

Participation in the General Curriculum

IDEA '97 mandates that the IEP address a student's participation and progress in the general curriculum in several specific ways. First, the statement of the *child's present level of educational performance* must now include how the child's disability affects the child's participation and progress in the general curriculum (614[d][1][A][i]). Second, the IEP must include "measurable annual goals, including benchmarks or short-term objectives, related to meeting the child's needs that result from the child's disability, to enable the child to be involved in and progress in the general curriculum" (614[d][1][A][ii]). Third, the *special education, related services, and supplementary aids* for the child, and the *program modifications and supports* for school personnel provided for the child, must be designed to enable the child to be involved and progress in the general curriculum (614[d][1][A][iii]) (italics not included in the original). Each of these IEP components—present level of performance, IEP goals and short-term objectives, special education and related services for the student, and program modifications and supports for school personnel working with the student—must address the student's involvement and progress in the general curriculum. Congress clearly intended that careful thought be given at each step in the development of the IEP to the child's participation in the general curriculum.

Participation in State and District Assessments

At the state level, IDEA '97 requires that "children with disabilities be included in general State and district-wide assessment programs, with appropriate accommodations, where necessary" (612[a][17][A]) and "as appropriate, the State or local educational agency: (i) develops guidelines for the participation of children with disabilities in alternate assessments for those children who cannot participate in State and district-wide assessment programs; and (ii) develops and, beginning not later than July 1, 2000, conducts those alternate assessments" (612[a][17][A] [i-ii]).

As of July 1, 2000, states also were required to report the numbers and performance of children participating in the alternate assessment (612[a][17][B][ii-iii]). Further, states must ensure that IEP teams individually address how students will participate in large-scale assessments (either via the general assessment, including the possible use of accommodations, or through an alternate assessment (614[d][1][A][v]). Finally, states must consider the performance of all students with disabilities, including those students participating in the alternate assessment, in the State Improvement Plan performance goals and indicators required under IDEA '97 (612[a][16][D]).

At the individual student level, the IEP must include a statement of any individual modifications needed for the student to participate in the state and/or district assessments. Moreover, if the IEP team determines that the student is unable to participate in any part of the state- or district-level assessment, the IEP must include a statement as to why the assessment is *not* appropriate for the student, and how the student will be assessed (614[d][1][A][v]).

In short, although some students may be excluded from participating in all or parts of the regular state- or district-level educational assessments, every student must be assessed in a manner appropriate to that student. Furthermore, the results of that student's assessment are to be included in the learning results reported for all students at the state and/or district level.

The new requirements for explicit participation in the general curriculum and inclusive educational assessments are closely interrelated. State and district educational assessments are designed to measure learning *as a function* of instruction in the general curriculum. Students with disabilities are to be included both in the curriculum itself and in the state and district measures of how well students have mastered that curriculum. Although IDEA '97 does not explicitly require that alternate assessments for students with disabilities be based on the general curriculum, it is the authors' position throughout this book that it does not make sense to require that all students be included in the general curriculum (including students with significant disabilities) and then *not* have their learning measured in the context of that same curriculum.

THE RELATIONSHIP BETWEEN CURRICULUM AND ASSESSMENT

As an integral part of standards-based reform, states and local school districts are increasingly identifying educational outcomes or content standards for all students. These standards become, in turn, the basis for the development of curricular frameworks, both at the local district and state levels, of what is to be taught, as well as a yardstick of what students have learned and can do as a result of their participation in that curriculum. Within standards-based reform, districts and schools are accountable for ensuring that their students have learned and can do what the standards say they should have learned and be able to do, and educational assessments increasingly are being designed to focus on measuring the extent to which those standards have been mastered.

The new requirements of IDEA '97, which are centered on students with disabilities participating and progressing within the general curriculum as well as being included in large-scale measures of educational performance, are meant to ensure that these students also participate in the benefits of standards-based reform. Too often, students with disabilities, especially students with more significant disabilities, have been viewed as a wholly separate population by schools, as a group who is not part of the larger picture of educational reform for "all students." The new requirements of IDEA '97 are designed so that educators give careful thought as to how they can remedy this problem and so that they reconsider whether they have made their curricular approaches for students with significant disabilities too specialized or too divorced from what is expected of all students.

Two Caveats

We should note here two critical caveats in our discussion about the inclusion of students with significant disabilities in educational reform. The first caution deals with the educational standards themselves; the second focuses on the individualized needs of the student.

Avoid Narrowly Defined Standards   Narrowly defined standards do not promote the development of good, inclusive curriculum practices. The flip side of this is that a number of authorities have noted that broadly developed educational standards, as opposed to narrow statements requiring the attainment of specific academic skills, foster the development of inclusive general curriculum approaches (Elliott, Ysseldyke, Thurlow, & Erickson, 1998; McLaughlin, Nolet, Rhim, & Henderson, 1998). For example, a content standard that requires all students "to use mathematical models to solve problems in everyday life" allows for considerably more variation in how a student may demonstrate that standard than one that requires all students "to master the principles of trigonometry and the properties of algebraic functions." Broadly conceptualized standards also require students to *apply* the content they have learned; higher order thinking and problem-solving skills (so important throughout all students' lives) clearly are required (McLaughlin et al., 1998) to master these new content standards.

Kleinert (1999) noted the following factors as critical to the inclusion of students with significant disabilities within the general curriculum:

- Broadly defined content standards as an integral piece of standards-based reform
- Alternate assessment tied to those same standards
- Inclusive curriculum design approaches

Although teachers may have only indirect influence over the first two factors (because these factors are state- or district-level decisions), teachers nevertheless have direct control over the third factor of inclusive curricular design because collaboration occurs at the school and classroom levels. Nevertheless, teachers should attempt to ensure, to the extent that they can, that the new content standards being adopted by their districts and states are sufficiently broad to encompass all students, including students with more significant disabilities. So, too, should they work toward having their state alternate assessments reflect at least a subset of those content standards for all students.

Focus on Other Educational Needs   The second caveat is that when creating IEPs, educators should not lose sight of students' unique needs related to their disabilities. Balancing the education of students with disabilities by focusing on the general curriculum that forms the core learning experience for all students, while at the same time considering the unique learning needs arising from the child's disability, is a challenging but essential task for all educators (Erickson, Ysseldyke, Thurlow, & Elliott, 1998; Hehir, 1998).

IDEA '97 provides a *balanced* framework in which the IEP team is to structure the student's educational program. The team must not only consider how the student will participate and progress in the general curriculum but also how the IEP will address "the child's other educational needs that result from the child's disability." Educators cannot afford to ignore this critical component: Students with disabilities have individualized educational needs related to their disability, which must be addressed *in addition* to aligning their learning with the general curriculum. For some students with disabilities, these individualized needs (e.g., instruction in braille for a student with a significant visual impairment) are *prerequisites* to accessing the general curriculum. For other students, these individualized needs represent a focus on *additional* learning experiences (e.g., systematic, community-based instruction for high school–age students with significant disabilities).

MAKING THE PROCESS WORK

Having considered these two caveats, we come to a critical juncture. How *are* students with significant disabilities going to participate in the general curriculum? How *will* it be proven that these students are progressing within the context of that curriculum? There are at least three essential strategies for ensuring the inclusion of all students with disabilities, even students with the most significant disabilities, in the general curriculum. Each of these strategies, described with examples throughout this chapter, has implications for the development and implementation of alternate assessments.

Embedding Priority IEP Objectives Across
General Classroom, School, and Community Environments

The first strategy for including students with significant disabilities in the general curriculum is to ensure that they have the opportunity to learn their *individually* determined IEP objectives in the context of a broad array of school, home, and community environments, including the general classroom. Although a student's IEP objectives may be the overriding learning focus for that student, providing him or her with the opportunity to practice those objectives in the context of the general classroom and to receive instruction on those objectives in the context of general education activities represents one fundamental way of ensuring that students with significant disabilities do participate in the general curriculum. This approach has much to recommend it, and it also ensures that educators will not lose their focus on the individualized needs of students with significant disabilities. However, this approach does not ensure that anything has been done to align the instructional objectives of students with significant disabilities with the learning outcomes or standards that have been set for all students. That is why the next approach is equally important.

Translating Content Standards for All
Students into Underlying Critical Functions

In a second approach to including students with significant disabilities in the general curriculum, we directly align the IEP objectives—written as generalizable, critical skills—with the learning standards we have identified for all students. We do this through an approach Owen White (1980) originally called a *critical function.* In other words, we look beyond the *form* of the behavior through which students typically demonstrate the state's or district's learner standards, and instead focus on the *function* of that standard in enhancing the student's life. In brief, we ask, "How does this standard apply for students with significant disabilities?" For example, the content standard "Student communicates ideas through speaking to various audiences" embodies an underlying critical function of the student "communicating his or her basic needs across environments, situations, and people." The standard "Uses computers and other kinds of technology to collect, organize, and communicate information and ideas," could be expressed, in terms of an underlying critical function, as "Uses necessary supports, including adaptive and assistive technology, to control own environment and to communicate effectively."

When the critical functions approach is used to align students' individually determined IEP objectives to the learning standards themselves, this process ensures that students with significant disabilities are not viewed as somehow being engaged only in their own curriculum, although they are physically present with the other students. Rather, this second approach enables all students to be viewed as working toward the same content standards, even though some students may demonstrate acquisition of those standards in unique and very creative ways. This approach, thus, allows the inclusion of students with significant disabilities in general class activities to be viewed not merely as an afterthought to the learning focus of the other students but as part of the broader enterprise of mastering an essential content of core learning for all students.

The weakness of this approach, however, is that the student's goals in the general curriculum may be limited only to the critical functions identified for each standard, and not to the higher level achievement indicators of those standards as they were intended for other students (Kleinert & Kearns, 1999).

Addressing the Academic Core of the Content Standards

The third strategy for enabling students with significant disabilities to gain access to the general curriculum, and the most typical strategy, is to address the educational standards for all students, not just through a translation process of critical functions but through the academic core itself. Thus, students with significant disabilities are included in the general curriculum and in general class activities neither just as a vehicle to learn and generalize their own individualized objectives (the first approach) nor just to learn the critical functions underlying the educational standards for all students (the second approach) but to learn the academic content itself. To be a part of a middle school science class is to learn at least some of the science. To be a part of a high school French class is to learn at least a little of the language and the culture of that nation.

How do we determine which part of science or French class, for example, is most important for the student to learn? This process is discussed in more detail in Chapter 4 through examples of more inclusive curriculum design. Although others have described this approach in greater detail elsewhere (see Onosko & Jorgensen, 1998), the approach discussed here pertains to its application for alternate assessment of significant disabilities. This final strategy presents tremendous potential not only for the inclusion of students with significant disabilities in the general curriculum but in the formulation of alternate assessment activities that best mirror the intent of IDEA '97. In the next section we describe the "essential questions" of alternate assessment.

THE PARAMETERS OF ALTERNATE ASSESSMENTS: THE WHO, WHAT, WHY, AND HOW

Why assess? As with all forms of assessment, the most central question regarding alternate assessments is their purpose. A central tenet of IDEA '97 is that special education must be directly linked to school reform for all students. The question of the assessment's purpose, then, should always be framed in the context of comprehensive statewide general education reform, in which schools are increasingly held accountable for clearly delineated student outcomes. The purpose of the alternate assessment should mirror the purpose of the regular assessment. Thus, if the purpose of the regular assessment is to give schools a "report card" on what students are learning and the ways that learning can be improved, then the alternate assessment should provide similar information for students with significant disabilities. Their performance on the alternate assessment should "count" toward their school or district accountability index in the same way that the performance of any other student counts in the regular assessment.

Lost in the Accountability Landscape

It should be noted here that IDEA '97, although requiring that all students be included in state- and districtwide educational assessments, does not specify that their scores be included in school and district measures of accountability. That is to say, IDEA does not mandate how the scores of students with disabilities will be used, or whether their scores will be used at all, in determining school rewards or sanctions. This is an important point, and for many who advocate for improved results for students with disabilities, it represents a limitation in the scope of the law. We would agree; to exclude the assessment scores of students with disabilities specifically from school accountability measures, though technically not prohibited under IDEA, seems to violate the principle of equal treatment while excluding students with disabilities from the public visibility of the "accountability landscape."

Who Should Be Eligible for Alternate Assessments?

IDEA '97 requires that states develop alternate assessments for those students who cannot participate in large-scale general assessments, even with accommodations. How should those students be defined? Is this strictly a decision to be made by the student's IEP team? Clearly, IDEA '97 places the ultimate authority for the decision of how a student will participate in state or district assessments with the student's IEP team. Yet, what eligibility criteria should IEP teams use to ensure consistent application? Should this decision be based solely on *diagnostic* labels (i.e., those diagnostic categories representing students with the most significant cognitive disabilities)? Yet, as has been noted elsewhere, a criterion for participation in the alternate assessment based solely on diagnostic labels would violate fundamental principles of due process and individualization because individual student decisions can never be based solely on such categorical labels (Kleinert, Haigh, Kearns, & Kennedy, 2000).

Should the decision be based on the student's *course of study*, such that the alternate assessment would be used for those students not earning a general high school diploma (e.g., those students in a certificate-of-completion program)? This criterion also presents a number of issues. First, how do you (or should you) determine for elementary-age students the likelihood that they will earn a general diploma? Furthermore, some educators have forcefully argued that *all* students who complete their prescribed course of studies should receive a general diploma (Shapiro-Barnard et al., 1996; Tashie, Malloy, & Lichtenstein, 1998).

Finally, should eligibility for the alternate assessment be based on decisions about whom we *think* would do poorly on the general assessment? Such a subjective criterion presents even more fundamental problems. IDEA '97 speaks of the alternate assessment as being specifically for those students for whom the regular assessment cannot be accommodated. There are students, however, who can take the regular assessment with reasonable accommodations but who nevertheless will do poorly for a multitude of reasons, including poor teaching and lack of exposure to the general curriculum. A criterion based on how educators think students would perform in the regular assessment would give schools an incentive to place into the alternate assessment those students they had failed to teach.

Individual states, of course, have approached eligibility policies in a variety of ways. For example, Kentucky chose to define eligibility in terms of *student instructional needs* occurring as the result of the severity of cognitive disability. Alternate assessment eligibility criteria in Kentucky include students whose limitations in cognitive functioning prevent the completion of the state's regular program of studies (mastery of a required set of Carnegie units) even with extended school services and other program modifications and adaptations, and who require *extensive* instruction in *multiple, community-referenced* settings to ensure skill acquisition, maintenance, and generalization to "real-life contexts." (Kleinert et al., 2000, pp. 53–54) Kentucky's eligibility requirements also state that the students in the alternate assessment at the high school level cannot pursue a general high school diploma.

Maryland, another state with extensive experience in large-scale alternate assessments, has approached eligibility somewhat differently. In Maryland, students eligible for the alternate assessment are those students "who are not pursuing the state's general education *outcomes* as specified" (i.e., students in Maryland's alternate assessment require significant alterations in the outcome itself or in the indicators for measuring that outcome) (Kleinert et al., 2000, p. 53). Students participating in the alternate assessment in Maryland *are* permitted to work toward a general diploma. As noted elsewhere, "Maryland's approach also has the distinct advantage of not establishing or reinforcing an existing duality of high school students—those pursuing general diplomas, and those who will only receive a Certificate" (Kleinert et al., 2000, p. 53).

Issues of eligibility for alternate assessments will be, unquestionably, at the forefront of educational policies for students with significant disabilities for years to come. These issues are complex and relate not only to the characteristics of each student's disability and the impact of that disability on performance but also to the nature and format of the assessments themselves. For example, it would appear far more problematic to accommodate students with disabilities in more traditional, multiple-choice achievement tests than in assessments that involve collections of the student's best work, such as portfolio assessments. Authorities also have argued extensively about students in the "gray area" who are learning the same content as other children, but who often "need a different way to show what they know" (Elliott et al., 1998, p. 26). We agree that such "gray area" students should be included, with appropriate accommodations, in the regular assessments, but we do not underestimate the challenges of doing so. Other authorities (Kearns et al., 1998) have noted that, based on a student's particular strengths, limitations, and learning profile, it might be very appropriate for that student to participate in the regular assessment in certain areas (e.g., math), but to participate in the alternate assessment in other content areas.

What Should Be Assessed?

To what extent can the content standards (or learning outcomes) for all students form the basis for the development of the alternate assessment? Can these same learning outcomes—or a modified set or subset of those outcomes—be used in constructing the alternate assessment? If the same content standards do apply to all students, can we specify differential benchmarks or performance indicators for each of these outcomes for students in the alternate assessment? Or, conversely, should alternate assessments be based on a different, more "functional" set of learner outcomes, and even more specifically, on the individualized learning objectives in the student's IEP itself? These questions affect the extent to which students with significant disabilities are active learners and participants in the general curriculum (Kleinert et al., 2000; Kleinert & Kearns, 1999).

States are again taking a wide range of approaches to this question. For example, Kentucky's alternate assessment is based on a subset of the state's Learner Outcomes (since renamed Academic Expectations) for all students. An important step in this process was identifying for each Academic Expectation a critical function conveyed by that outcome, so that students with significant disabilities might show the targeted outcomes in a variety of adapted ways. For example, a student with significant disabilities could demonstrate the expectation of "using patterns to understand past and present events and predict future events" by managing his or her own daily printed or pictorial schedule of activities. This approach has the advantage of aligning the alternate assessment with the content standards for all students. However, care must be taken not to limit the learning of students with significant disabilities only to the functional interpretations or critical functions underlying the content standards (see Kleinert & Kearns, 1999).

Other states, such as Maryland, have worked from a merged set of adapted academic and skills outcomes, addressing a comprehensive set of life domains. This approach likewise grounds the alternate assessment in the core content standards, yet provides an additional set of life outcomes that may lie outside the priorities of the core academic standards.

A third approach being considered by several states is to base the alternate assessment directly on the IEP; students who are achieving high percentages of their individual short-term objectives would score higher than students who had made little progress on their specific objectives. This approach certainly makes the alternate assessment directly relevant to the student's educational program, but in no way does it ensure that the student's learning will address the content standards underlying the general curriculum for all students.

Similar to the question of *whom* to assess, the question of *what* to assess poses considerable challenges. This question cannot be divorced from the context of the state or district content standards that are the framework for the general curriculum and the regular assessment. As noted previously in this chapter, broadly stated content standards—focused on the broad application of core content to "real-life" contexts—are clearly more suited to inclusion in the alternate assessment than are more narrowly written standards that focus on only a prescribed set of academic content.

Though it is not always easy to articulate the relationship of a state's learning standards for all students to the requirements of its alternate assessment, we find ourselves very much in agreement with the position of Elliott et al.:

> Let us be clear—it is not the intent of the new IDEA for district and state assessment requirements to have students eligible for an alternate assessment working toward a different set of standards or learning expectancies. The best of all worlds is to have a broad set of standards for all students. Creating a second set of standards for students who take the alternate assessment simply perpetuates a fractured system of service delivery to students with disabilities. (1998, p. 25)

How Should Assessment Be Done?

A key issue for states and local districts in the development of alternate assessments is, of course, what these assessments will look like—how they will be structured, and what the sources of data will be. Ysseldyke and Olsen (1999) described a range of possible options, including performance "event" tests (e.g., structured problems that require a student to create a solution or develop a product), adaptive behavior skills or performance checklists (i.e., a listing of standardized or criterion-referenced critical skills that a student has mastered), interviews with significant others knowledgeable about the student's performance, analyses of progress on current IEP objectives, portfolios (collections of student work that reveal what students can do), or some combination of these measures. We believe very strongly that alternate assessments should be *performance-based* ("testing methods that require students to create an answer or product that demonstrates their knowledge or skills," U.S. Congress, 1992, p. 18), as opposed to more "paper-and-pencil"–based measures (e.g., multiple choice, reiteration of academic facts). Because alternate assessments, according to IDEA '97, are for those students for whom the regular assessment is not appropriate, even with modifications and accommodations, more traditional, paper-and-pencil assessments hardly seem appropriate as accurate gauges of learning for these students.

A number of states (e.g., Kentucky, Maryland, Rhode Island, New Hampshire, Tennessee, South Carolina, New York) are developing and/or implementing portfolio methods of assessment for students with significant disabilities. Portfolio assessments, which are performance-based collections of student products, are especially suited for alternate assessments because 1) portfolio assessment enables the student to showcase what he or she can do and is not a delineation of what the student cannot do, 2) portfolio assessment enables students and teachers to use multiple measures (e.g., student products and student self-evaluations, instructional programming data, peer and family reflections), and 3) portfolio assessment can provide a broadly defined assessment structure capable of accommodating a very diverse student population. Given the heterogeneity within the population of students with significant disabilities, a broad and flexible structure for collecting student learning samples over time is very important for demonstrating student performance (Kleinert, Kearns, & Kennedy, 1997). Elliott et al. have further noted that the portfolio approach "allows several components or entries to be included that directly reflect the standards and the curriculum that the students are learning" (1998, p. 25). Finally, as Ezell, Klein, and Ezell-Powell (1999) have observed, portfolio assessment can provide opportunities for students to take more control over their own learning and to gain critical practice in skills related to self-determination. For all these reasons, this book reflects examples of student work that are easily adaptable to a portfolio assessment format. It is hoped that the examples in this text are helpful to any teacher whose state or district alternate assessment is performance-based, however, even if that work is not collected specifically within a portfolio format.

WHAT DO WE BELIEVE?
PRINCIPLES OF ALTERNATE ASSESSMENTS

Each of us operates not only from what we know from our experience and from the research base of our field but also from what we believe. As researchers and as educators who have worked with students with significant disabilities, we believe that the new IDEA requirements for the inclusion of all students in large-scale educational assessments, including the advent of alternate assessments for students with significant disabilities, present not only tremendous challenges but

a singular opportunity as well. Below are our principles of what constitutes effective alternate assessment strategies—principles that we believe will result in
improved programs and outcomes for students with significant disabilities:

1. Alternate assessment must be integrally tied to effective instruction,
    including direct student engagement; high rates of student responses;
    and structured, systematic teaching opportunities specifically designed
    to elicit those responses.
2. Alternate assessment should be based on authentic instruction—
    instruction that focuses on real-life skills taught across essential life
    environments.
3. Alternate assessment should allow the student to apply what he or she
    has learned; skills are not used in isolation. Instead, they are parts of
    complex performances that integrate skills across developmental and
    academic areas.
4. Alternate assessment should not be a one-time test or single snapshot of
    student performance. Rather, alternate assessment should be based on
    continuous assessment of student performance.
5. Alternate assessment should reflect what the student can do in the pres-
    ence of optimal student supports. Providing education to students with
    significant disabilities is not only about teaching skills leading to inde-
    pendence and community participation, but about building the supports
    in students' lives that will enhance that independence and participation.
    Natural supports are a critical part of this equation.
6. Alternate assessments must be integrally tied to the individualized cur-
    ricular focus for students with significant disabilities as well as related to
    the general curriculum. In no case should the alternate assessment
    merely be a "watered-down" version of the regular assessment, any
    more than the curricular focus for students with significant disabilities
    should be a watered-down version of the general curriculum. The indi-
    vidualized instructional priorities for a student with significant disabili-
    ties, thus, should be an essential (but only one) component of that stu-
    dent's alternate assessment. How those individualized priorities are
    realized in the context of the general curriculum is the other critical part
    of the alternate assessment.
7. The core strategies for developing alternate assessments cannot be
    viewed in isolation; rather, they are "all of one cloth." For example,
    performance-based assessment for students with significant disabilities
    should focus on the acquisition of meaningful skills across multiple
    environments and contexts, with opportunities for students to exercise
    control over their own learning and to monitor and evaluate that learn-
    ing. Supports for performance should be, to the maximum extent pos-
    sible, those that are naturally occurring within the environment, and
    friendships and the development of a rich fabric of social relationships
    are themselves a fundamental outcome of the educational process. To
    focus on one or two of these concepts while neglecting the others is ulti-
    mately to fragment our expectations for the students we serve.
8. The ultimate purpose of alternate assessments for students with signifi-
    cant disabilities is to improve instruction and results for these students.

This cannot happen, however, unless teachers learn specific strategies for embedding assessment into effective instruction. Teachers must learn to use alternate assessment not only to document what the student has learned but also to enhance and extend that learning. It is for this reason that we have written this book, and it is for this reason that it is addressed primarily to educators.

REFERENCES

Allington, R., & McGill-Franzen, A. (1992). Unintended effects of educational reform in New York. *Educational Policy, 6*(4), 397–414.

Carnegie Council on Adolescent Development. (1989). *Turning points: Preparing American youth for the 21st century.* New York: Author.

Elliott, J., Ysseldyke, J., Thurlow, M., & Erickson, R. (1998). What about assessment and accountability: Practical implications for educators. *Teaching Exceptional Children, 31*(1), 20–27.

Erickson, R., Ysseldyke, J., Thurlow, M., & Elliott, J. (1998). Inclusive assessments and accountability systems: Tools of the trade in educational reform. *Teaching Exceptional Children, 31*(2), 4–9.

Ezell, D., Klein, C., & Ezell-Powell, S. (1999). Empowering students with mental retardation through portfolio assessment: A tool for fostering self-determination skills. *Education and Training in Mental Retardation and Developmental Disabilities, 34*(4), 453–463.

Goals 2000: Educate America Act of 1994, PL 103-227, 20 U.S.C. §§ 5801 *et seq.*

Hehir, T. (1998, April). *Conversations with OSEP.* Presentation to the Council for Exceptional Children Annual Convention, Minneapolis, MN.

Individuals with Disabilities Education Act Amendments of 1997, PL 105–17, 20 U.S.C. §§1400 *et seq.*

Kearns, S., Kennedy, S., Warren, S., Bechard, S., Kleinert, H., Farrell, M., Haigh, J., Cippoletti, B., & Meiczkowski, M. (1998, December). *Alternate assessments: Innovative state approaches.* Full-day TASH TECH workshop presented to the International Association for Persons with Severe Handicaps (TASH) Conference, Seattle, WA.

Kleinert, H. (1999, July). *Access to the general curriculum for students with severe disabilities.* Unpublished paper presented at the U.S. Department of Education Research in Education Individuals with Disabilities Project Directors' Meeting, Washington, DC.

Kleinert, H., Haigh, J., Kearns, J., & Kennedy, S. (2000). Alternate assessments: Lessons learned and roads to be taken. *Exceptional Children, 67*(1), 51–66 .

Kleinert, H., & Kearns, J. (1999). A validation study of the performance indicators and learner outcomes of Kentucky's alternate assessment for students with significant disabilities. *The Journal of The Association for Persons with Severe Handicaps, 24*(2), 100–110.

Kleinert, H., Kearns, J., & Kennedy, S. (1997). Accountability for all students: Kentucky's Alternate Portfolio assessment for students with moderate and severe cognitive disabilities. *The Journal of The Association for Persons with Severe Handicaps, 22*(2), 88–101.

McGrew, K.S., Thurlow, M.L., & Spiegel, A.N. (1993). An investigation of the exclusion of students with disabilities in national data collection programs. *Educational Evaluation and Policy Analysis, 15*(3), 339–352.

McLaughlin, M., Nolet, V., Rhim, L., & Henderson, K. (1998). Integrating standards: Including all students. *Teaching Exceptional Children, 31*(3), 66–71.

National Commission on Excellence in Education. (1983). *A nation at risk: The imperative for educational reform.* Washington, DC: Author.

National Governors' Association. (1986). *Time for results.* Washington, DC: Author.

Onosko, J.J., & Jorgensen, C.M. (1998). Unit and lesson planning for the inclusive classroom. In C. M. Jorgensen, *Restructuring high schools for all students: Taking inclusion to the next level* (pp. 71–105). Baltimore: Paul H. Brookes Publishing Co.

Shapiro-Barnard, S., Tashie, C., Martin, J., Schuh, M., Malloy, J., Piet, J., Lichtenstein, S., & Nisbet, J. (1996). *Petroglyphs: The writing on the wall.* Durham: University of New Hampshire, Institute on Disability.

Smith, R.C. (1988). *America's shame. America's hope: Twelve million youth at risk* (ERIC Document Reproduction Service No. ED 301 620). Chapel Hill, NC: MDC, Inc.

Tashie, C., Malloy, J., & Lichtenstein, S. (1998). Transition or graduation: Supporting all students to plan for the future. In C.M. Jorgensen, *Restructuring high schools for all students: Taking inclusion to the next level* (pp. 233–260). Baltimore: Paul H. Brookes Publishing Co.

U.S. Congress (1992, February). *Testing in American schools: Asking the right questions* (Report No. OTA-SET-519). Washington, DC: U.S. Government Printing Office.

White, O. (1980). Adaptive performance objectives: Form versus function. In W. Sailor., B. Wilcox, & L. Brown (Eds.), *Methods of instruction for severely handicapped students.* Baltimore: Paul H. Brookes Publishing Co.

William T. Grant Foundation. (1988). *The forgotten half: Non-college youth in America.* Washington, DC: Commission on Work, Family, and Citizenship.

Ysseldyke, J., & Olsen, K. (1999). Putting alternate assessments into practice: What to measure and possible sources of data. *Exceptional Children, 65*(2), 175–186.

Zlatos, B. (1994, November). Don't test, don't tell. *The American School Board Journal,* 25–28.

chapter 2

*Can performance goals
be set for all students?*

CREATING STANDARDS-BASED INDIVIDUALIZED EDUCATION PROGRAMS

Jennifer Grisham-Brown and Jacqui Farmer Kearns

Individualized education program (IEP) teams are charged with the task of determining how individual students will participate in their state and/or district educational assessment(s), and, at an even more fundamental level, how the students' disabilities affect their *involvement and progress in the general curriculum*. Specifically, the Individuals with Disabilities Education Act (IDEA) Amendments of 1997 (PL 105-17) state, "The IEP must include (i) a statement of the child's present levels of educational performance including (ii) how the child's disability affects the child's involvement and progress in the general curriculum" (614[d][1][A]).

In order to make this determination, IEP teams must, at a minimum, examine the performance goals and indicators (also called standards) established for *all* children in their state, as these goals typically form the foundation or framework for the general curriculum and, in turn, the basis for large-scale assessments. *Instruction* refers to the activities that teachers use to provide students with access to the curriculum content that will be assessed. This chapter outlines a process for developing IEPs that articulates the relationship of these individualized programs to those standards set for all students.

THE RELATIONSHIP BETWEEN STANDARDS
AND THE INDIVIDUALIZED EDUCATION PROGRAM

Giangreco, Cloninger, and Iverson (1998) provided an example of the relationship of the IEP to curricular activities. These authors suggested that the IEP represents a prioritized subset of skills that the learner's family and his or her instructional team believe must be accomplished. Although students with significant disabilities may need to learn many things, the process of developing a student's IEP requires the team to narrow down the priorities for the student. This is consistent with the idea that teaching fewer skills in multiple environments increases the chances that the skills will be acquired. The IEP is "nested" into the general curriculum content and in the routine classroom and school activities in which most students in school participate (e.g., locating classrooms, putting away coats, following teacher instructions, locating desks, getting out materials, walking in a line). The standards-based curriculum represents those directly planned instructional activities—such as writing a personal narrative, reading about the solar system, or making a papier-mâché planet—that articulate learning associated with specific content standards. Figure 2.1 takes the Giangreco et al. (1998) model one step further by incorporating the standards that correspond to particular IEP skills. Standards are articulated through instructional activities. In this way, students can work on skills that are appropriately individualized and the curriculum standards can assist IEP teams in determining what the student should be learning in relation to what other students are expected to learn.

To further illustrate how this process works, think of a baker making a dessert. The IEP skills represent the ingredients for the recipe, the instructional activities and techniques represent the cooking process, and the standards represent the finished dessert (the end product of learning). The more authentic the cooking process, the more standards get represented (or included) in the dessert (and the more delicious it tastes). For example, students conducting a science experiment work not only on science content but also on reading, writing, and speaking. This overall model forms the basis of the discussion of how standards and the IEP can inform each other. This chapter outlines how IEP goals and objectives can be written so that student learning is maximized.

DEVELOPING THE IEP

Even with the changes made to IDEA '97, the IEP remained the mechanism for guiding service delivery for students with disabilities who receive special education services. According to IDEA '97, the plan must include

- A statement of the child's present level of performance
- A statement of annual goals and criteria for judging whether those goals have been achieved (i.e., short-term objectives or benchmarks)
- A statement identifying the required educational supports and related services needed to achieve goals and objectives
- Identification of who will be responsible for implementing those services
- A description of where the plan will be implemented
- A rationale for how the student's disability affects his or her involvement and progress in the general curriculum

IEP

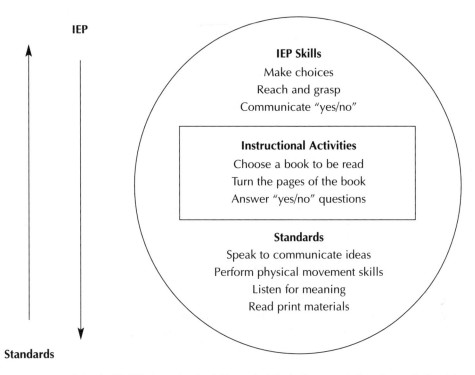

Standards

Figure 2.1.   Articulating the IEP skills, instructional activities, and standards. The arrows indicate that standards and the IEP inform each other.

When delivering services to students with disabilities, given the importance of the IEP in determining what they should learn, it is essential that there be a merger of the IEP process with the development of standards-based curricula and assessment. Figure 2.2 illustrates the relationship among standards, instruction, and assessment. Essentially, what is taught (i.e., curriculum standards) should align with what is assessed. Instruction represents the process by which students learn the standards.

For this synthesis to occur, three important pieces must be present in the IEP. First, the goals/objectives identified in the IEP must be *critical skills* that can be taught in a variety of contexts. Second, given that students with significant disabilities require instruction that is provided in meaningful, functional contexts in order to acquire skills (Gast & Schuster, 1993; Heward, 2000), the strategies for assessing performance must also be aligned with the context in which the student is learning. The IEP must then reflect the context in which the critical skills will be taught. Third, the IEP must sufficiently identify the supports, modifications, and adaptations needed for the student to learn the critical skills within the identified contexts. Each of these issues is described in detail below.

Determine Critical Skills

Often, when IEPs are developed, the following process occurs. First, the teacher completes some type of criterion- or norm-referenced assessment. Following the completion of the assessment, the teacher determines where the student has

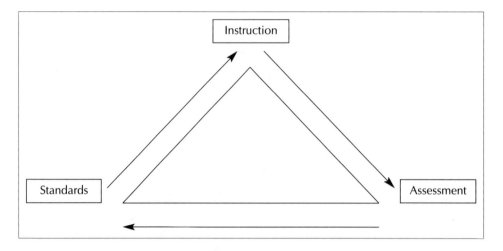

Figure 2.2.　The relationship among standards, instruction, and assessment.

incorrectly performed or answered assessment activities or items. Based on that information, the teacher develops an IEP objective for that "missed" item. The following is an example of an IEP objective created using this process.

> When presented with a four-piece inlaid puzzle and the task direction, "Put together the puzzle," the student will match the piece to its corresponding spot on the puzzle in five of five trials over 3 consecutive days.

A number of problems are apparent with this objective: 1) The objective "putting together a four-piece inlaid puzzle" is probably not appropriate for many students, particularly those who are older than preschool age; 2) this objective might result in isolated instruction of repeated practice in working puzzles; and 3) it is doubtful that the attainment of this objective articulates any general learner outcome or standard as identified for all students. In fact, this task might be only one of many a student could do (if it was age-appropriate for the child) to demonstrate that he or she was able to match shapes, solve problems, or demonstrate eye–hand coordination.

To develop instruction that promotes achievement for *all* children, another process must be in place to link the IEP to standards-based curriculum and assessment. An understanding of critical skills and why goals and objectives must be based on them is essential. These skills have several features:

1. **Critical skills are required to complete part or all of an activity; they are not the activity itself**. This differs from the ecological model that has been advocated as an approach for planning IEPs for students with significant disabilities in recent years (Snell & Brown, 1993). In the ecological model, a domain (e.g., domestic) might be the annual goal statement "to improve domestic skills," with corresponding "domestic"

activities serving as the short-term objectives (e.g., sweeping, taking out trash, washing dishes). Although these activities are functional contexts for some learners, they do not represent critical skills. Instead, numerous critical skills across several traditional developmental areas are required to complete each of these domestic activities (e.g., communicate need for materials associated with the activity, use both hands together to complete a task, initiate social interactions with others involved in the activity).

2. **Critical skills should result in repeated use throughout all daily activities and routines.** Unless a student is a custodian's assistant or an intensely clean person, it is unlikely that he or she will have multiple opportunities to sweep throughout the day, particularly if that student spends the majority of his or her time in a general education class. The critical skills as described previously, however, can be taught across a variety of activities and routines that are available in a general education class. Such skills might include expressing concerns, bilateral coordination, and social initiations.

3. **Critical skills are not components of the curriculum.** IEPs sometimes contain objectives that are *too* specific to the students' curriculum. For example, saying that a child will answer questions related to stories in the third-grade basal reader is too specific to the reading curricular area. It limits instruction on that objective to having students answer questions only during the time in which they are reading the third-grade basal reader instead of also practicing reading in other content areas. Rather, the objective should indicate that the child will answer comprehension questions related to course content, which could include language arts, science, and social studies. Therefore, critical skills should be considered as broad classes of behaviors that can be taught across curriculum content areas (e.g., answering comprehension questions, reading sight words, calculating addition problems).

4. **Critical skills identified on the student's IEP should be linked to the state standards designed for all learners.** Chapter 4 presents several examples at each age level for how critical skill instruction for students with significant disabilities can be embedded into general class activities and related to the state learning standards for all students.

Function Versus Form　　Imagine educational practices in which learners with significant disabilities have the same learner outcomes as students without disabilities. Closely related to the notion of teaching critical skills to students of all abilities is an understanding of the concept of form versus function or, in this case, function versus form (White, 1980). White indicated the need to identify the "function or purpose the behavior is supposed to serve, rather than the specific form or the motor act used to achieve the effect" (p. 49). Often, students with significant disabilities are penalized on standardized assessments because they cannot perform the motor, communicative, or sensory behaviors required to complete certain items on the assessment (e.g., putting together a four-piece inlaid puzzle requires vision and fine motor skills).

White (1985) has challenged us to determine what the outcome of such a task is and then to determine alternate behavioral forms a student might use to demonstrate his or her capacity to achieve that outcome. For example, let's say that the function for putting together a four-piece inlaid puzzle is to demonstrate problem-solving behaviors. The student might show that she or he knows where the piece belongs by using an eye-gaze system, in which another person holds up each puzzle piece and asks the student to look at the place on the puzzle where the piece belongs. With this alternate behavioral form (e.g., eye-gaze), the student can demonstrate the same outcome as a student who can manually put the pieces in the correct places on the puzzle.

Likewise, students with disabilities might demonstrate that they can achieve the same standards as all students if the following are determined: 1) the function of those standards, and 2) alternate behavioral forms a student might use to achieve those outcomes. Figure 2.3 shows an example of a standard, its critical function, and one way a child with significant disabilities might achieve that standard.

For example, let's say that a standard for all students is as follows:

> Students speak using appropriate forms, conventions, and systems to communicate ideas and information to different audiences for different purposes.

Although some students with significant disabilities may be unable to speak (behavioral form), these students might be able to communicate information such as their basic wants and concerns (function) through an augmentative or alternative communication system (e.g., body movement, gestures, sign language) to various communicative partners. Expressing wants and concerns, then, is a critical skill because it is one that can be taught across multiple environments and can be linked to a learner outcome for all students.

Involve Students in Authentic Activities and Environments

Authentic assessments involve tasks that we value; simulate challenges facing workers in a field of study; require application of knowledge; and are multimodal, requiring the student to demonstrate an integrated performance that incorporates several skills into a single activity (Wiggins, 1991). For example, grocery shopping

Standard	Critical Function	Alternate Form
Speak to communicate ideas	Communicate ideas	Use augmentative and alternative communication system (e.g., sign language)

Figure 2.3.   Standards, critical function, and alternate behavioral form.

requires reading, math, and communication skills. The reading and math skills are applied, and multimodal responses are required. Similarly, standards-based instruction involves instructional/assessment activities that require students to evince a variety of standards within a single assessment product. The instruction/assessment products for grocery shopping might include examples of the student's grocery lists as well as instructional data for selecting items on the list, choosing cheaper items, or using a calculator to budget purchases. Instructional activities may be designed to address a variety of critical skills as well as curriculum standards in a meaningful context. In that case, authentic assessment suggests that the student must demonstrate the use of the standard within a variety of meaningful environments.

Most IEP objectives do not indicate where critical skills should be taught or they too narrowly define the conditions under which those skills should be taught. For example, an objective might read:

> When presented with a red, blue, green, or yellow 1-inch cube and given the task to answer the question, "What color is that?," the student will identify the cube's color in 10 of 10 trials over 3 consecutive days.

Color identification might be considered a critical skill; however, when an objective is written in this manner, the instructor will not necessarily teach the critical skill in a environment in which the child will need to demonstrate knowledge of colors (e.g., when playing a game with colored game pieces, when putting on socks that are the same color, when setting the table with various colored dishes). In addition, if we teach students to identify colors only with 1-inch color cubes, there is no guarantee that the student can identify other objects of the same color because many students with disabilities have difficulty generalizing skills across stimuli (Rainforth, York, & York-Barr, 1997). The development of a standards-based IEP should include a variety of authentic contexts in which the critical skill can be taught, as well a variety of stimuli that can be used for teaching the critical skill.

Determine Appropriate Supports, Adaptations, and Modifications

A standards-based IEP should include a detailed account of the supports, adaptations, and modifications that are needed for the student to achieve the critical skill within the various environments. In the IEP, there is a required section entitled "Specially Designed Instruction" in which these components are described. This section should include information about materials, assistive technology, instructional modifications, and perhaps even people who will facilitate the student's acquisition of the skills across various contexts. These adaptations may be essential for some students to demonstrate certain standards, such as the example provided in Figure 2.3 (e.g., communicating ideas and information with an augmentative or alternative communication system). In addition, supports often are an integral part of alternate assessments for students with significant disabilities. In fact, the use of natural supports and appropriate adaptations are essential components of any performance assessment. For example, in a vision examination for a driving test, the driver may use his or her eyeglasses in the vision test if he or she regularly uses eyeglasses. The eyeglasses in this case are an appropriate accommodation. Without the glasses, the individual would most likely fail the vision examination. Yet very often, students with significant disabilities are expected to perform without the most basic accommodations.

Avoid Mislabeling Objectives　　The authors frequently note that IEPs are void of information on adaptations, modifications, and supports that are needed to plan a student's educational program. In some situations, these important components of an IEP are stated as IEP objectives. For example, a student's IEP might state "The student will be positioned for 30 minutes a day in a prone stander." The prone stander is an important adaptation that might facilitate a child's participation in a variety of activities while the child learns trunk control (perhaps a very critical skill!). However, this statement is not an objective. In an analysis of IEP objectives, Weisenfeld (1987) found that many IEP "objectives" inform the teacher of what to do instead of indicating what the student will learn. If a student requires the use of various positioning equipment throughout the day, that information should be reported in the "specially designed instruction" component of the IEP, and not as an objective. Figure 2.4 illustrates the areas of needs and of supports that an IEP might address in order to help a student succeed (Giangreco et al., 1998).

PUTTING IT ALL TOGETHER

Grisham-Brown and Hemmeter (1998) developed a process for writing IEP goals and objectives for young children with disabilities that is easily modified for a standards-based IEP model. The first three steps of the model are particularly pertinent to the discussion of a standards-based IEP.

IEP priorities	Curriculum	General supports
Communication Socialization Personal management Vocational	Classroom routines and activities Reading Math Social Studies Science	Personal needs Physical needs Teaching others Sensory needs Access and opportunity Assistive technology

Figure 2.4.　Relating IEP priorities to the general curriculum and student support needs. (Adapted from Giangreco, M.F., Cloninger, C.J., & Iverson, V.S. [1998]. *Choosing outcomes and accommodations for children [COACH]: A guide to educational planning for students with disabilities* [2nd ed., p. 46]. Baltimore: Paul H. Brookes Publishing Co.)

Step 1: Identify Critical Skills and Priority Activities

The critical skills and activities identified for the IEP should be those that are a priority to the family and other members of the student's educational team. This means that the student's teacher must work with the family *before* the IEP meeting to determine their priorities for student learning. Many methods exist for gathering this information. Some of these are highly structured and formal, although others are less structured and informal. *Choosing Outcomes and Accommodations for Children (COACH): A Guide to Educational Planning for Students with Disabilities, Second Edition* (Giangreco et al., 1998), is one approach that yields priority information from families. It is a highly structured interview process that gathers pertinent information by asking families questions about 1) quality of life issues (e.g., the amount of choice and control in their child's life), 2) their perception of how their son or daughter performs skills across various domains (e.g., communication, socialization, school), and 3) priorities regarding what skills should be included in the child's IEP. In addition, COACH has a process for gathering information from members of the child's educational team with regard to supports and adaptations. Although COACH is only one method for gathering priority information, it fits nicely with the standards-based assessment because it identifies critical skills that then can be easily practiced in a variety of instructional activities that address those standards.

If the teacher actively involves the family in the development of the student's IEP and facilitates an effort that assists the family in identifying critical skills, it will be easier for the family to understand how their son or daughter might work on the same standards as all students. In addition, it is absolutely essential that special education teachers review the standards that have been identified for students in their state. For example, several school districts with whom we work have included on their IEP skill prioritization worksheets a column to indicate the relation of each prioritized skill to one or more of the state standards for all students.

Step 2: Write Annual Goal Statements

Annual goals "are broad general statements that help focus on the general areas in which individualized services will be provided" (Blackhurst & Berdine, 1993, p. 60). With standards-based IEPs, the IEP should address the major areas of concern for the student as well as a variety of contexts in which those skills can be taught. Therefore, the annual goal statements should contain the developmental domain that will be the focus of instruction as well as the environments in which skills from those domains will be taught. An example of an annual goal statement written in this format is the following:

> Increase communication skills at home, at school, and in the community.

This statement implies that instruction will occur in various locations, including those in which the students' family and peers participate. Many content and per-

Table 2.1.   IEP goal example for Meredith

Goal #1

To improve communication skills in the areas of receptive and expressive language in all environments.

Short-term objective

When involved in the following activities and given a choice between three objects, activities, or people per activity, Meredith will make her choice by activating a communication device during 9 or 10 opportunities across 3 consecutive days.

Sample activities

Choice of what to wear to school

Choice of friend to work with on class projects

Choice of enrichment classes to attend

Choice of classroom chore

Choice of book to have read during reading

Adaptations and modifications

Contrasting background without clutter

Proper positioning so that she can bring hands to mid-line

BIGmack switches with recorded messages paired with objects

Vertical presentation of switches and objects

Time-delay prompting procedure

Small motor preparation/assistance

Peer assistance

Implementers

General and special education teachers

Intervenor

Related services providers (physical therapist, occupational therapist, speech-language pathologist)

Vision consultant

formance standards address the application of knowledge and skills in real-life situations. Stating annual goals in this manner is in keeping with that broad approach to standards.

Step 3: Develop Short-Term Objectives

The short-term objective should tell the teacher *what* to teach, *where* to teach, and *how* to teach. Research indicates that IEPs typically do not provide teachers with enough information for program planning (Hilton & Liberty, 1992). To address this issue, short-term objectives should have three components. The first component is the *behavioral objective* written in generic terminology. The behavioral objective states the behavior the student will learn in measurable terminology, the conditions under which the behavior will be taught, and the criterion or standard for judging that the behavior has been learned. According to Grisham-Brown and Hemmeter (1998), the short-term objective should not be so specific that it limits where and under what circumstances the student will learn the desired skill. For example, if the objective indicates that a student should learn to use a pincer grasp by picking up raisins, a presumption is made that picking up raisins is the only time a student can use that skill and, furthermore, that time must be set aside for teaching the student to pick up a pencil, block, or other object. Rather, the objective should state that the student will pick up *objects* using a pincer grasp.

Table 2.2.   Meredith's critical skills related to the communication goal area

Annual goal	Associated critical skills for short-term objectives	Assessment products	Standards
Improved communication skills	Sequence daily events Make choices Answer yes/no Greet peers or adults Follow one-step commands	Photographs of calendar box Book selections for reading Instructional data and peer reports for greeting Modeling clay class-room demonstration Science experiment (sorting magnetic/non-magnetic objects)	Communicating ideas Science (magnetic objects) Reading Working with others

Second, the short-term objective should identify the activities in which the skill might be taught. All too often, students work on skills in isolation rather than at times when they need to use the skill. We know that this is an ineffective way to teach students with significant disabilities because of their inability to generalize and synthesize skills (Rainforth, York, & York-Barr, 1997). As such, a list of sample activities in which the student can practice the identified skill should follow the objective. These activities should be those that 1) are priorities for families, 2) address the range of environments mentioned in the annual goal statement, and 3) include activities that offer opportunities for social interactions with students who do not have disabilities. For example, a student can practice a pincer grasp when putting on clothes in preparation for coming to school, in art class when picking up art supplies, and when picking up items in a grocery store.

In addition to the objective and associated activities there should be listed adaptations, modifications, and supports that provide the educational team with information about how to teach the skill within the identified activities. When all of this information is in place, teachers are better equipped to facilitate the acquisition of generalized responses across activities and environments. Table 2.1 is an example of a short-term objective written in this manner.

Meredith   Meredith is a fourth-grade student with multiple disabilities who spends all day in a general fourth-grade class. Fourth grade is the year in which she participates in assessment. Table 2.2 presents an overview of the critical skills identified for Meredith's IEP in one goal area.

The critical skills on Meredith's IEP were identified by her family using the COACH process, with input from others on her educational team including the fourth-grade teacher, the physical therapist, the occupational therapist, and the speech-language pathologist. Each of the critical skills was then translated into a short-term objective, which, in turn, included examples of the times during the day when she could practice that critical skill. In addition, the needed supports and adaptations were included for each objective.

SUMMARY

The articulation of the IEP with the curriculum standards determined for all students is an important IEP team consideration. Determining the critical function, or outcome, of a particular standard represents an important understanding for IEP teams as they develop an IEP that moves the student within the framework of the general curriculum. The process of specifically identifying on the IEP the appropriate activities and environments in which particular skills can be practiced is essential to ensuring students' acquisition and generalization of skills. Identifying supports, adaptations, and modifications increases the opportunity to learn because the teacher can determine appropriate opportunities for instruction and the student can respond appropriately in learning activities. All of these are essential for IEP teams to consider as they define what students with disabilities should know and be able to do in a standards-based environment.

REFERENCES

Blackhurst, A.E., & Berdine, W.H. (1993). Issues in special education. In A.E. Blackhurst & W.H. Berdine (Eds.), *An introduction to special education* (3rd ed., pp. 37–75). New York: HarperCollins.

Gast, D., & Schuster, D. (1993). Students with severe developmental disabilities. In A.E. Blackhurst & W.H. Berdine (Eds.), *An introduction to special education* (3rd ed., pp. 455–491). New York: HarperCollins.

Giangreco, M.F., Cloninger, C.J., & Iverson, V.S. (1998). *Choosing outcomes and accommodations for children (COACH): A guide to educational planning for students with disabilities* (2nd ed.). Baltimore: Paul H. Brookes Publishing Co.

Grisham-Brown, J.L., & Hemmeter, M.L. (1998). Writing IEP goals and objectives: Reflecting an activity based approach to instruction for children with disabilities. *Young Exceptional Children, 3*, 2–10.

Heward, W. (2000). *Exceptional children: An introduction to special education* (6th ed.). Columbus, OH: Merrill Prentice-Hall.

Hilton, A., & Liberty, K. (1992). The challenge of ensuring educational gains for children with disabilities who are placed in more integrated settings. *Education and Training in Mental Retardation, 27*, 167–175.

Individuals with Disabilities Education Act (IDEA) Amendments of 1997, PL 105-17, 20 U.S.C. §§ 1400 *et seq.*

Rainforth, B., & York-Barr, J. (1997). *Collaborative teams for students with severe disabilities: Integrating therapy and educational services* (2nd ed.). Baltimore: Paul H. Brookes Publishing Co.

Snell, M.E., & Brown, F. (1993). Instructional planning and implementation. In M.E. Snell (Ed.), *Instruction of students with severe disabilities* (4th ed., pp. 99–151). New York: Macmillan.

Weisenfeld, R.B. (1987). Functionality of IEPs of children with Down syndrome. *Mental Retardation, 25*, 281–286.

White, O. (1980). Adaptive performance objectives: Form versus function. In W. Sailor, B. Wilcox, & L. Brown (Eds.), *Methods of instruction for severely handicapped students* (pp. 47–69). Baltimore: Paul H. Brookes Publishing Co.

White, O. (1985). The evaluation of severely mentally retarded populations. In D. Bricker & J. Filler (Eds.), *Severe mental retardation: From theory to practice* (pp. 161–184). Lancaster, PA: Lancaster Press, Inc.

Wiggins, G. (1991), Standards not standardization: Evoking quality student work. *Educational Leadership, 48*(5), 18–25.

chapter 3

How do I develop
standards that "fit" all of my students?

HELPING STUDENTS WITH SIGNIFICANT DISABILITIES GAIN ACCESS TO GENERAL CURRICULUM STANDARDS

Jacqui Farmer Kearns

One of the keys to ensuring that students reach high performance goals is to require that all students be included in standards-based assessment systems. Indeed, Congress recognized this need and enacted *Title II, National Education Reform Leadership, Standards, and Assessments,* calling for state assessment systems to include all students as a part of its Goals 2000: Educate America Act of 1994 (PL 103-227). Requiring that students with disabilities be included in assessment programs, however, represents only a small portion of the challenge. In order to qualify for funds under Goals 2000, states are required to identify standards on which to judge the performance of students under Title I of the Elementary and Secondary Education Act. Consequently, state legislatures and state boards of education across the nation have adopted learning standards that form the foundation for assessment systems. More significantly, the reauthorization of the Individuals with Disabilities Education Act (IDEA) in 1997 (PL 105-17) mandated that state assessment systems include children with disabilities, either through the use of accommodations or through an appropriate alternate assessment. Although IDEA '97 stopped short of including students with disabilities in accountability systems (i.e., what states actually *do* with the scores in terms of consequences for schools and districts), states must report assessment results for children with disabilities. This requirement is, in part, to determine if students with disabilities are indeed benefiting from special education services mandated under IDEA. IDEA '97 thus brought the requirements that states must have performance goals and indicators for all students (612[a][16]) and that all students must participate in assessment programs. These requirements were necessary to ensure the "effectiveness of efforts to educate children with disabilities" (Sec. 601 [d]).

SO, WHAT IS A STANDARD, ANYWAY?

Merriam-Webster's Collegiate Dictionary, Tenth Edition, defines a standard as "something established by authority, custom, or general consent as a model or example" (1998, p. 1145). According to Lewis, there are four types of standards under discussion:

1. *Content standards* establish what should be learned in various content areas such as science, social studies, or mathematics. Generally, content standards are clear and measurable and describe what students should know.
2. *Performance standards,* often described as that which "a student should be able to do," define the degree to which students achieve at particular levels.
3. *Opportunity-to-learn* standards focus primarily on the conditions and resources necessary to level the playing field so that *all* students have an equal chance to achieve both content and performance standards. (Opportunity-to-learn standards are of particular importance to the discussion of inclusive assessment and accountability systems, in which decisions about student promotion, retention, or graduation may result from assessment.)
4. *"World Class"* standards are defined by examining and comparing the curricula in other countries that exemplify high levels of achievement in particular content areas. (1995, pp. 746–747)

How Standards Are Determined

Standards may be determined through open forums, such as town meetings, in an effort to develop a broad consensus on what students should know and be able to do. Standards-setting events may involve a significant number of content area teachers who evaluate tasks and develop standards for judging what constitutes high-quality student work or performance.

Generally, few special education teachers participate in standards-setting events at any level. Reasons for this vary; however, special education has operated historically as a separate educational system predicated on the notion that the general education curriculum is not for students in need of a special education (Skrtic, 1991). In fact, the field of special education is itself divided on the notion of whether students with significant disabilities should participate in the general curriculum and, if so, to what degree (Boundy, 2000; Kleinert & Kearns, 1999). This is no doubt related to the fact that special education has been focused primarily on *how* to teach students with significant disabilities. Curricular approaches for students with significant disabilities have ranged from developmental to functional, or a combination of these approaches. With the advent of inclusive school practices in the late 1980s and 1990s, determining how students with significant disabilities could gain access to the general curriculum became much more important (see Chapter 4 for specific examples of this access). Later in this chapter we present a curriculum planning framework for students with disabilities based on work done by Sizer (1992) and Wiggins and McTighe (1998) and articulated by Jorgensen (1995, 1998). This curriculum planning model explicitly links standards to the curriculum design process and considers how standards-based curriculum can be differentiated (Tomlinson, 1999) for those with diverse learning needs.

The Standards Dilemma

The notion of standards-based reform focuses on standards that, ideally, not only are high and rigorous but that also are sufficiently broad to provide flexibility at the local school level (Jorgensen, 1998). Standards should communicate to a variety of publics what students should know and be able to do, but they should not limit the ways in which learning occurs. In his book *The Schools Our Children Deserve*, Alfie Kohn (1999) argued that higher standards often get translated into "harder standards"; harder standards, in turn, offer less flexibility than do broader standards in terms of instructional strategies used to help students achieve them. Similarly, in an interview, Glickman commented, "It's a bit scary when narrow standards are established for every academic area; there are single-format tests; and a level of mastery is established [based on] one group's idea of what every student should learn by a certain time" (2000, p. 7). Sarason (1990) poignantly suggested that our current educational system fails children by mandating that everyone learn the same thing, at the same time, regardless of individual concerns.

Sizer (1992) posited that different types of skills, including *habits of mind* (e.g., diligence, tolerance, collaboration, critical thinking) as well as *content area* knowledge (e.g., science, social studies, language arts) and *basic academic* skills (e.g., reading, writing, mathematics) are needed by students to survive in our world. Ford, Davern, and Schnoor (1992) suggested that a common curricular framework helps teachers to identify what is important for all learners, including those with disabilities. This represents a broad standards approach, in which standards address a variety of life outcomes. Such broad standards as thinking and problem-solving are rarely included in assessments because of the difficulty in designing assessments that measure them appropriately using traditional paper-and-pencil formats.

It is important, then, to consider the ways in which standards are written in order to identify their ultimate purpose. Defining their ultimate purpose is in keeping with Owen White's (1980) concept of critical function described in Chapter 2. The following examples represent one approach to standards for mathematics:

1. Students demonstrate understanding of number concepts.
2. Students demonstrate understanding of concepts of mathematical procedures.
3. Students demonstrate understanding of concepts related to space and dimensionality.
4. Students demonstrate understanding of measurement concepts.
5. Students demonstrate understanding of change concepts of patterns and functions.
6. Students demonstrate understanding of concepts related to mathematic structure.
7. Students demonstrate understanding of data concepts related to certain and uncertain events.

These standards statements reflect broad outcomes that include the purpose of the concepts in real-life learning situations, and can be used in a variety of content applications across grade levels. They represent the ceiling of the learning, leaving the floor open to a variety of entry points. This is important because rarely do all students enter instruction at the same level of understanding. In contrast to these broad standards, the following is an example of a narrowly articulated standard from algebra:

> Students will solve linear and quadratic equations.

In this second example, the standard doesn't illuminate the ultimate result of learning algebra. In fact, the broad standards shown in this example indicate that students should understand change concepts of patterns and functions, which represent at least one of the *outcomes* of applying principles of algebra. If you ask most adults about their experiences with algebra, few will be able to articulate the important skills (e.g., quadratic equations, solving for roots). If, however, instruction focuses on the actual application of algebra in everyday life—such as identifying patterns and functions or using a quadratic equation to make a prediction about a phenomenon—one can identify a number of daily situations in which those skills are used. In addition, algebra generally is thought of as a high school course, when indeed, the foundations for algebra can begin as early as the primary school years.

Finally, a third set of examples represents standards that are narrowly defined for a particular age or grade level.

> **Grade 3**
> 1. The student will solve story problems involving one-step solutions and using basic addition and subtraction facts.
> 2. The student will count, compare, and make change using coins and bills.
> 3. The student will determine the value of a collection of coins and bills up to $5.00.

Standards that are defined in this way represent skills that students should acquire, but such standards fail to illuminate the purpose or function of these skills in a real-world application. Although third-grade students should make change for coins and bills up to $5.00, the real-world application of counting change occurs when the student purchases an item or service. It is important in this case to consider from a developmental point of view how typical third-grade students purchase items and within what range their purchases usually occur. A typical third-grade student may purchase school supplies from a machine and lunch or snacks from the cafeteria, or he or she may save for a special item. In any event, however, third-grade students are not likely to purchase items without the direct supervision of an adult, so the level of independence of counting change is very tied to the age of the student. In addition, in many cases an educator's interpretation of how to teach students to count change will be based on the third-grade math textbook, instead of authentic activities in which money is really exchanged. In this way, narrowly defined standards for grade levels may conflict with the developmental process of learning—particularly for young learners.

Narrow standards tend to be skills based instead of outcome based, which in effect may limit teachers to using skill-based instruction rather than instruction that considers the outcome of learning through authentic experiences and real-life tasks. Another problem with narrowly defined standards is that there generally are an overwhelming number of such standards. Because students with significant cognitive disabilities typically learn at a slower rate, it becomes more important to identify those skills (or standards) that are likely to be used in multiple environments and across daily activities. In cases in which standards have been broadly defined in terms of the outcome instead of the skill, it is easier to find appropriate content and performance indicators for a variety of learners, including those with significant disabilities. Standards that have been narrowly defined not only present difficulties in terms of finding alternative entry points to the standard, but also they often fail to illuminate how instruction might focus on the ways the standards are used in real life. IDEA '97 requires individualized education program (IEP) teams to document the extent to which students with disabilities progress in and have access to the general education curriculum. Because students with disabilities must be included in assessments to determine their benefit from special education as well as their progress in the general curriculum, the central issue becomes how to meaningfully articulate those standards (that determine the general curriculum) for students who have significant disabilities.

APPLYING CURRICULUM STANDARDS IN EVERYDAY LIFE

The key to accessing general curriculum standards for any student has to do with designing instructional activities that require him or her to demonstrate authentic or real-life performances. Table 3.1 illustrates instructional activities designed for typical students at the elementary, middle, and high school levels who might be asked to address the same standard of accessing information. Activities that address this standard include retelling a news broadcast, investigating the purposes behind school rules, and surveying community support services. In each of these cases, the student takes on discipline-based roles including a television broadcaster, leader of school committee, or social worker, and produces useful authentic materials such as oral presentations, brochures, and databases. These instructional activities represent a universal curriculum design (Meyer & Rose, 2000). Universal designs increase the probability that the curriculum becomes a continuum in which a variety of learners with diverse needs can be accommodated.

Although some students with significant learning needs may not be able to do these activities independently, they can participate in these activities by working in cooperative learning groups, which in turn maximize opportunities to practice those critical skills (e.g., communication, social, and motor skills) that already exist in most instructional activities. Partial participation refers to the assumption that a person has the right to participate in any and all activities to the maximum extent possible. This principle further suggests that it is better for students with diverse learning needs to participate partially than to be denied access altogether.

For example, a student can participate in the science lesson about the solar system when the lesson for all learners is making papier-mâché planets. She or he may be working on reach and grasp, focusing attention on the papier-mâché materials, or choosing a partner to work on the project. In addition to reach and grasp, the student may also be working on appropriate social interaction skills such as turn-taking or complimenting others. Furthermore, as a part of content learning she or he may also differentiate planets, such as Earth, Mars, or Saturn.

How Students with Significant Disabilities Participate in General Activities

Thousand (1986) identified four ways in which students with significant disabilities learn in the context of regular curricular activities. Students may participate 1) in curricular activities in the same way as other students; 2) in the same activities, but at a different level in that subject than other students (multilevel); 3) in the same activities, but with different educational goals that are embedded into classroom activities and routines (embedded or overlapping curricular objectives); and 4) in different activities with different goals, but related to the classroom activities. Figure 3.1 illustrates four different ways students with diverse learning needs may participate in the curriculum.

By combining the work of White (1980) regarding the form and function of behavior with the work of Thousand (1986) in determining how children with disabilities are included in general education classrooms, we describe a model of how children with disabilities gain access to general curriculum standards—whether those standards are narrowly or broadly determined.

Students with disabilities can gain access to the general curriculum standards in at least four ways. First, some students with disabilities may demonstrate a particular standard—whether narrowly or broadly stated—exactly as it is written. For example, a third-grade student may count change up to $5.00. For students with disabilities in particular, it is more likely that they will respond appropriately

Table 3.1.   Examples of activities across grade levels to help students meet the standard "Accessing Information"

Elementary school grade levels

Watch a news broadcast on television and retell it for a student audience.

Middle school grade levels

Investigate the reason behind a school rule by interviewing teachers, principal, parents, and students. Organize the information using a database. Prepare a report for the school newscast.

High school grade levels

Create a database of student support services in the community. Publish your findings in a brochure for student use.

From Kentucky Department of Education (1994). *Transformations.* Frankfort: Author; adapted by permission.

within a natural context in which the skill is required rather than on a multiple-choice test or a workbook page.

The second way a student with a disability may gain access to the standards is through an alternate form (White, 1980). The alternate form requires the same level of cognition, but a different response format is necessary. For example, a student may give a presentation by using an augmentative or alternative communication system if she or he cannot speak.

A third way to gain access to the general curriculum standards is to determine the critical function (White, 1980) of the standard. The skill of estimation is used in making purchases. Teaching the student to count the correct number of dollars and then add a dollar for change (next-dollar strategy) accomplishes the purpose of the standard (estimation), and then the function or outcome of the standard has been accomplished. Generally, the critical function represents a modification of the level and complexity of the standard but accomplishes the same purpose or outcome.

The fourth way in which a few students with disabilities will gain access to standards is through *critical* (see Chapter 2) or *access* skills (e.g., requesting assistance, making choices). These students are working on very basic skills that are embedded in standards-based activities. In these cases, the opportunity to learn alongside peers, even though the student may have very different learning goals, maximizes the opportunities to practice these critical access skills. In addition, practicing these skills within the context of standards-based activities increases the probability that students may learn incidental content information. In this

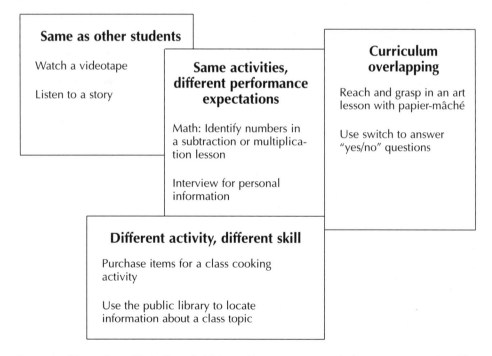

Same as other students

Watch a videotape

Listen to a story

Same activities, different performance expectations

Math: Identify numbers in a subtraction or multiplication lesson

Interview for personal information

Curriculum overlapping

Reach and grasp in an art lesson with papier-mâché

Use switch to answer "yes/no" questions

Different activity, different skill

Purchase items for a class cooking activity

Use the public library to locate information about a class topic

Figure 3.1.   Ways students with significant disabilities could participate in general education activities. (Adapted from Thousand, J. [1986]. *The homecoming model: Educating students who present intensive educational challenges within regular education environments.* Burlington: University of Vermont.)

way, opportunity-to-learn standards play a critical role in the acquisition of skills for these students. Simply practicing critical or access skills in isolation of general curriculum activities does not achieve the same level of access to the general curriculum. The opportunity to learn the content, along with the natural supports readily available in general education classrooms, maximizes the probability that skills will be acquired. Figure 3.2 illustrates the four ways of accessing the curriculum standards for all students

USING STANDARDS TO GUIDE CURRICULUM

Chapters 2 and 3 have discussed in detail the importance of instructional activities that articulate standards. This task is made easier, as noted, when the teacher is working from broadly stated standards. Yet, what if your state has developed highly subject-specific or narrowly stated standards? When working with standards that represent narrowly defined skills, it is necessary to first convert those standards into instructional activities. The example in Table 3.2 illustrates how to articulate standards and skills into activities.

A real-life context for solving story problems with one-step solutions might be one in which educators choose to act out a story or picture problems for elementary-age students; they also could choose to practice solving story problems during regularly occurring activities such as snack time or lunch time. High school students with disabilities may solve one-step problems while their peers complete more complex math problems, but within a naturally occurring context (e.g., ordering items for the school store, accounting for yearbook sales). Once an instructional activity has been determined, a number of critical skills selected from the student's IEP or the curriculum itself can be identified and practiced within the context of that selected activity. Consequently, those critical skills can be viewed alternately as *access skills* because they provide students with significant disabilities a way to access the standards-based curriculum.

In Kentucky, to facilitate the inclusion of students with disabilities in standards-based learning activities, Dyer and Kearns developed a companion docu-

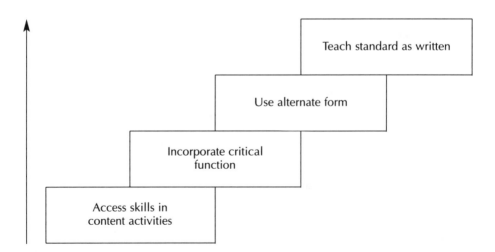

Figure 3.2. Good practices for helping all students access general curriculum standards. The arrow shows how each step builds on the one before it.

ment to highlight the ways in which activities and skills can be combined: *TASKS: Teaching All Students in Kentucky Schools* (1998) provided many examples of activities that articulate the standards and the "critical" or "access" skills for both general and special education teachers. Figure 3.3 highlights the academic expectation or standard: "Students organize information through development and use of classification."

Developing Rich Instructional Activities

From the *TASKS* (Dyer & Kearns, 1998) examples you can see that students with diverse abilities can work together in standards-based frameworks, albeit with varying degrees of sophistication. The instructional activities make all the difference. By having students participate in rich, engaging instructional activities that include a range of standards, educators demonstrate a key understanding of how students with significant disabilities gain access to the general curriculum. In effect, these instructional planning techniques bridge the views about curriculum in special education. They allow teachers to address functional learning as well as developmental learning; for example, a student may work on personal information practices by developing a personal narrative in Language Arts, while another student may use a switch to answer "yes/no" to personal information questions.

Jorgensen (1995) has suggested that students with disabilities can be meaningfully included at any level provided that the following three conditions are met:

1. Teachers plan collaboratively.
2. Curriculum design planning occurs backward from expected outcomes to a final student exhibition ending with lesson design, rather than beginning with lesson design.
3. Overarching or essential questions are used to guide performance-based curriculum development.

Similarly, curricular units should be planned with the end in mind (Jorgensen, 1995, 1998; Tyler, 1949; Wiggins & McTighe, 1998). Stephen Covey (1989) suggested that beginning with the end in mind means starting with a clear understanding of your destination. This backward planning process requires that the desired results be identified first, that acceptable evidence of mastery be determined next, and that planning the learning activities or instruction occur as the

Table 3.2. Articulating skill-based standards

Standards area: computation and estimation	Instructional activities; real-life applications	Related critical access skills
Solve story and picture problems involving one-step solutions	Serve snack	React to objects
	Divide into teams	Express more
	Pass out materials	Reach and grasp
		Count with one-to-one correspondence (e.g., passing out papers: each person gets one piece of paper)

One activity/project that could be shared with elementary school learners:

GOAL 1: Use basic communication and mathematics skills.

Academic expectation 1.10: Students organize information through development and use of classification.

A. One sample instructional activity/project for elementary learners that incorporates this academic expectation could be

Each student is asked to bring a stuffed animal to school. The class then identifies a classification system and places the stuffed animals on the shelf. Then, three groups of students are each asked to determine an alternative way to organize the stuffed animals on the shelf.

B. Ways students with diverse educational abilities and instructional needs could demonstrate this academic expectation within this sample class activity:

(1) The student will correctly respond to "same or different" question with either "yes" or "no" when a peer holds up two stuffed animals and asks the question, "Are these bears the same color?"

(2) Given a varied set of animals, the student will find all the "bean bag animals."

(3) The student will state how two animals are the same (e.g., same color, both bears have big eyes).

(4) The student will choose between three options to determine which animal would be the best to hug.

(5) After observing a stuffed toy, the toy will be placed in a box out of view and the student will answer "yes/no" questions about characteristics of the stuffed animal.

(6)

(7)

(8)

(9)

(10)

C. Ideas for providing students with diverse educational abilities and instructional needs with opportunities to practice basic skills and critical activities found on their IEPs while participating in this class activity:

(1) The student will hold a stuffed animal in each hand and walk to the shelf without losing balance or significantly altering normal gait. [Targeted skills: communication skills, motor skills] {COACH: COMMUNICATION #7}

(2) The student will play with another student with the stuffed toy in the house-keeping center. [Targeted skills: social skills, critical recreation/leisure activity] {COACH: COMMUNICATION #3, #5 #8; SOCIALIZATION #13, #14, #15, #19, #20, #22; LEISURE/RECREATION #40}

(3) The student will use a series of phrases including nouns, verbs, and adjectives to describe a stuffed animal. [Targeted skills: communication skills] {COACH: COMMUNICATION #11}

(4)

(5)

Figure 3.3. Examples of activities that articulate standards and the critical or access skills for general and special education teachers. (From Dyer, L., & Kearns, J.F. [1998]. *TASKS: Teaching all students in Kentucky schools.* Lexington: University of Kentucky; reprinted by permission.) (*Note:* Mentions of COACH refer to Giangreco, M.F., Cloninger, C.J., & Iverson, V.S. [1998]. *Choosing options and accommodations for children [COACH]: A guide to planning inclusive education,* [2nd ed.]. Baltimore: Paul H. Brookes Publishing Co.)

One activity/project that could be shared with middle school learners:

GOAL 1: Use basic communication and mathematics skills.

Academic expectation 1.10: Students organize information through development and use of classification.

A. One sample instructional activity/project for middle school learners that incorporates this academic expectation could be

> *Each student will construct a genealogical chart of his family depicting at least three generations.*

B. Ways students with diverse educational abilities and instructional needs could demonstrate this academic expectation within this sample class activity:

  (1) The student will verbally answer questions about the identity of members of his or her family (e.g., "What is your father's name?" "Is your sister's name Elizabeth?")

  (2) Given pictures of individual clearly in one of three generations, upon verbal request by peer, the student will point to the boy or girl, mother or father, or grandmother or grandfather.

  (3) The student and a peer will record the voices of the student's immediate family members.

  (4) Given a number of photographs of family members and unfamiliar individuals, the student will point to members of his family.

  (5) The student will respond in a positive manner, to the presence of his mother's and/or father's voice.

  (6)

  (7)

  (8)

  (9)

  (10)

C. Ideas for providing students with diverse educational abilities and instructional needs with opportunities to practice basic skills and critical activities found on their IEPs while participating in this class activity:

  (1) Working with a peer without disabilities, student will follow one-step verbal directions to construct a chart of his immediate family using photographs [Targeted skills: communication skills, motor skills] {COACH: COMMUNICATION #7; SOCIALIZATION #19}

  (2) The student will travel into the community and purchase the items necessary to construct a bulletin board display of each student's genealogical chart. [Targeted skills: critical community activity] {COACH: COMMUNITY #73, #76}

  (3) With the assistance of a peer, the student will write the names of family members on his genealogical chart. [Targeted skills: communication skills, socialization skills, functional academic skills, basic motor skills] {COACH: COMMUNICATION #7; SOCIALIZATION #19; APPLIED ACADEMICS #42, #44, #45, #46, #47, #55; SCHOOL #67}

  (4)

  (5)

(continued)

Figure 3.3. *(continued)*

Classifying

One activity/project that could be shared with high school learners:

GOAL 1: Use basic communication and mathematics skills.

Academic expectation 1.10: Students organize information through development and use of classification.

A. One sample instructional activity/project for high school learners that incorporates this academic expectation could be

    Students will collect videotape samples of television advertisements, define characteristics, develop a scheme for classification strategies used to convince the buyer, and make a visual documentation of the classification system.

B. Ways students with diverse educational abilities and instructional needs could demonstrate this academic expectation within this sample class activity:

    (1) When viewing a television program at home with peers from school, the student will discriminate between entertainment ("television show") and commercial, when asked by the peer, "What are you watching?"

    (2) When shown two commercials, and asked how they are the same, the student will answer correctly (e.g., "They are both selling cars." "They are selling soap.").

    (3) Shown a television advertisement for a product and given three picture symbols defining different products (e.g., breakfast cereal, toothpaste, cars) the student will point to the correct picture symbol.

    (4) The student will identify techniques used in the television advertisement (e.g., music, singing, dancing, children, celebrities), when asked "How are they selling the product?"

    (5) The student will respond to a preferred song, slogan, or individual on the television by changing activity level, specific body movements, expression, or vocalization.

    (6)

    (7)

    (8)

    (9)

    (10)

C. Ideas for providing students with diverse educational abilities and instructional needs with opportunities to practice basic skills and critical activities found on their IEPs. While participating in this class activity:

    (1) The student will operate the videocassette recorder so peers can view videotapes of commercials. [Targeted skills: motor skills, critical recreation/leisure activity] {COACH: COMMUNICATION, #7; SELECTED ACADEMICS #44, #45, #46}

    (2) During classroom group activities, the student will participate in the discussion of each commercial. [Targeted skills: communication skills, social skills] {COACH: COMMUNICATION #2, #8, #9, #10, #11; SOCIALIZATION #13; SCHOOL #66]

    (3) The student will use next-dollar strategy to purchase videocassettes at three different community stores. [Targeted skills: functional academic skills, critical community activities] {COACH: SELECTED ACADEMICS #52; COMMUNITY #73, #76}

    (4)

    (5)

More ideas and examples:

Goal 1: Use basic communication and mathematics skills

Academic expectation 1.10: Students organize information through development and use of classification.

General demonstrators of this academic expectation that may be appropriate for students with diverse educational and instructional needs and might be adapted to a variety of age-appropriate activities or projects:

The student will

(1) Find two items that are the "same," given a set of items.

(2) Find the item that is different, given a set of items.

(3) Sort items into two groups by category (e.g., foods, animals, toys).

(4) Put items into sequence by size.

(5) Sort items into groups by one physical characteristic (e.g., color, shape, texture).

(6) State whether a peer is a boy or girl.

(7) Go to the correct section of a grocery store to find a specific item.

(8) Proceed to the appropriate location in the community to complete an assigned task (e.g., mail a letter, do laundry, purchase a banana).

(9) Sort laundry at the launderette.

(10) State verbally how two objects are the "same."

(11) Find a source of community services in the city, state, county, and federal sections of the telephone book.

(12) Find the telephone number of a taxi in the yellow pages of the telephone book.

(13) Put materials away in their appropriate location in the classroom.

(14) Make a choice to use a fork or spoon with a specific food at lunch.

(15) Distinguish between and act differently with familiar people, acquaintances, and strangers.

(16)

(17)

(18)

(19)

(20)

If you are using COACH 2nd ed., the following COACH activities might fall within this academic expectation:

SOCIALIZATION: #16, Distinguishes between and interacts differently with familiar people, acquaintances, and strangers.

SELECTED ACADEMICS: #44, Differentiates/discriminates between various things final step (Wiggins & McTighe, 1998). Using this reverse planning process forms the foundation from which a unified curriculum can be designed that is inclusive of all students.

The first step involves identifying the unit organizers. Organizers should focus on a real-life issue, problem, or question that the students will encounter as a part of the learning. Below are examples of the three types of organizers:

Life Issue: Saving our environment
Problem: How can we control the effects of pesticides?
Question: Is your lunchbox hazardous to your health?

Organizers, with essential or guiding questions, (Jorgensen, 1995; Wiggins & McTighe, 1998) have common characteristics. They are open ended yet focus on inquiry; they are nonjudgmental, but answering them requires high-level cognitive work; they "hook" students or provide "intellectual bite"; and they are succinct but demanding. Jorgensen (1998) suggested that these types of organizers can be answered on multiple levels, which means any student can provide answers. Here is an example of an organizer with essential questions:

Is your lunchbox hazardous to your health?
- What are nutritious foods?
- What do nutritious foods do for your body?
- Do people in your school choose nutritious foods?

According to Jorgensen (1998) and Wiggins and McTighe (1998), the important criteria for teachers to consider when developing standards include the following: 1) Does it have value beyond the classroom? 2) Does it involve creating a context for real-life learning? 3) Can it be discovered by students? 4) Is it interesting and engaging? 5) What will students remember once the work is done? (Jorgensen, 1998).

To answer these questions about nutrition, teachers should begin to consider which standards could be addressed within the context of such instruction. Some examples may include communicating through a variety of media, expressing ideas clearly in writing, gaining access to information from a variety of sources, and solving problems. In addition, making healthy nutritional choices may fall under content standards for maintaining physical health.

For students with significant disabilities, the question "What do I expect the student to remember?" is even more important but does not mean that what other students are learning is not an important context for their learning. Indeed, the social context of learning with typical students provides an added bonus for students who need multiple opportunities to practice social and communication skills. The question becomes more focused and the learning more individualized.

For example, at one urban school the fourth grade includes science inquiry standards. The team of teachers decides to use electricity as the context for teaching science inquiry. They design an instructional unit about electricity that includes building a complete circuit as a culminating activity. Alan, a student who has autism, also learns about electricity in the unit. His learning targets include 1) identifying the components of a circuit (content vocabulary), 2) following verbal two- and three-step directions to assemble the circuit (critical skill) and 3) practicing safety in working with electricity (functional skill). Because Alan works with other students, he also works on social and communication skills in natural contexts. Figure 3.4 presents a worksheet for teachers that is based on Jorgensen's "essential questions" unit design.

KEEPING THE END IN MIND: CULMINATING PERFORMANCES

Determining a final product or culminating performance increases the probability that students will practice a variety of skills from a variety of standards areas. This signifies the end of the instructional unit and includes the demonstrators that students should accomplish. The culminating performance should reflect that students have acquired genuinely useful skills and knowledge and raises issues that are both personal and real-world. A culminating performance should challenge students by requiring persistence, organization, and inquiry (Jorgensen, 1998; Wiggins & McTighe, 1998). In addition, it should prompt students to stretch their minds and make connections to real-life situations.

Teachers should consider how to allow adequate time and flexibility for students to accomplish serious and comprehensive work. A culminating performance or final exhibition for the instructional unit "Is your lunchbox hazardous to your health" could be a nutrition fair with student-developed posters and exhibits on various aspects of selecting nutritious foods. Students might develop posters, pamphlets, or videotapes about healthy eating. Students might also use research tools to find out about the eating habits in their school. Students with disabilities or diverse learning needs may participate in these culminating performances either through group or individual work.

The following examples suggest how students with learning challenges can participate in this unit of study:

- Sarah, a student with significant disabilities who is participating in the nutrition unit, may select pictures of milk for her poster. She may use a micro-switch to blend milk shakes for the nutrition fair. She may sort nutritious and non-nutritious food by answering "yes/no" questions using her Big Button switches (AbleNet, 1991).
- Lyle, a high school student with a moderate disability, may prepare nutritious lunches and snacks for weight management.
- Amy may work with a peer, Amanda, to develop a computer slide show about the special diet that Amy needs. Amy may select the pictures of the foods for the slide show while Amanda writes the copy for the slides. During their presentation, Amy might also use a switch to change the slides while Amanda reads the copy.

Planning Guide

Topic of Instruction: _____

Unit: _____

Step 1: Determine essential questions.

What do we want students to remember about this unit (core content)?

What should they be able to do once they have forgotten the details?

Step 2: Determine academic standards to be incorporated into this unit.

- Language Arts

- Mathematics

- Science/Technology

- Social Studies

Step 3: Develop culminating performances.
- Reflect useful knowledge and skills
- Demand intense student work and preparation
- Require persistence, organization, and inquiry
- Put knowledge and skills in sensible context
- Allow student to accomplish serious comprehensive work

Step 4: Determine instructional and assessment activities.
- Instructional activities serve as assessment activities
- Should incorporate student learning styles and modalities
- Should address multiple intelligences

Step 5: Determine accommodations for learners with special needs.
- Locate high interest–low vocabulary reading materials
- Locate extension materials for gifted learners
- How will students with more significant challenges participate?
    - Same as everyone else
    - Same activities/different materials
    - Same activities/different skills
    - Related activity/different skills

Figure 3.4.   Planning guide for instructional unit development.

Student #1:

Student #2:

Student #3:

Student #4:

Student #5:

Student #6:

Step 6: Determine evaluation methods.
- Scoring rubrics
  - Evaluative criteria
  - Quality definitions
  - Scoring strategy
- Basic skill data collection

Step 7: Locate community resources.
What community resources are available?

Step 8: Determine roles and responsibilities.
Who will do what? When?

- Jeremy's group is tracking healthy foods in lunchboxes. As the group investigates the lunches by asking the other students to volunteer a list of what they have brought, Jeremy may tally the number of healthy foods by using a bingo stamp and a specially designed tally sheet.

It is important to note that although the topic of the instruction is health and fitness, a number of standards including those found in language arts, math, and technology can be practiced in the context of these rich activities.

MERGING INSTRUCTION AND ASSESSMENT

Instructional activities refer to the daily instructional tasks that incorporate the standards and that address individual student learning styles, talents, and interests. Wiggins and McTighe described the assessment process as a continuum of assessment types that are reliable and valid, authentic, feasible, sufficient, and student-friendly (1998). Instructional activities may also serve as assessment activities and yield performance tasks and projects, systematic instructional performance data, or other means of verifying skills. Daily instructional activities also serve as assessments in that they require students to perform skills that are inclusive and applicable to real-life problems. Consider learning styles, reading levels, and special accommodations that provide an opportunity to learn. There is a wider range of assessment options for typical students than for students with disabilities. Assessment strategies for students with disabilities are merged with instruction through the following:

- Assessment products (performance tasks and projects or work samples)
- Systematic instructional data on specific skills
- On-demand or prompted performance using videotape
- Peer/outside observer reports

Performance tasks or projects represent authentic tasks that include the real work of the content area discipline (e.g., mathematician, writer, scientist) (Wiggins & McTighe, 1998). Systematic instructional data yield tried-and-true results for students with significant disabilities and are similar to the type of data that might come from quizzes or tests. Peer or observer reports provide an added dimension of validity. For example, a parent may write a note or a peer may interpret a student's action and write about it. A peer may describe his or her role in the project or activity and also identify what the student with a significant disability gained from the experience.

All of the activities in the nutrition unit yield assessment products. Sarah's poster about milk required choosing appropriate pictures, placing them on the poster, and choosing appropriate captions. Systematic instructional data (see Wolery, Bailey, & Sugai, 1988) on sorting healthy foods and the use of Sarah's switches, along with a videotape showing her choosing healthy snacks and a note from her partner in the poster project, clarify what Sarah knows and is able to do for her IEP goals while they highlight her understanding of the health concepts, as well. The pieces of evidence triangulate to improve the validity of the assessment. In addition, they represent authentic work, are feasible, and are student-friendly.

Lyle may include assessment products such as his food intake log, his weight chart, and his exercise log. The teacher might collect performance data on Lyle's food preparation safety (e.g., washing hands, using clean utensils, wrapping food correctly, making sure that cold foods stay cold).

A printed copy of the slide show produced by Amy and Amanda, along with the teacher's instructional data of the number of prompts required to activate the switch during the slide show, highlights Amy's work. Amanda adds a note detailing what she and Amanda have learned. Likewise, Jeremy's tally sheets from investigating the lunchboxes are included as an assessment product; systematic instructional data on reaching and grasping the bingo stamp and following instructions also clarify how Jeremy is participating in the work and document his performance.

All of these products are the result of daily instructional activities designed for this unit of study over a period of a few weeks. Instructional data, work samples, peer reports, videotapes, and audiotapes provide rich data sources from which to document skill acquisition and the access to the general curriculum for students with significant disabilities. Organizing these materials in a portfolio allows the student and his or her family to see tangible evidence of progress and performance. Portfolios further provide holistic data for making decisions about future learning opportunities.

SUMMARY

In a survey of educators who teach individuals with significant disabilities regarding outcomes they believe are most important for these students, Kleinert and Kearns (1999) found that the following five outcomes were rated as most important: 1) social skills, 2) communication skills, 3) physical wellness, 4) emotional wellness, and 5) choice-making. Social and communication skills are best taught in natural environments in which students have the opportunity to practice those skills. Social skills are best learned in social relationships, and students improve their communication skills when they have opportunities to communicate with peers. All of these can be taught within the context of interesting, engaging instructional activities that are based on authentic activities requiring real-life learning.

In special education there is a longstanding debate about what students with disabilities should and do know. We believe strongly that the general curriculum should be the first consideration for IEP teams. Standards thus represent the framework that supports the body of instructional/assessment activities. The four ways that students with disabilities gain access to the standards-based curriculum help to cut through the instructional barriers. The features of instructional design that we have discussed make it easier to include a wide variety of learners in learning activities. In the next chapter, we provide specific examples—at the elementary, middle, and high school levels—of how students with significant disabilities can access the general curriculum based on the standards that are identified for all learners.

REFERENCES

AbleNet, Inc. (1991) Big Button Switches. Minneapolis, MN: Author. http://www.ablenet.com.

Boundy, K. (2000). Including students with disabilities in standards-based education reform. *TASH Newsletter 26*(4), 4–21.

Covey, S. (1989). *Seven habits of highly effective people.* New York: Simon & Schuster.

Dyer, L., & Kearns, J.F. (1998). *TASKS: Teaching all students in Kentucky schools.* Lexington: University of Kentucky.

Ford, A., Davern, L., & Schnor, R. (1992). Inclusive education: Making sense of the curriculum. In S. Stainback & W. Stainback (Eds.), *Curriculum considerations in inclusive classrooms: Facilitating learning for all students* (pp. 37–61). Baltimore: Paul H. Brookes Publishing Co.

Glickman, C. (2000). The good and bad of standards. *ASCD Education Update, 42*(4), 7.

Goals 2000: Educate America Act of 1994, PL 103-227, 20 U.S.C. §§5801 *et seq.*

Individuals with Disabilities Education Act (IDEA) Amendments of 1997, PL 105-17, 20 U.S.C. §§1400 *et seq.*

Jorgensen, C.M. (1995). Essential questions, inclusive answers. *Educational Leadership, 52* (4), 52–55.

Jorgensen, C.M. (1998). *Restructuring high schools for all students: Taking inclusion to the next level.* Baltimore: Paul H. Brookes Publishing Co.

Kentucky Department of Education (1994). *Transformations.* Frankfort: Author.

Kleinert, H.L., & Kearns, J.F. (1999). A validation study of the performance indicators and learner outcomes of Kentucky's alternate assessment. *Journal of The Association for Persons with Severe Handicaps, 24*(2), 100–110.

Kohn, A. (1999). *The schools our children deserve.* New York: Houghton-Mifflin.

Lewis, A. (1995). An overview of the standards movement. *Phi Delta Kappan, 76*(10), 746–750.

The Merriam-Webster collegiate dictionary (10th ed.). (1998). Springfield, MA: Merriam-Webster.

Meyer, A., & Rose, D. (2000). Universal design for individual differences. *Educational Leadership, 58*(3), 39–43.

Sarason, S. (1990). *The predictable failure of educational reform: Can we change course before it's too late?* San Francisco: Jossey-Bass.

Sizer, T. (1992). *Horace's school: Redesigning the American high school.* Boston: Houghton-Mifflin.

Skrtic, T. (1991). *Behind special education.* Denver, CO: Love Publishing.

Thousand, J. (1986). *The homecoming model: Educating students who present intensive educational challenges within regular education environments.* Burlington: University of Vermont.

Tomlinson, C. (1999). *The differentiated classroom: Responding to the needs of all learners.* Alexandria, VA: Association for Supervision and Curriculum Development.

Tyler, R. (1949). *Basic principles of curriculum and instruction.* Chicago: University of Chicago Press.

White, O.R. (1980). Adaptive performance objectives: Form versus function. In W. Sailor, B. Wilcox, & L. Brown (Eds.), *Methods of instruction for severely handicapped students* (pp. 47–69). Baltimore: Paul H. Brookes Publishing Co.

Wiggins, G., & McTighe, J. (1998). *Understanding by design.* Alexandria, VA: Association for Supervision and Curriculum Development.

Wolery, M., Bailey, D., & Sugai, G. (1988). *Effective teaching: Principles and procedures of applied behavior analysis with exceptional students.* Needham Heights, MA: Allyn & Bacon.

chapter 4

*What does alternate assessment
"look like" in real classrooms?*

INTEGRATING ALTERNATE
ASSESSMENT IN THE
GENERAL CURRICULUM

Mike Burdge, Vanessa Burke Groneck, Harold L. Kleinert,
Amy Wildman Longwill, Jean Clayton, Anne Denham,
and Jacqui Farmer Kearns

This chapter provides readers with a clear picture of how general education activities can give students a meaningful context for learning targeted individualized education program (IEP) objectives. It also shows how educators can document that learning in the format of an alternate assessment. To meet these objectives, this chapter includes a series of examples that span grade levels and subject areas, as a well as a framework for achieving them. Many excellent texts and resources describing the process for including students with significant disabilities in general education classes are available (Cole, Horvath, Chapman, Deschenes, Ebeling, & Sprague, 2000; Falvey, 1995; Giangreco, 1997, 1998; Giangreco, Cloninger, & Iverson, 1998; Jorgensen, 1998), and it is not our intent to duplicate those materials. Rather, the following examples—and the framework described here—are intended to give the reader a perspective on how teachers can use the kinds of performance data they may already be collecting as a rich source of evidence for their state's or district's alternate assessment. We have drawn our examples either from actual students who have participated in statewide alternate assessments or from composites of students with whom we have worked. Because we have found that teachers struggle most with issues of high school inclusion, we have provided the greatest level of detail in the high school examples. We describe our examples within a useful planning format.

RELATING STUDENT OBJECTIVES TO
GENERAL EDUCATION UNITS AND STANDARDS-BASED ASSESSMENTS

Figure 4.1 presents a blank planning form for adapting a general education lesson or unit, which allows collaborating teachers to identify the academic standards and classwide learning objectives that will be addressed for a specific general education unit. This form provides a place for teachers to identify each of the
major activities within the unit, the IEP goals/objectives that will be addressed for
the target student, the person(s) responsible for providing instruction on those
objectives, and Additional Learning Outcomes (that may also be addressed for
that student in the context of each activity. For a complete description of
Additional Learning Outcomes, the reader is referred to *COACH, Second Edition.*
(Giangreco et al., 1998). Briefly, they are the second-highest set of learning priorities for a student (after the IEP objectives have been chosen). These comprise
academic outcomes identified from the general education curriculum and sec-
ond-priority skills identified from *COACH.* Additional Learning Outcomes, thus,
are a means to ensure that a student with a significant disability receives targeted
instruction not only on priority embedded skills (e.g., goals for communicating,
making choices, initiating and sustaining interactions) but also on at least a portion of the academic content. To illustrate this process, let's consider the example
in the following section of how Marcie, a student with a significant disability, participates in her fourth-grade geography class.

Elementary School Examples

Here are some examples of ways to integrate elementary school students with
disabilities into the general curriculum.

Learning About Geology in Fourth-Grade Social Studies   One state includes a
social studies standard for students to "recognize and understand the relationship
between people and geography and apply their knowledge in real-life situations."
A fourth-grade class in that state is working on a unit in geography, Changing
Landforms, toward achieving this standard. The students are reading from the
textbook, looking at maps, watching a videotape on earthquakes and volcanoes,
and creating a culminating project. The unit objectives are to develop a vocabulary of 15 related terms such as *plates, fault line, magma,* and so forth and to
demonstrate a knowledge of the basic concepts related to changing landforms.
Performance will be assessed by having students complete an open-ended
response explaining the process of how landforms change and taking a multiple-
choice test on terms and concepts.

Marcie, who has a significant disability, is working on identifying sight words
and writing simple sentences using capital letters and appropriate ending punctuation. Class activities consist of teacher lecture, class discussion, small-group
research, worksheets, and a culminating project. To work on her identified IEP
goals in reading and written expression, Marcie participates in all class activities.
See Figure 4.2 for a detailed description of how Marcie participates in this unit.

During lecture and classroom discussion, the general education teacher
delivers the primary instruction for Marcie and her classmates. The special education and general education teachers have collaborated before the unit begins to
identify Marcie's content and learning objectives (e.g., exhibiting appropriate

Student: _____ Date: _____

Level: _____

Class: _____

Standard: _____

Learner objectives (for all students): _____

Classroom activity	IEP goal:	Who	IEP goal:	Who	IEP goal:	Who	Additional Learning Outcomes:	Who

Figure 4.1. Form for adapting a general education lesson or unit.

51

Student: _Marcie_ Date: _March 14_

Level: _Elementary (fourth grade)_

Class: _Social Studies_

Standard: _Understanding relationships between people and geography and applying this knowledge in real-life situations_

Learner objectives (for all students): _Develop 15 related-word vocabulary (plates, fault line, magma, etc.), understand basic concepts of how landforms change._

Classroom activity	IEP goal: Identify sight words	Who	IEP goal: Write simple sentences with beginning capitals and ending punctuation	Who	IEP goal:	Who	Additional Learning Outcomes: Exhibit appropriate classroom behavior	Who
Lecture							Raise hand; stay on topic; listen actively.	Gen. Ed. T. (GT)
Class discussion							Raise hand; stay on topic; listen actively.	GT
Small-group research	Read words on computer, printouts, references, text, etc.	GT, Spec. Ed. T. (ST), Asst., Peers etc.	Write sentences on computer; take notes.	GT, ST, Asst., Peers			Group behavior: take turns; stay on topic; demonstrate job responsibility.	GT, Peers
Worksheets	Highlight sight words on worksheets.	GT, ST, Asst., Peers	Write on worksheets.	GT, ST, Asst., Peers			Learn five related vocabulary words.	
Project	Read selected part of class presentation.	Peers, Mom, Dad	Label poster.	Peers			Identify two basic principles of how landforms change.	

Figure 4.2. Sample form for Marcie: Adapting a general education elementary school unit on geography.

classroom behavior, such as raising her hand before speaking; staying on topic; listening actively; developing her geography vocabulary and understanding of landform concepts).

During small-group research, Marcie is in a group of four students (randomly assigned by the teacher). Throughout the year, instructional staff (general and special education teachers and instructional assistants) have modeled and prompted ways of facilitating Marcie's involvement in activities. Therefore, her group members have learned to include her appropriately in completing assigned tasks. Her group members make sure that she participates in the tasks (e.g., taking turns, operating computer software, choosing pictures).

In the context of participating in the group research task and completing the worksheets, Marcie is expected to work on her IEP goal of identifying sight words. She reads the words that she knows on the computer, printouts, reference books, textbooks, and so forth. She demonstrates her performance by using a highlighter on printouts and worksheets or a dry erase marker on a sheet protector slipped over book pages to mark the words she can read. The special education teacher reviews these words with her, and uses these student products as data collection devices and portfolio assessment evidence. Instruction on new words (including geography words) can also be delivered at these times by the general education or special education teacher, instructional assistant, or peers. Adaptations such as picture symbols representing geographic concepts, simplified worksheets, and individualized study guides help Marcie master the content identified under the Additional Learning Outcomes.

In these same group tasks, Marcie not only works on her targeted reading goal but she also works on her writing objective. She does this on the computer and by answering questions on worksheets. The computer printout and worksheets are used by the special education teacher for data collection and portfolio assessment evidence.

During the culminating activity, Marcie works with her small group to select, plan, and complete the project. Her group chooses to create a poster and classroom presentation illustrating a working volcano. To work on her writing goal, Marcie types her part of the presentation on the computer and helps label the poster. She works on her reading objective by reading her part of the presentation. She also practices her presentation at home and with peers prior to the event. Her final presentation includes her explanation of two important principles of land-form changes (an Additional Learning Outcome for her).

Mixed-Age Primary Group Math Class: Learning Number Concepts   A mixed-age primary classroom (kindergarten and first grade) is working toward the state standard of understanding number concepts. The class is working with a variety of manipulatives including dinosaur counters, interconnected blocks, and place-value cubes. Student objectives include computing numbers, stating place value, and exploring multiples. Student performance will be assessed by a performance test, worksheets, and student work samples.

Taylor, who has an IEP, is working on the expressive communication goal of initiating three- to five-word sentences by using the Picture Exchange Communication System (PECS; Bondy & Frost, 1994) as his augmentative and alternative communication system. He has the same math goals as all of the other students. Taylor also works on the *curriculum access* skill of augmentative communication in the context of his math activities.

Learning centers provide weekly activities, such as counting a specified number of objects, calculating story problems, and completing worksheets. Daily calendar math provides opportunities for instruction on place value, sequencing, and computation.

The general and special education teachers collaborate on instructional unit design. The general education teacher initially leads the whole-group instruction. The special education teacher then guides instruction in learning centers while the general education teacher provides small-group and individual instruction. All students rotate through the centers and small-group instruction.

During the center activity of counting a specified number of objects, each student receives an egg carton with numbers ranging from 1 to 20 written in the bottom of each section of the carton. Taylor is provided with a larger version of the egg carton so that he can use his preferred manipulatives—dinosaur counters—instead of the counting beans that the other students are using. During the activity of calculating story problems, students are expected to read the problems, write them in mathematical form, and then solve them using their manipulatives and egg cartons. Taylor listens as a peer reads the story problem. Then, he uses his counters to solve the problem and stamps the number for his answer on his worksheet. The *form* (i.e., stamps versus writing) of his response is different from his peers because Taylor is not writing independently, but the *content* of the learning (and the standards) he is demonstrating in math knowledge and application is the same as everyone else's.[1]

During daily calendar math activities, each student adds the current date to his or her individual calendar. Taylor uses his PECS communication system to convey "Yesterday was ... [date]," "Today is ... [date]," "Tomorrow will be ... [date]." A photocopy of the PECS is used within Taylor's alternate assessment, along with teacher data or notes, as evidence of his performance.

Second-Grade Science: Learning About the Weather   A second-grade class is working toward the state standard of using appropriate and relevant scientific skills to problem-solve. The instructional unit is about weather and involves a variety of classroom activities: reading selected books, researching on the computer, looking at weather maps, charting and predicting the weather, and discussing topics in the classroom. The culminating activities include announcing the daily weather forecast over the school's public address system and creating a hallway bulletin board called "All About Weather." General education student objectives include learning ten weather-related terms, describing the types of clouds and the concept of weather prediction, and demonstrating how to chart and interpret data. Student performance is assessed by a variety of student products, a test on definitions, open-response questions, and teacher observation.

José, a student with significant disabilities, is completing this unit with his class. José's IEP goals include improving his oral communication, attending to task, and visual scanning skills. While the class is reading selected books, the stu-

---

[1]Because Taylor is learning the same math content as the other students in his class, some may question his participation in his state's alternate assessment. Taylor participates in the alternate assessment because the content of his learning is substantially modified for his other subjects (most notably reading and language arts), and the decision in his state for participation in the alternate versus the regular assessment is not made on a subject-by-subject basis but rather holistically for all subjects. Some states (e.g., Colorado) are considering a more individualized assessment model, however, in which a student may be placed in the regular assessment for some subjects and in the alternate assessment for others.

dents take turns reading orally and silently. Prior to beginning the unit, the general and special education teachers have collaboratively identified expectations for José. Strategies have also been identified (e.g., assigning him to his preferred seating, pairing him with a peer knowledgeable about how José communicates, prompting him periodically, giving him more teacher attention) to facilitate José's performance on IEP goals. Alternate assessment evidence for José includes data collected on his attending skills.

While the class is researching weather on the computer, José copies and pastes the daily weather graphic from the Web using IntelliKeys (IntelliTools, 2000), a programmable keyboard with a custom overlay, and single-switch access that enables the student to produce his own report (see Chapter 7 for a complete discussion of this device and software). The graphic is printed, cut out, and displayed in chart form on the bulletin board. When the class activity requires writing, José uses IntelliKeys with a custom overlay and IntelliTalk (IntelliTools, 1996) to describe the day's weather. José's custom overlay is designed to address his goal of visual scanning. Copies of typical peer work and José's overlay also can be used as assessment evidence. During small-group work, a peer models the weather-related word; remembering to use initial sounds, José repeats that word. The speech therapist monitors and collects data during this activity; her data can be used as assessment evidence as well.

The students are required to predict the weather for 3 days based on information from the web, television forecasts, and classroom discussion. They prepare a newspaper-style forecast while using symbols that José has printed for them. Using the computer to copy and paste graphics, José completes this activity with the group. A copy of the graphics is included as another part of his assessment evidence.

The culminating activity includes a forecast over the public address system. José's responsibility is to announce a one-word description of the daily weather. (He must be sure to use the initial sound!) Assessment evidence may include a videotape or audiotape of José performing this task, or teacher data. Peer notes and general education teacher notes may also be used as assessment evidence.

Fourth-Grade Science: All About Insects!   A fourth-grade class is doing a science unit on insects that emphasizes a student-generated research question: What kinds of insects do certain foods attract (Kearns, Kleinert, & Kennedy, 1999)? The unit is designed to address the state's Academic Expectations in the areas of the nature of scientific activity, classifying, patterns, and quantifying. Adam, a student with autism, is working on the same academic expectations in science as all the other students, though he may demonstrate these expectations in somewhat different ways. Along with his partner, Elly, Adam assembles the insect traps. Elly reads the directions and checks off each step as Adam completes it. They place a food sample in each of their traps, and find a particularly "buggy" location outside the building. Later in the unit, they participate in a cooperative learning activity in which the students classify their insects with the aid of an insect identification chart. Adam matches the picture of the biggest insect on the identification chart to their "prize catch" in the insect trap, and draws a picture of it.

At the end of the unit, everyone must complete a final exam, which includes short-answer or multiple-choice items and two performance activities. For the short-answer part of his exam, Adam must identify and draw pictures of insects; for the performance portion, he assembles an insect trap.

In his portfolio, Adam includes such items as an insect graph (which foods attracted which insects, and how many insects?), pictures of the insects that were collected, and photographs of his insect trap assembly. His portfolio also includes his teacher's probe data on the number of steps he completed independently while assembling his insect trap. Finally, Adam includes a self-evaluation/reflection sheet in his entry, in which he evaluates his own progress and the areas in which he needs to improve.

General Education Units and
Standards-Based Assessments: Middle School Examples

Here are some examples of ways the general curriculum can be made accessible to middle school students with disabilities.

Understanding Novels in Eighth-Grade Literature One of the state standards in language arts is to make sense of printed material (i.e., reading comprehension). The eighth-grade class is reading and discussing novels. The students and teacher read the novel together in class. Student objectives are vocabulary development, comprehension (e.g., identification of plot structure, major and secondary characters) and an understanding of literary forms, such as symbolism. Performance is assessed by anecdotal recording of student responses in class, and by worksheets and vocabulary tests. Joe, who has a significant disability, is working on adapted computer access, single-switch usage, and the ability to hold his head up. Figure 4.3 illustrates how Joe is participating in this unit.

Students take turns reading orally, answering comprehension questions, participating in classroom and small-group discussions, and creating story maps. While the students are reading the novel together in class, the general education teacher facilitates the group. The general and special educator collaborated prior to the beginning of class to establish expectations for Joe, as well as procedures that the general education teacher can implement to provide multiple opportunities for instruction and to document Joe's learning. For example, as the teacher circulates throughout the room, he periodically elicits Joe's attention by saying his name as he would for any other student in the class. This becomes Joe's cue to hold his head up. The special education assistant or teacher may physically prompt him as needed; a peer can assist in providing this prompt at naturally occurring times. During this activity, Joe uses his single switch to operate a tape player with recorded selections from the book. Duration data on Joe's ability to maintain head control, as well as a frequency count of his switch use, are recorded by special education staff and submitted as alternate assessment evidence.

In designing the lesson, the general and special education teachers have identified a single question per chapter that has two probable answers. For example, the teacher may ask, "Did the girl feel sadder because of the weather or because she missed her friend?" The answers, paired with pictures, are then placed on an adapted keyboard such as IntelliKeys (IntelliTools, 2000). The teacher then calls on Joe, asks the targeted question, and observes Joe touching one of the two areas on the keyboard to activate a recorded response. Recorded responses and the printout of keyboard overlays can be submitted as portfolio evidence. To aid Joe in understanding the plot, while other students are working on a story map, a typically developing peer who needs additional practice with event

Student: _Joe_   Date: _April 4_

Level: _Middle School (eighth grade)_

Class: _Language Arts_

Standard: _Reading comprehension_

Learner objectives (for all students): _Develop 20-word vocabulary from novel; understand plot and character development, concept of symbolism._

Classroom activity	IEP goal: Adapted computer access	Who	IEP goal: Single switch usage	Who	IEP goal: Hold head up.	Who	Additional Learning Outcomes: Choice making	Who
Oral reading			Play tape-recorded selection from the book.		Pick head up when teacher calls name.	GT, Asst., Peers		
Comprehension questions	Use IntelliKeys to answer questions.	GT, ST, Asst., Peers			Pick head up when teacher calls name.	GT, ST, Asst., Peers	Choose preferred answer; respond to questions about plot and character feelings.	GT
Classroom and small-group discussion	Use IntelliKeys to answer questions.	GT, ST, Asst., Peers			Pick head up when teacher or peers say name.	Peers	Choose preferred answer.	GT, Peers
Story map					Pick head up when peers say name.	Peers	Choose preferred symbol or picture; respond to questions about plot and character feelings.	Peer

Figure 4.3.   Sample form for Joe: Adapting a general education middle school unit on language arts.

recall and sequencing helps Joe complete a story timeline using pictures or symbols relating to the book. This timeline also can be included as assessment evidence. Joe's responses to questions about plot and character feelings are noted as Additional Learning Outcomes on the Lesson Unit Plan.

Learning about American Folk Culture   A sixth-grade class is working toward the state standard of developing an understanding of the influence of time, personality, and society on the arts and humanities through productions, performances, and interpretations. The instructional unit is on American folk culture and involves a variety of classroom activities—lectures, class discussions, a field trip, student products, and small-group presentations. General education student objectives include identifying art and music of the American Folk style and understanding its history. Performance is assessed by replicating that style through art, dance, and music production, open-response and multiple-choice tests, and a choice of classroom presentations illustrating facts about the American Folk style.

Sujata, a student with multiple disabilities, is completing this unit with the class. Her IEP goals include reaching and choice making. The general education teacher and special education teacher collaborate to identify objects related to the content material that Sujata can hold and show to the class during classroom discussion. A peer assists Sujata in reaching toward and holding new objects appropriate to the content of the class. During a trip to the Folk Art exhibit at the art museum, which encompasses art, dance, and music, all students are required to record information about five works of their choice to use in the development of their classroom presentation. Using the museum's special access provisions for individuals with disabilities, Sujata uses a texture pad to indicate her like or dislike of the works that she can touch or hear, and a peer records her responses.

For her culminating activity, Sujata creates a PowerPoint presentation with her partner. The partner chooses the visuals and Sujata chooses different pieces of folk music to accompany the visual presentation. Sujata works on her goal of reaching to operate the switch to run PowerPoint. Both the PowerPoint presentation and her choices at the museum are included as assessment evidence.

Sujata's group chooses to create and perform a folk dance. Her peers, who are familiar with Sujata's mode of choice making, include her in group decisions as these decisions naturally occur. Sujata participates in the dance by reaching for a partner's hand. Additional assessment evidence includes photographs of Sujata participating, and peer notes.

Special Area Class: Learning About Careers   Learning About Careers, a middle school class, is required as part of a rotation of special area classes, and meets for a 9-week period. Other classes in the rotation include art, music, and life skills (formerly called Home Economics). Each homeroom goes through this rotation of classes together so that the student grouping remains the same for the school year. The students' goal for this unit of study is the state-assessed learner outcome of "using strategies for choosing and preparing for a career by gathering information about different career areas."

Gary, who has multiple disabilities, is working on improving his vocational and writing functioning by stamping his name and improving his head and neck control (specifically, holding his head up to acknowledge/attend to others). The regular and special educators confer twice weekly to make adaptations and modifications appropriate for Gary. Before going to class, Gary reminds himself of his targeted skill for the day in Learning About Careers by completing part of a planning, monitoring, self-evaluation sheet (see Figure 4.4, a sample of a blank form). A peer usually helps Gary complete this form during or at the end of class, and samples of it are used in the state's alternate assessment as evidence.

The students begin the unit by learning about 13 career clusters (e.g., manufacturing, office/technology, health care) and examples of careers within each cluster (e.g., packager, filing clerk, child care worker).

The teacher always begins class time by asking the students to hold up their student planners. This is Gary's cue to hold up his head while lifting up his planner for the teacher to see. The teacher records data one day each week to show how Gary is making progress on maintaining head control, and one of his peers goes over that progress with him. These data are used as evidence of working on targeted skills for his state's alternate assessment.

While studying each individual career cluster, the students learn to gather information and assess future outlooks for several careers by using four different sources: the web, *Career Information Center* reference books (Career Information Center, 1996), *Occupational Outlook Handbook* (United States Department of Labor, 2000–2001), and *Dictionary of Occupational Titles (DOT)* (USDOL, 1991). The teacher demonstrates how to use each of the reference sources and each student is asked to use the sources to find information about assigned careers.

The students complete this activity in small groups. The assignment sheet includes space for information to be filled in for each career chosen. Gary's group votes on the career on which it will report, and Gary indicates his choice by stamping his name on his preference from the list after a peer reads the choices. The group also has decided that Gary's part of the assignment is to choose the source for the information and the others will fill in the assignment sheet. Gary chooses, by eye gaze, which reference source the group will use first, second, and so on, after being asked to do so by another group member. Copies of the group assignment are used as evidence in the alternate assessment.

The class also participates in job site visits on two separate occasions, and develops a report about the job they shadowed for that 2-hour period. The report is based on criteria set forth by the Learning About Careers teacher. Gary completes a modified report (see Figure 4.5) to be used as evidence in the state's alternate assessment. The job-shadowing visits are planned by the teacher, and each student is assigned to the career cluster in which he or she is most interested.

In order to determine Gary's interest area, he completes a Reading-Free Career Interest Survey (Becker, 1981), in which he is given several series of three job-related pictures. He chooses his preferred job among the three jobs pictured by stamping his name on his choice. A two-page example from the inventory is used as evidence in the alternate assessment, along with a sample of a peer's written interest surveys and aptitude tests to show the relationship between Gary's work and that of his peers.

While job shadowing, Gary shadows the same job as do two other students. Gary's peers ask the employer his questions for his report, and Gary records the answers by stamping his name on the appropriate answer for each question. His two adapted reports also are included in the alternate assessment as evidence of Gary's use of his name stamp to indicate his choice and/or to record a response to a question. This example also illustrates the concept of instruction and performance across settings, which we explore in much greater detail in Chapter 9.

Career Choices Form

Name: _____ Date: _____

Today I will work on:

Stamping my name   Holding my head up to see   Staying on task to finish

I will practice this skill by:

Working with peers   Myself   Teacher reminder   Worksheets

Teacher/peer comments and initials:	Compare last time and this time:
	Tally the number of cues given:
Needs more practice on skill? Y N	

Self-evaluation:

Based on tallies in this box
I did:

☺   😐   ☹

Better   The same   Not as well

Last date   Today's date

Next time I plan to work on:

Stamping my name   Holding my head up to see   Staying on task to finish

Figure 4.4.   Career choices form using planning, monitoring, and self-evaluation format.

Job Shadowing Report

Name: _Gary Johnson_   Date: _3/16/00_

Answer the following using information from a job-shadowing experience.

1) Name of occupation: _Restaurant manager_

2) Name of business (or attach business card):
Donnelli's

3) Can you ride a bus to this job? (Circle one.)

    (Y)   N

4) Do you work nights? (Circle one.)

    (Y)   N

5) What days do you work? (Circle those that apply.)

    S   M (T) (W) (Th) (F) (S)

6) Is training for your job: On the job   Videotape training

7) Is your job (circle one):   (Full time)   Part time

8) Use a magazine to cut out pictures associated with two job duties for this occupation.

9) Starting pay for this job is approximately: $_25,000_

10) Do you wear a uniform for this job? (Circle one.)

    (Y)   N

11) How old must you be to hold this job? (Circle one.)   16   18   (21+)

12) Does this job require a high school diploma? (Circle one.)

    (Y)   N

Signature/title _Mary Ramirez_   Date _3/16/00_

Figure 4.5. Job shadowing report for Gary.

High School Examples

The following are examples of ways to include senior high school students in the general curriculum.

Social Studies: World Civilization from 1500 to the Present   Students in a social studies class are receiving instruction focused on the state standard of "recognizing continuity in historical events, conditions, trends, and issues in order to make decisions for a better future." The current instructional unit focuses on 18th and 19th century civil rights movements and the individuals and groups that began them. The unit involves lecture; classroom discussion; videotape presentations; paper/pencil tests and quizzes; and a culminating activity of the students' choice—which may be a term paper, oral presentation, or other approved project. General education objectives include learning facts about civil rights movements, preceding historical events, and the characteristics of such movements, as well as understanding their impact on the people involved and on society as a whole.

Kayla, who is a senior, has IEP goals of looking at people, objects, and materials to which her attention is directed; using a cheek switch; and operating her electric wheelchair. See Figure 4.6 for a description of how Kayla is participating in this unit.

The general and special education teachers confer biweekly to establish daily and weekly goals, adaptations/modifications, and activities for Kayla. Responsibilities for the implementation of those decisions are divided among the general education teacher, the special education teacher, and the paraprofessional, with the explicitly stated expectation that peers will assist whenever possible.

On quiz days (every Friday), Kayla's physical therapist takes Kayla to the special education classroom to provide direct therapy, assess her progress, and make wheelchair adjustments; all other days, Kayla takes part in her World Civilization course. At other times throughout the unit when general education peers are taking tests over the material, Kayla, along with classmates who have received 100% on related quizzes, goes to the public library to check out videotapes on the lecture topics for the next few days. At these times, the special education teacher who accompanies the group takes ongoing data on Kayla's progress in visual attending to her classmates and the videotapes, as well as in her use of her electric wheelchair. Data, photographs, and peer notes, along with Kayla's own self-evaluation forms (see Chapter 6 for examples), provide evidence of her performance, access to general education standards and curriculum, instruction in multiple environments, and opportunities to develop sustained relationships with peers.

During lecture and classroom discussions, the classroom paraprofessional collects data on Kayla's visual attending to videotaped presentations, to speakers (both the teacher and peers), and to instructional materials (mostly photographs in texts and other research materials). When the teacher assigns discussion questions to small groups, Kayla is expected to look at the members in her group and shift her gaze as appropriate. The reporter for each group changes daily. When it is Kayla's turn to be the reporter, her group members record the answer(s) to their question(s) on Kayla's CheapTalk (Enabling Devices/Toys for Special Children, 1999), which she then activates with her cheek switch to present the material to

Student: _Kayla_   Date: _November 1_

Level: _High School (eleventh & twelfth grades)_

Class: _Social Studies_

Standard: _Recognizing continuity in historical events, conditions, trends, and issues in order to make decisions for a better future_

Learner objectives (for all students): _Learn facts about civil rights movements, preceding historical events, and characteristics of movements_

Classroom activity	IEP goal: Look at people/objects/materials	Who	IEP goal: Use cheek switch	Who	IEP goal: Operate electric wheelchair	Who	Additional Learning Outcomes: Use appropriate classroom behavior	Who
Lecture	Look at speakers (teacher, peers), videos, print/photos.	GT, Asst.			Go to and from class.	Asst., Peers	Listen quietly.	Asst.
Class discussion	Look at speakers (teacher, peers), videos, print/photos.	GT, Asst., Peers	Presenting small-group material to class.	Peers, Asst.			Listen quietly.	Asst.
Small-group discussion	Look at peers, print/photos.	Asst., Peers	Recording material on CheapTalk	Peers	Move to areas of classroom.	Asst., Peers	Listen quietly.	Peers
Quizzes/tests	Look at peers, videos.	ST, Peers			Work with PT; move within the community and public library.	PT, ST, Peers		
Project	Look at partners, research materials.	Peers	Operating PowerPoint presentation.	Peers	Move to front of the room and within school building.	Peers, Asst.	Listen quietly.	Peers

Figure 4.6. Sample form for Kayla: Adapting a general education high school unit on Social Studies.

her class. Assessment evidence for this skill again includes data, photographs, and notes, along with Kayla's planning, monitoring, and self-evaluation forms.

In preparation for the culminating project, two of Kayla's friends (who are also in "Tech. Ed." class with her) ask Kayla to be involved in their project, which is concerned with the disability rights movement. During their research, which they do mostly in the library and computer lab, Kayla looks at materials they have found on the topic. Because her friends are very familiar with her goals and her needs, they are able to provide Kayla with an appropriate amount of assistance for each activity, although they expect her to do her part!

Kayla and her partners decide to give an oral presentation to the class with an accompanying PowerPoint presentation illustrating significant points. To make it even more interesting, they decide to include *JPEGs* (digitized photographs that can be viewed on a computer screen) of themselves in period clothing and surroundings demonstrating different eras in the disability rights movement. They use costumes, props, and the school's digital camera to take their pictures. The digital photographs also are included in Kayla's assessment portfolio.

After 2 days of practice, Kayla and her partners present to their class, with Kayla operating the PowerPoint slides with her cheek switch while her friends present orally. The general education teacher's evaluation of the project is part of Kayla's assessment evidence, along with printouts of other PowerPoint slides.

Language Arts Class: Reading and Writing   A high school language arts class is working toward the state standard of reading ("constructing meaning from a variety of printed materials") and writing ("communicating ideas and information to a variety of audiences through writing") by reading and interpreting various novels throughout the semester and by a variety of writing assignments. The lesson objectives include making sense of these different readings, writing with a purpose, and using technology to communicate ideas. Class assessments are conducted through open-response items, student work samples, quizzes, and objective tests.

Lester (who has a significant disability) is working on improving his functional language in the skill areas of expressive language (i.e., writing ideas) and receptive language (i.e., improving comprehension, word-recognition skills).

The classroom teacher uses a variety of teaching methods including lecture, reading aloud, independent/group work, culminating videotape and student/teacher individual writing conferences. The general and special education teachers confer before the unit begins to establish learner outcomes for Lester, with the special educator making most of the adapted/modified materials.

The unit begins with the teacher introducing the novel and writing activities. Students complete some readings aloud in class; however, most readings are completed independently and class time is used to discuss the novel's content. Each student also receives a study guide at the beginning with a vocabulary list and questions to be discussed as the reading progresses. Lester's study guide is modified and used as evidence in the alternate assessment, along with a planning, monitoring, and evaluation form where he graphs and keeps track of his ongoing progress. (Planning, monitoring, and evaluating are discussed in detail in Chapter 6, and a copy of Lester's planning, monitoring, and self-evaluation sheet is included in that chapter.)

The teacher begins class discussions by asking Lester which chapter/question number will be discussed that day. Lester keeps track of the class's progress by marking off each question as it is discussed, and putting a bookmark at the end of each chapter as it is completed. This motivates Lester to listen and participate. He uses an audiotape format for reading, and listens to the book in his special education class or at home.

During class discussion, Lester uses a modified form for class notes (see Figure 4.7), and his unit examinations come from items on these class notes. The general education teacher prints important ideas on the chalkboard so that Lester can copy them onto his class notes form. These notes are then used to develop activities to reinforce word recognition and comprehension. Samples of the forms are used as evidence in the alternate assessment. The general education teacher also writes a narrative report of Lester's progress toward targeted skills, and a copy of this narrative and his report card for the class are included as assessment evidence as well.

The writing activities for this class include a summary of the novel (similar to a book report) and a reasoned response to ideas related to the novel, with the teacher writing topic suggestions on the board. The summary is modified for Lester (a copy of that modification is included as Figure 4.8). This blank form has space to write vocabulary and other ideas brought up during discussion.

For the second writing activity (responding to ideas presented in the novel), students can work together on prewriting activities to develop their work. Lester works with a group that is brainstorming ideas; one student in the group records the responses and gives everyone in the group a copy. Lester has to come up with two ideas to include in the brainstorming list, and another student marks Lester's ideas with an asterisk to be included as evidence of Lester's ability to plan his writing.

Instead of the two- to three-page writing assignment given to the other students, Lester's adapted assignment is to compose one paragraph (to be typed and included in the alternate assessment). Lester is required to develop five different ideas for this paragraph, which a peer helps him to commit to paper. The peer also helps Lester number these sentences in a logical sequence, and Lester writes the appropriate numbers next to each sentence (this draft and peer comments at the bottom will be included as evidence in his assessment portfolio, as well).

The general education teacher confers with Lester on his writing before it is typed to help him evaluate his work and to identify how he can improve (a copy of the conference form is included as evidence in the alternate assessment). These suggestions are checked off as Lester makes improvements to his writing piece. He then types the final product on the computer. Finally, it is worth noting that although Lester writes and types his work, these activities could be further modified through more pictorial information or through assistive technology for students who had not yet attained Lester's skills in these areas.

Tenth-Grade World Studies   Mark is a 15-year-old sophomore who has a moderate disability. Mark has been in an inclusive program since middle school and has a group of friends that he has known for several years. Mark's IEP goals address the following: improving his communication, using assistive technology (primarily IntelliKeys), increasing his sight-word vocabulary, and improving his ability to use money (prioritized through *COACH*, Giangreco et al., 1998).

Mark is taking World Studies 101, a course required for all sophomores, which addresses the state standards related to cultural heritage and historical perspective. The class currently is comparing different ancient civilizations. As part of

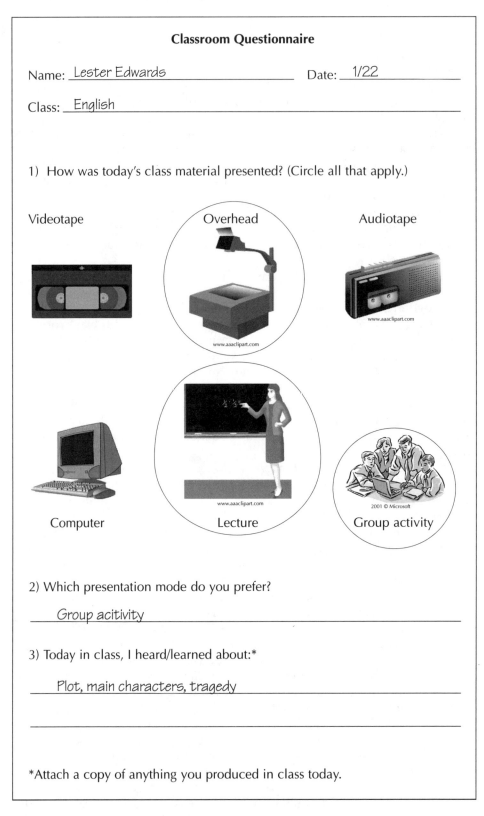

Classroom Questionnaire

Name: Lester Edwards   Date: 1/22

Class: English

1) How was today's class material presented? (Circle all that apply.)

Videotape   Overhead   Audiotape

Computer   Lecture   Group activity

2) Which presentation mode do you prefer?

Group acitivity

3) Today in class, I heard/learned about:*

Plot, main characters, tragedy

*Attach a copy of anything you produced in class today.

Figure 4.7.   Lester's classroom questionnaire for listening/participation skills inquiry.

Book Journal/Report

Name: _____ Date: _____

Book title: _____

Book author: _____

Main characters: _____

New words I learned (5): _____

_____

How I chose to complete the book (circle one):

With a buddy   Audiotape   On my own   Videotape

The book ended (circle one or both):

    Happily   Sadly

The book was (circle one):

    Great!   Good   Okay   Poor (not so good)

    ****   ***   **   *

Next time, I will use this strategy (circle one):

With a buddy   Audiotape   On my own   Videotape

Does this book discuss anything you heard in class? (Circle one.)   Y   N

It discusses: _____

_____

Write a short summary of the story on the back of this sheet (*over*).

Figure 4.8.   Book journal/report form.

the classroom unit, each student has to use a graphic organizer prepared by the general education teacher. The organizer is in the form of a word table. The students, through various methods of research, are to fill in the table independently or work with a partner (student choice). Mark has chosen to work with a partner. Mark and his partner's table have various columns/rows to be completed, with designated headings such as *clothing, money, family, religion,* and *jobs.* For this unit of study, Mark's vocabulary words are the same as the headings (e.g., *family, religion*) used by all the students. Using research methods identical to the rest of the class, Mark finds pictures that can go with each word/heading. These pictures also are used for the poster presentation that Mark and his partner will make. Mark is responsible for pointing to the correct word and introducing (verbally) each section (heading) of the presentation. As part of Mark's assessment for this unit, he completes a worksheet matching the correct picture to each vocabulary word; he also has to locate each word on a computer screen from a verbal cue and then retype the word below. During this time, Mark is learning to use IntelliKeys (IntelliTools, 2000); this format is used for additional practice on the keyboard and also to reinforce the words he has learned.

Mark uses a similar strategy in cooperative small groups in the World Studies class that is learning about ancient religions. Each group is responsible for designing a PowerPoint presentation at the end of the unit of study. As he did previously, Mark uses the headings *prayer, worship, church,* and so forth as his vocabulary words for this unit. As part of the PowerPoint presentation, each group must create a specific number of slides as well as a set number of sounds and pictures, for example. Mark's primary responsibility is locating pictures from ClipArt and other sources on the Internet. He has to cut and paste the pictures into the presentation. Mark's group members also decide that Mark needs to take additional responsibility with the sounds, so Mark selects the sounds used with each heading. Another group member, Christy, selects sounds used for the transitions between slides. Mark uses his adaptive keyboard to enter the headings for the slides and to select the format for each heading. Mark also enters the entire text for one slide by using his keyboard.

When the rest of the class is involved in taking notes, Mark takes notes (arranged previously with general and special education teachers) from a copy of the overhead used by one of the teachers. Specific words or phrases are highlighted with a highlighter pen. Mark chooses whether to copy the information into his binder or to use the adapted keyboard and then make a computer printout to put in his binder.

General and special education teachers collect progress data and so, of course, does Mark. Mark's planning, monitoring, and evaluation sheets are part of his alternate assessment, as are his work samples (including completed tables, photographs of poster sessions, copies of PowerPoint slides, and his end-of-the-unit tests).

Physical Science Class: Learning about Physical/Chemical Properties and the Periodic Chart   A high school physical science class is working toward the state standard of applying core scientific concepts and principles by studying the physical and chemical properties of matter and learning about the structure of basic elements. The specific student objectives include identifying differences in chemical and physical properties of matter and using information from the periodic chart to report information about the elements. Jane, who has a significant disability, is working on improving her social skills in the areas of needs verbalization and socially appropriate behavior (through gaining access to information and making eye contact with others) and improving her math skills in the areas of counting and number concepts. She also is responsible for learning a portion of the science content.

The general education teacher uses a variety of teaching methods including lecture, lab experiments, group activities, and quizzes/tests. The general and special education teachers confer on the appropriate modifications for Jane for this unit. They decide that Jane will be tested orally and that she will choose the correct answer from two choices on examinations and quizzes. Jane also will only complete questions on the exam that assess her performance for the skill areas in which she is working. The general education teacher will modify the regular exam by omitting/marking off items that need not be completed. Another modification for Jane includes allowing her to use a calculator, which will be provided by her special education teacher, for mathematical operations.

The unit is introduced with a lecture and group activity to learn more about physical/chemical properties. Jane uses a modified form of note taking for class (refer to Figure 4.7). A smaller Post-It paper containing three or four concepts the teacher will cover in class is attached to the modified class notes form as well. Jane highlights or marks each concept as the teacher covers it in class. The teacher prints the terms on the board as she discusses them. Jane counts the words covered for her daily physical science assignment and lists the number covered on her planning, monitoring, self-evaluation form for science (see Figure 4.9). This sheet is included as evidence in her alternate assessment. After class, Jane looks up the definition of these words in the glossary of the book and copies them (students have had instruction on how to use the glossary). A peer from class reads the words/definitions before class begins and initials Jane's definitions page. Jane uses these definitions as her adapted assignment, in lieu of the end-of-chapter questions that other students complete. A copy of Jane's and a peer's chapter assignment is included as evidence for the alternate assessment.

During lab experiments, the students discover the difference in chemical and physical properties of matter. The students divide into groups of three, follow the specific procedures for combining or changing different forms of matter (e.g., mixing solutions together, heating solutions in test tubes), and record what happens in the procedures. Jane's part of the assignment is to gather the materials needed for the experiment and to state what happens in one of the parts of that experiment, as prompted by a peer. The peer circles Jane's response and Jane initials it at the end of lab time (the teacher also asks a peer to write at the bottom of the lab report whether or not Jane uses eye contact with her team members during lab time, as this is an important communication objective for her). The experiment sheet (listing each team member's duties for the day as well as the lab results) is used in the portfolio as evidence of using eye contact in social exchanges. Jane's self-evaluation sheet for physical science also includes space for the general education teacher to provide input as to whether Jane is using this social skill in her class.

Part of this physical science unit deals with using the periodic table and drawing pictures of atoms. Students use the periodic table to determine the number of protons, electrons, and neutrons (using a formula) that make up each element, and then they draw pictures of how the elements look. Jane uses parts of

Planning, Monitoring, and Self-Evaluation Form

Name: _____ _____ Date: _____

Today I will work on:

Looking/listening   Math/counting   Finishing working/asking for help

How will I practice this skill?

Working with peers   Working on my own   Working with my science teacher

Teacher/peer initials: _____

Evaluation: My performance (circle one):

Improved

Remained the same

Needs to be better

New science words:

1. _____
2. _____
3. _____
4. _____

100	100
90	90
80	80
70	70
60	60
50	50
40	40
30	30
20	20
10	10
% of questions Last time	% of questions Today

Compare the percentage of study questions correct today with last time by shading in blocks above.

Next time I plan to work on:

Looking/listening   Math/counting   Finishing working/ask for help

Figure 4.9.   Example of planning, monitoring, and self-evaluation form for physical science.

this assignment in her assessment as evidence of counting and number concepts. The general education teacher has decided that Jane will draw models of basic elements only, so as not to be concerned with positive and negative charges. Using a chart, the students compute the number of protons and electrons (the element's atomic number) and neutrons (the element's atomic number subtracted from the atomic mass number—after that mass number is rounded to the nearest whole number). The students are permitted to work in pairs for this assignment; it is adapted for Jane by a peer rounding off all the atomic masses for her on her periodic chart, so that Jane computes the numbers using a calculator. This assignment is included as evidence in the alternate assessment.

After completing the chart, Jane draws the atoms on a modified worksheet that already contains a series of circles for her to draw electrons onto and on which she can label each element (see Figure 4.10). Jane has learned that there is a limit to the number of electrons that she can draw on each circle (otherwise known as the atom's shell). Knowing the total number of electrons from her chart, Jane continuously subtracts the maximum number of electrons as she draws them on each circle. This adapted assignment, along with the assignment of a peer without a disability, is included in her alternate assessment.

To show how to individualize student objectives (and instruction and assessment activities) within such a challenging subject area, one final example is given.

A Second Example from High School Physical Science   Samantha is a 15-year-old sophomore with a moderate disability who is enrolled in Physical Science, a required class for sophomores. Samantha's IEP goals/objectives addressed in this unit include calculator use for math, communication/speech, basic reading, and vocabulary.

Calculator use is addressed regularly through density calculations as well as atomic weight/mass, protons, electrons, and so forth. Communication objectives are embedded daily through interactions with peers and teachers. Basic reading and vocabulary are addressed nearly every day, as well.

The Physical Science class is just completing a basic 1-week unit on calculating density. Once the basic terms have been introduced, the class works individually and in groups to master calculating density and related applications. Samantha quickly learns the "triangle" along with the other members of the class:

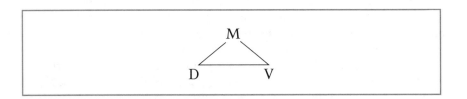

From this equation model (in which D = density, M = mass, and V = volume), students can derive the following equations: $m = dv$, $d = m/v$, $v = m/d$. Given any two of the variables, students need to complete the steps to calculate the third variable. The only modification that Samantha requires is to have the numbers highlighted in the word problems and applications. For the unit assessment, Samantha works with two typically developing peers, Bobbi and Heidi. Bobbi and Heidi read the problems out loud, and Samantha attempts to identify the two correct variables needed to calculate each problem. Bobbi and Heidi then either con-

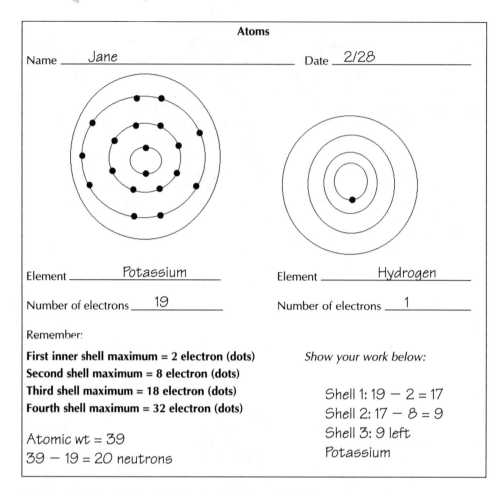

Figure 4.10. Jane's modified worksheet for calculating the number of electrons.

firm Samantha's responses or make their own guesses as to the correct variables for that problem. Once consensus is reached, Bobbi and Heidi are accountable for the correct variables being included in the formula, and Samantha is responsible for performing the correct calculation with her calculator. For the assessment, Samantha uses an index card with the triangle and the formulas. Other students are expected to apply the formulas from memory.

Students also complete a unit of study on nuclear energy for this course. Various learning activities occur, including guest speakers, web-based research, labs, and so forth. The final project/culminating activity is to put together a proposal *for* or *against* the use of nuclear energy in the students' home state. Samantha again works with Bobbi and Heidi. Samantha locates web sites and looks for information pertaining to the cost of nuclear energy compared with the cost of current energy sources in the state. Once the figures are compiled, Samantha's portion of the assessment is to "calculate" the costs. Samantha, Bobbi, and Heidi work as a group to put the information together. Bobbi and Heidi assist Samantha in determining what figures to put in the calculator and which operations need to be used (addition, subtraction, multiplication, or division).

Samantha keeps a weekly log/notebook of her calculator use. She uses the data collected in science, as well as other school and community settings (shopping, bank account at school, lunch account) in which she is expected to master calculator use. Each week she examines the areas in which she is making improvement and the areas in which she needs to improve. She then makes a plan for improving for the following week. Samples of the calculator log, work samples, and the portfolio piece completed with Bobbi and Heidi in Physical Science are all a part of Samantha's math entry for her alternate assessment. Bobbi and Heidi use the final project (proposal) for their writing portfolios as a content area piece, required as part of the state's regular high school assessment. In this way, all three students complete an important part of their school accountability portfolios together. (We should always remember that alternate assessment never has to mean "separate" assessment!)

On-Line Clip Art for Planning, Monitoring, and Self-Evaluation Forms
A number of web sites include free, downloadable* symbols that are useful when designing assessment forms. For a virtual tour, visit these sites on the Internet:

Modified Job Shadowing Report
http://www.coolarchive.com
http://www.aaaclipart.com
http://www.teacherfiles.com/clip_art.htm
http://www.artclipart.com

Career Choices Planning Sheet
http://www.aaaclipart.com
http://www.artclipart.com

Technology (computers, audio/video, overhead)
http://www.aaaclipart.com (click on office, computers, or technology)

TVs, VCRs, Cameras
http://www.clipartgallery.com (click on electronics)

Team/group work (people at tables)
http://www.coolarchive.com (click on clipart, office)

Domestics/food
http://www.barrysclipart.com (click on clipart, agricultural or assorted black and white, or fruit in Images by Jacci)

Science/math
http://www.iband.com/clip (click on clipart)
http://www.barrysclipart.com (click on chemistry)

*Check each site carefully for copyright and usage guidelines.

SUMMARY

Throughout this chapter, we have shown how students with significant disabilities can address priority IEP objectives in the context of general education activities, and in the process of that instruction, can demonstrate what they have learned in the framework of their state's alternate assessment. Although each state is developing its alternate assessment in its own way, our work across the country has given us a broader perspective of the commonalities in those alternate assessment systems. We have thus tried to select examples that apply to the kinds of authentic, performance-based alternate assessments that many states are developing. While some states are referring to these assessments specifically as student portfolios, other states are calling the content of their alternate assessments *bodies* or *collections* of student work. What this chapter illustrates is the kinds of performance evidence that can be included in those bodies or collections of work. Ideally, that evidence should provide a clear picture of the skills the student has learned, the context and settings in which the student has learned those skills, and the relationship of those skills to the state standards for all students.

Raising the Bar—The Power of Higher Expectations

Raynetta had learned the names of a few letters by the time she reached second grade, but still couldn't identify any words except her first name. Before school began, I was collaborating with her new general education teacher. The teacher asked about Raynetta's reading level and what we could expect her to accomplish in that area on the IEP. I said that she was never going to be a "reader" but could probably learn some functional sight words as she grew older. Ms. Armstrong emphatically stated, "Everyone in my class learns to read." When I left the classroom that day, I thought, "I'll give her 2 months...then she'll understand." The next few times I was in the classroom, Raynetta always seemed to be in one reading group or another. Her teacher ability grouped for reading but, in her commitment to see Raynetta read, had placed her in every group, regardless of the level. After about 6 weeks, I came into the room and Ms. Armstrong said, "Raynetta, bring your book over here and read for Mr. Burdge." Raynetta read straight through, stumbling a few times, getting distracted by the pictures, but reading just the same. Now Raynetta is in seventh grade and is still reading. Although she does not read at grade level, she is able to read adapted texts and leisure books. Higher expectations in general curriculum classes are providing us with lots of new information about what children with disabilities can do.

—Mike Burdge, Kentucky State Coordinator of Alternate Assessment

---

REFERENCES

Becker, R. (1981). *Reading-free vocational interest inventory.* Columbus, OH: Elbern Publications.

Bondy, A., & Frost, L. (1994). The Picture Exchange Communication System. *FOCUS on Autistic Behavior, 9*(3), 1–19.

Career Information Center (1996). *Career information center occupational profiles.* New York: Macmillan.

Cole, S., Horvath, B., Chapman, C., Deschenes, C., Ebeling, D., & Sprague, J. (2000). *Adapting curriculum & instruction in inclusive classrooms: A teacher's desk reference* (2nd ed.). Bloomington: University of Indiana, Indiana Institute on Disability and Community, Center on Education and Lifelong Learning.

Enabling Devices/Toys for Special Children (1999). *CheapTalk.* Hastings-on-Hudson, NY: Author.

Falvey, M. (1995). *Inclusive and heterogeneous schooling: Assessment, curriculum, and instruction.* Baltimore: Paul H. Brookes Publishing Co.

Giangreco, M.F. (Ed.). (1997). *Quick guides to inclusion: Ideas for educating students with disabilities.* Baltimore: Paul H. Brookes Publishing Co.

Giangreco, M.F. (Ed.). (1998). *Quick guides to inclusion 2: Ideas for educating students with disabilities.* Baltimore: Paul H. Brookes Publishing Co.

Giangreco, M.F., Cloninger, C.J., & Iverson, V.S. (1998). *Choosing outcomes and accommodations for children (COACH): A guide to educational planning for students with disabilities* (2nd ed.). Baltimore: Paul H. Brookes Publishing Co.

IntelliTools (1996). *IntelliTalk* (Version 1.0) [Computer software]. Novato, CA: Author.

IntelliTools (2000). *IntelliKeys.* Available: http://www.intellitools.com/index.html

Jorgensen, C.M. (1998). *Restructuring high schools for all students: Taking inclusion to the next level.* Baltimore: Paul H. Brookes Publishing Co.

Kearns, J., Kleinert, H., & Kennedy, S. (1999). We need not exclude anyone. *Educational Leadership, 56*(6), 33–38.

Microsoft Corporation (2000). *Microsoft PowerPoint 2000* [Computer software]. Redmond, WA: Author.

United States Department of Labor. (1991). *Dictionary of occupational titles (Rev. 4th ed.).* (GPO Stock No. 029-013-00094-2). Washington, DC: U.S. Government Printing Office.

United States Department of Labor. (2000–2001). *Occupational outlook handbook* (GPO Bulletin 2520). Washington, DC: U.S. Government Printing Office.

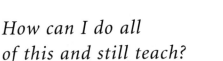

chapter 5

How can I do all
of this and still teach?

INTEGRATING
ALTERNATE ASSESSMENT
WITH ONGOING INSTRUCTION

Jean Clayton, Mike Burdge, and Harold Kleinert

Few people would doubt the importance of including the educational outcomes of all students, including those of students with significant disabilities, in measures of school effectiveness and accountability. Yet, teachers express serious concerns about the impact of still another procedural requirement on what many perceive to be an already excessive burden of paperwork (Kleinert, Kennedy, & Kearns, 1999). Several authorities have noted the growing pressures on special education teachers in general resulting from increased paperwork and documentation (Special Educators Share Their Thoughts, 1999; Heward, 2000). In their statewide survey of teachers participating in Kentucky's alternate assessment, Kleinert et al. (1999) found that a number of teachers reported that the effort to document performance in the alternate assessment took time away from teaching and added greatly to their paperwork load. A number of teachers with whom we work, however, have noted that the issue is not so much one of finding the time to do this extra work but of learning to integrate portfolio assessment into the context of ongoing, regular instruction. In fact, Kampfer, Horvath, Kleinert, and Kearns (in press) found that the amount of time outside of class that teachers spent on student portfolios only weakly predicted student scores; a far more powerful predictor was the extent to which the alternate assessment was integrated into daily instruction. Another strong predictor was the extent to which students were integrally involved in the construction of their own portfolios.

The responsibility for collecting and evaluating performance data need not rest solely on the teacher, then. In fact, by emphasizing the role of the *student* in managing and evaluating his or her own learning, educators can teach valuable skills that are vital to developing students' self-determination (Browder & Bambara, 2000; Ezell, Klein, & Ezell-Powell, 1999). Integrating alternate assessment strategies into the context of ongoing instruction is the focus of this chapter; teaching students to take ownership for their own learning, in the broader context of self-determination, is the major focus of Chapter 6.

This chapter is organized into two sections. The first section opens with a framework developed by Jean Clayton, a teacher at White's Tower Elementary School in Independence, Kentucky, for integrating instruction with the performance requirements of her state's alternate assessment. Her framework clearly indicates how planning for assessment must be considered in the broader context of the student's entire educational program. In this section, teachers are presented with strategies for integrating authentic assessment into daily instruction, as well as with examples of ways in which they can collect assessment data as a part of their teaching. The second part of this chapter presents strategies that we have found particularly useful for adapting curricular materials and instruction.

SIX STEPS TO EMBEDDING ALTERNATE ASSESSMENT INTO DAILY INSTRUCTION FROM DAY ONE: A TEACHER'S EXPERIENCE

The following account by Jean Clayton shows firsthand how alternate assessment requirements can be integrated into the students' individual educational programs.

Step 1: Getting Started (August 16, the First Day of School)

I sit down with each student's individualized education program (IEP) and review the objectives to determine where I can work on identified skills within the daily routine of the general education class. I don't limit my thinking to those objectives obviously related to the subject area (e.g., working on number concepts only in the context of math class) or to the content area to which they were assigned on the IEP. For example, I may work on what traditionally is thought of as a language arts objective in science or social studies. In reality, I will need to work on each skill in *several* settings or activities to facilitate the needed generalization. At this point, all I am doing is prioritizing a time and subject area for each targeted skill. This process is not time consuming but may require "out-of-the-box" thinking. For example, Meg's objective states that she will hold her head up for 30 seconds with only verbal cues. I decide that science has a lot of opportunities for colorful graphics, 3-D materials, and hands-on experiments (all of which provide incentives for holding up one's head), so I identify science as a primary setting to teach that objective. Another one of her targeted skills is to work on identifying common pictures (paired with printed words). I choose social studies because of its close link to daily living. In social studies class, she will be able to work on this second skill in two ways:

1. Pictures of daily materials, such as a book, pencil, paper, map, and so forth, will be used as a subset of her schedule/planning sheet during social studies time. She will look at the schedule to determine what materials she needs for social studies, and a peer can help her get the materials together.

2. Pictures that are coordinated with the current unit in social studies will be provided to help her gain access to the curriculum being taught in the class. These may be limited to a few key concepts taught in the unit and will also be used to evaluate her understanding of the material.

Another student, Mark, has goals in writing, sight-word identification, and reading comprehension. I determine that he will have many opportunities to work on writing within the context of science. Rather than focusing only on writing for his language arts class (which often takes the form of creative writing), he can write about what the class is studying in science. This allows him to review the science material an additional time and to put the science content into his own words, while simultaneously working on his objective of writing a complete sentence starting with a capital letter. Sight-word identification is emphasized, especially in the context of social studies. I will ask Mark to locate all of the high-frequency words within the variety of social studies materials used in class. This will allow us to embed the words into age-appropriate material, as well as provide a time to work on the skill without pulling him from regular class work.

Step 2: Developing Data Collection and Monitoring Sheets

Once I have identified the primary settings and classes in which each student's objectives will be covered (while making sure that all subject areas and IEP objectives are covered), I develop data sheets and student planning, monitoring, and self-evaluation forms (see Chapter 6 for a complete description of these forms). In developing these, I review the standards of our state's alternate assessment to see if I can include ways to "prompt" students and teachers to address each of the standards, and to provide ongoing evidence that they are doing so! Performance across multiple environments is a standard in our state's assessment, so somewhere on the planning sheet or data form I want to document environments. I usually add a row on my data sheets that simply reads *settings*. Each time I record data, I write down the setting and/or activity in which we worked on the skill. This also becomes a visual reminder to me to work on the skill in other environments. Including the data sheet along with work samples, peer notes, pictures, or videotapes provides evidence that the student performed the skill across multiple environments.

On the planning, monitoring, and self-evaluation sheet, I also provide a place to document the alternate assessment standard of "The student is able to make choices both within and across entries" (e.g., did the student have a choice about how to begin an assignment, with whom to work, what resource book to use?). Not only does this standard promote self-determination for students but it also can provide powerful motivators for student learning. As I create these monitoring sheets, I save them on the computer so that I can revise them as needed.

By this time, you may be saying, "I just want to teach," or, "I don't have time to do all of this performance monitoring and still teach what my students need to learn." Yet, we know that students with significant disabilities learn best when presented with carefully planned and continuously monitored instruction, that variables such as multiple environments are essential for the generalization of skills, and that making choices is an essential building block of the critical outcome of self-determination (Browder & Bambara, 2000). Instructional variables that are essential to achieving ultimate outcomes for our students are worth monitoring on a daily basis!

Of course, I cannot do this planning in isolation. Rather, I work as part of a team. The general education teachers with whom I work have a yearly calendar available for easy and speedy access to their general plans for the entire year, and they develop detailed lesson plans for each day as well. My planning is closely related to theirs. I find myself at times at the mercy of starting some of my planning only after the general education teachers have some things put together; thus, I often have to wait until school actually has started before I can complete some tasks. When you observe the general education classroom, you will find that the first week is spent mostly setting the stage for classroom behavior, work habits, and routine. This is important for the students I am serving, and my physical presence may not be so greatly needed during these first days to modify instruction or materials. Thus, often I can use this week to finalize many of the data monitoring and planning sheets. I have found that this planning should be a high priority, and that it will pay off in terms of increased instructional focus and student learning throughout the year.

I now have all my data sheets in place, which I needed in order to get that first month's data, and I feel ready! By aligning my data sheets with the evidence required for the alternate assessment, I also have forms that will help me fulfill the requirements of the assessment tool.

Step 3: Designing Instructional Strategies

At this point, I have to design my instructional methods. I find this easier than when I was planning the entire curriculum within a self-contained classroom. I now use the curriculum prescribed by our state and lesson plans designed by the general education classroom teacher. My job is to embed the student's targeted skills into the context of the general curriculum, and to provide the adaptations and instructional supports that lead to student success.

I begin this process by choosing a method that will easily generalize from unit to unit, in order to reduce the number of adaptations that the student needs to learn, as well as the number of adaptations that I need to make. For example, to practice sight-word identification in social studies, I have come up with a few basic strategies—no matter what the material. One such method is to open one side of a sheet protector and slip it over a page in the social studies book, give the student a dry erase marker, and ask him to mark each word he knows. Another strategy is to read the passage with the student and verbally fill in all the words that the student doesn't know. I have found that this helps the student pay attention, and the student usually begins picking up on frequently used terms, such as *mountain* or *city* in the context of a social studies unit. I monitor progress in a variety of ways; one is to use flash cards and the other is to circle the words in the text and ask the student to identify each of the circled words. Other teachers have used short, daily sight-word sessions to teach both sight-word and content-word vocabulary. Constant time delay, in which a specific time interval (e.g., 3 seconds), is inserted between the task request and the prompt, is an excellent teaching strategy here (Snell & Brown, 2000; Wolery, Ault, & Doyle, 1992). Simultaneous prompting (Fickel, Schuster, & Collins, 1998), in which all teaching trials are taught at a 0-second delay, has also had excellent results. These sessions can be conducted as part of individual and small-group work, and there is preliminary research showing the effectiveness of simultaneous prompting for heterogeneous groups of students with significant disabilities and students without disabilities (Fickel et al., 1998; Parker, 2000).

Other examples of ongoing instructional methods may be more specifically designed for individual students. For example, Tim, one of my students, is learning to operate a multifunction switch with voice output. Tim's objective, which he is working on within science class, is to choose the correct switch according to color, number, or picture symbol. In preparation for his work in this class, I make four envelopes with colors or numbers corresponding to those on the switch. With each unit, the other students in this class write study questions and divide their questions into four categories such as definition, real-life examples, concepts, and "What do you think will happen?" questions. Within the context of this activity, Tim chooses a color or number and activates the switch corresponding to that color/number. His classmates then have to choose a question out of the correct colored or numbered envelope and answer. We often do this in a game format and keep our scores!

For Tim, at least three skills can be practiced within this activity: the motor skill of activating the switch, recognizing colors or numbers, and understanding science concepts. In addition, Tim's peers have a chance to practice the content twice, once when creating cards and then again when playing the game.

Step 4: Adapting Materials

Once I have an ongoing instructional method for each objective in each subject area, I look at individualized adaptations (e.g., pictorial study guides) that I need to make for the student to benefit the most from each unit of study. Reading and math usually require weekly changes. I find that social studies, arts and humanities, music, physical education, and science units last closer to 2–3 weeks. I usually have a fairly standard method of adapting the material, but the actual content changes with each unit. For example, for some students, I have summarized each chapter of the class novel to about one page, and have found that I can reduce the required reading level significantly by doing so. I also have typed questions on the same page so the student can reference the reading. I have made an accompanying vocabulary list in which the student matches the word to a corresponding picture symbol, and have added a picture-symbol word box at the top of the page to help the students with word identification.

Step 5: Embedding All of This into Classroom Routines

The next task is to teach all of the other people who will work with the student the knowledge and skills they will need. I keep my data and planning sheets in a three-ring binder. I begin by showing the classroom teacher and the instructional assistant these forms and describing how I plan to use them. I try to explain why I am doing things a certain way, and yet I still try to be responsive and open to feedback from other people. When I come into the classroom, I can pick up the notebook and see what has been accomplished, what needs to be modified, where I need to fine tune, what I need to explain again, and so forth. I also include a Getting to Know You sheet in the beginning that includes important information, paraphrased objectives, health and vitality issues (e.g., allergy alerts), and general instructional hints.

I take a somewhat different approach to facilitating peer support. I don't want other students taking on a teacher role, so I mostly model how the student with a disability works on a skill. When asking peers to help the student with a specific skill, I am careful to word it so that I am asking them to work together on science or reading. Then I show the other students how my student can work on the activity *with* them. I use requests such as, "Sue, will you and Marcia work together? Marcia, you need to circle the words that you know in the social studies questions while Sue answers. Talk about the questions and answers together." I find that requests such as these go a long way toward modeling the idea of children learning together, as opposed to some students always being in the role of learner and others always providing assistance.

Step 6: Monitoring and Revising the Programs as Necessary

Once data and planning, monitoring, and self-evaluation forms are completed and objectives are embedded into the general education curriculum, I begin to 1) monitor the progress of instructional data, 2) collaborate with the general education teacher about upcoming activities and lessons, and 3) cross-check student performance with the assessment standards to ensure I am covering all necessary elements.

Monitoring student progress isn't unique to alternate assessment, of course, and has long been required as part of the IEP process. With the onset of alternate assessment (and especially performance-based alternate assessment), progress data take on an additional dimension and often include student self-monitoring. (Student self-monitoring and evaluation are discussed in much greater detail in Chapter 6.)

What Happens When Progress Is Not Made?   When instructional data do not indicate progress, it is essential to modify instruction. I always try to tie the instructional modification to the student's self-evaluation; my modification should reflect the area in which the student also has identified a need to improve. For example, one particular student was not making progress in his oral reading objectives. He identified a need to work harder on looking at the individual letters to improve his word discrimination skills. I chose 5–10 words he missed in the reading passage from his social studies book and listed them. He formed the words with magnetic letters at home and traced them at school in order to practice looking more closely at each letter. In addition, he practiced with flash cards and filled in word-shape boxes on worksheets. In this way, my strategies were directly tied to what the student believed he most needed to do to improve his oral reading skills. The effectiveness of the approach would, of course, be documented by improved oral reading, and the student would have the added satisfaction of knowing that his own ideas were part of that improvement!

On an ongoing basis, I meet with the classroom teacher at least once per week. In ideal situations, we plan unit activities together. In these situations, we are able to ensure at the onset that the unit will meet the instructional needs of all of the students. More often, though, I find out from the teacher what the lesson plans already are, what information is going to be covered, and when the students are going to be assessed. One routine adaptation is to provide picture study guides and tests. Saving or copying pictures from the web and then inserting them into a word-processing document is one efficient way of creating individualized study guides. Once the pictures are part of a word-processing file, each picture can easily be copied to form a test from the study guide. Because science and social studies units are generally 2–3 weeks long, usually it is not necessary to do this every week. The most important and relevant information is chosen for the student to learn and included in the instructional material. Both hard and electronic copies are saved to be re-used the next year.

In addition to making these adaptations, I look at the materials and activities used by the general class and determine how students with disabilities can use them. For example, if the class is going to make a presentation on the computer, then collaboration with the speech-language pathologist enables us to get assistive technology in place for a child with an augmentative and alternative communication (AAC) system to communicate what he or she has learned. Subject-specific communication board overlays also are generated in collaboration with the speech-language pathologist.

Step 7: Organizing Ongoing Instructional Data

To organize my data for the alternate assessment, I collect work samples and completed student planning, monitoring, self-evaluation sheets and file them by student and subject area. Every month I review these and identify and target areas of weaknesses or gaps. These can include the need to document natural peer support or to demonstrate skill acquisition across multiple environments. The easiest way to evaluate the thoroughness of collected evidence (which reflects instruction) is to design a cover sheet reflecting your state's or district's alternate assessment requirements. Figure 5.1, based on my state's requirements, is one that I have found very helpful. Each of the dimensions identified in Figure 5.1 are important elements of our state alternate assessment. Moreover, we are finding that these same dimensions, precisely because they represent dimensions of best practices for students with significant disabilities (see Kleinert & Kearns, 1999, and Kleinert, Kearns, & Kennedy, 1997), are reflected in the content requirements and scoring rubrics of other states as these states develop their alternate assessments.

DEVELOPING ADAPTATIONS TO INCLUDE STUDENTS WITH SIGNIFICANT DISABILITIES IN GENERAL EDUCATION

Throughout Jean's discussion, she presents examples of how students with significant disabilities can be included within age-appropriate general education activities, how individualized learning objectives for students with significant disabilities can be incorporated into those lessons, and how student work can be collected and organized from these activities as an integral part of ongoing educational assessment. It is obvious from these examples that an important part of this planning process is designing student adaptations that foster participation and progress in the general curriculum. Although the creativity of adaptations may greatly expand students' learning opportunities in general education classes, there are important practices that educators should—and should not—employ when designing those adaptations. By keeping in mind the following five essen-

	Reading	Math	Science	Social studies	Physical education	Arts and humanities
Targeted skill						
Student planning						
Student self-monitoring						
Student self-evaluating						
Evidence of progress						
Multiple settings						
Peer interactions						
Appropriate adaptations						
Natural peer support						
Embedded choices						
Age-appropriate activities						

Figure 5.1. Cover sheet reflecting alternate assessment requirements for Kentucky.

tial questions when developing adaptations, educators can ensure that the adaptations they devise are appropriate.

Five Questions to Ask When Developing Instructional Adaptations

When developing an adaptation so that the student can participate in another instructional activity or setting, it is easy to get swept away by the anticipation of the new opportunities that will be available to him or her. Sometimes in the excitement, however, teachers overdevelop and come up with adaptations that are unusual-looking, cumbersome, activity/environment specific, and require lots of new learning on the part of the student just to use the tool. Too much time and energy is expended on things that are not really practical or effective. Then it is back to the drawing board to come up with something else, and by that time, the activity is over!

To avoid spending instructional time (or worse yet—your own time after school) on developing adaptations that really cannot be effectively used, it may help to keep the following questions in mind:

1. **Does it look like what everyone else is doing?** By using the same materials as the other students you do not have to search for different materials, and the student is less stigmatized than he or she would be by separate work. For example, if the class is reading a literature book or content text, the text for each page could be simplified to the reading level of the student, typed on the computer, and inserted over the original text on each page. Students without disabilities could even read this modified text and enhance their understanding by summarizing the content in their own words. (This adaptation also answers Questions 2, 3, and 4 that follow.) Assessment evidence might include copies of the original and adapted texts (with correctly read words identified), and peer and student notes to accompany these pages. In another example, when students are reading handouts, newspapers, or other consumer publications, the student with a disability could highlight with a marker those words she or he can read independently. (This adaptation answers Questions 2, 3, 4, and 5, as well.) Assessment evidence can include the highlighted material and the teacher data on sight-word recognition.

2. **Does it use a skill the student already has or can it be used to teach a new, essential skill?** If a student already has a skill he or she can use in one situation, the most effective use of time would be to transfer or generalize that skill to another meaningful activity. For example, the student who uses the skill sequence of reach/grasp/release on a squeeze stick to play music could use that same skill sequence to operate an audiotape recorder in order to "read" tape-recorded passages from the social studies text. (Questions 3 and 4 that follow can be answered by this adaptation, as well.) A student who has not yet mastered reach/grasp/release could, in addition to the previous two examples, receive instruction on this embedded skill throughout the school day in such activities as moving manipulatives in math class, passing out equipment in biology lab, using colored chalk in art, paying for lunch,

building a solar system model in science, and so forth. Assessment evidence might include teacher data on skill development, peer and teacher notes, and videotape.

3. **Does it enhance or facilitate a greater degree of independence for the student?** Sometimes adaptations require more educator time and the intervention of others than is needed. For example, there is usually quite a bit of "up front" time on the part of adults to prepare materials for a student who requires large print. And, as usually happens, some materials are overlooked, resulting in the necessity of assistance from an adult or peer. Teaching the simple skill of using a magnifier would significantly increase the independence of a student with visual impairments (and answer Questions 1, 4, and 5, as well). Photographs would be assessment evidence of this adaptation.

4. **Can the same adaptation be effective in several different activities/environments?** Devising adaptations that are activity- or setting-specific requires much more of educators' time than devising one adaptation that can be used across a variety of activities and in a variety of places. If a student is learning to communicate, the form or mode of his communication should remain constant across settings. Using a switch in language arts, line drawings in social studies, eye gaze at lunch, and vocalizations in math would likely be too confusing, not only for the student but also for the receiver of the messages. A more effective instructional strategy would be to pick one augmentative adaptation that has the greatest flexibility across settings. If a student is using line drawings to communicate, they should be available for instruction across all settings, activities, and times. Of course, some environments may need sets of symbols to convey messages within a particular context (e.g., geography versus fine arts). (Questions 2, 3, and 5 can also be answered by this adaptation.) Copies of symbols, teacher data, peer notes, and videotape may constitute assessment evidence of adaptations being used across environments.

5. **How easy is it for the student to use or learn the skill?** Sometimes in our efforts to design the best, most flexible adaptations, we devise systems that are much too complicated for students to use (or at least initially learn to use). A student who is just learning to use symbolic communication skills may not initially need an AAC system requiring three steps to open, two steps to indicate the need for a change of overlay, and symbols that may have several different meanings according to the overlays used. In addition, carrying all those things around can be a task in itself and may require assistance from others in the management of the system. A simplified AAC system requiring the touch of a particular symbol or photograph would be much easier for the student to learn to use and for others to learn to interpret. (An adaptation such as this answers Questions 2, 3, and 4, as well.) Assessment evidence might include copies of the symbols, videotape or audiotape, peer notes, and teacher data.

Few things are as frustrating as having designed an impractical adaptation. By keeping in mind these five questions, educators should be able to devise adaptations that are immediately useful to the student, less stigmatizing, and flexible enough to facilitate learning and greater degrees of academic and social participation.

EMBEDDING ALTERNATE ASSESSMENT
ACTIVITIES INTO THE CONTEXT OF DAILY INSTRUCTION

It is essential that teachers understand the relationship between ongoing instruction and the kinds of learning evidence that should constitute the basis for their students' performance in the alternate assessment. If the Individuals with Disabilities Education Act Amendments of 1997 (PL 105-17) requirements for the inclusion of all students in large-scale educational assessments are interpreted by states, local districts, and teachers as something wholly new or as wholly different from what should *already* be effective instructional classroom practice, then alternate assessments may well be just another paperwork requirement for already overburdened practitioners.

Yet, alternate assessments can also bring instructional focus and clarity to a student's program (see Kleinert et al., 1997). Alternate assessments can themselves become instructional organizers for the student's overall program as well as a way of showcasing the student's important learning outcomes. Figure 5.2, developed by Mike Burdge, presents the ABCs of how to merge assessment with instruction. These are useful for any teacher interested in linking performance-based assessment to ongoing instruction.

SUMMARY

Through the process that Jean Clayton has described and the five questions related to effective instructional adaptations, this chapter illustrates how planning for the state alternate assessment can (and should) be incorporated into instructional programming from the start of the school year. We also hope that this chapter shows how planning for the alternate assessment can, in fact, *enhance* daily instruction to ensure maximum benefits for the student.

Table 5.1, which is based on a schedule developed by the Kentucky Statewide Alternate Assessment Project (1999), suggests a broad, year-long timetable that teachers may want to consider in creating alternate assessments that mirror the important elements of daily classroom instruction. Although we are very much aware that the individual timetables for alternate assessments will vary from state to state, the principle of planning for that assessment should always be integral to planning for the student's overall instructional program. Therefore, a timetable that reflects the entire school year, and the kinds of tasks in which teachers typically engage at different points throughout the year, generalizes very easily across all states requiring performance-based collections of student work.

Collaboration should center first around the state program of studies and the activities/units that will be covered in the general education setting. Second, the team should consider how the student with an IEP might take part in that instruction and what adaptations, assistive technology, and instructional support may be necessary to ensure meaningful participation and progress in the general curriculum. Third, thought should be given to how community-based instruction

ABCs of Merging Assessment and Instruction

A ssess, instruct, assess, instruct, assess, instruct, and so forth.

B egin with a clear expectation of what the student is to learn.

C ollaborate with others to develop meaningful instruction and assessment.

D esign adaptations/modifications to use across the curriculum.

E mbed skills into all activities to facilitate meaningful contexts and generalization.

F unctional skills include academics and literacy.

G eneralization occurs after a skill has been learned.

H ave instructional materials mirror things that are available during assessment.

I ntegrate skill instruction/application/generalization across the curriculum.

J udge your performance by that of your students.

K eep assessment tasks clear and concise.

L ook for other learning opportunities within an activity or lesson.

M ake adaptations that lots of students can use.

N ever say, "She won't get anything out of it."

O pportunities for instruction/assessment may occur outside of school for all students.

P repare the student and yourself well in advance of assessment activities.

Q uestion why a student's performance isn't as good as it should be.

R eview with the student how he did at the end of instruction and refocus on the expectations at the beginning of each lesson.

S ystematic instruction toward skill acquisition is essential.

T ake a look at the general education curriculum, content, and assessment first.

U tilize technology.

V ary instructional techniques and assessment modes to meet students' learning styles/preferences.

W ait for the student to respond.

X pect that your student will learn.

Y our instruction is reflected in your students' performance.

Z oom in on the most important parts of an activity/lesson/unit.

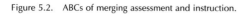

Figure 5.2. ABCs of merging assessment and instruction.

Table 5.1. Suggested timeline for alternate portfolio accountability year

	September	October	November	December	January	February	March	April	May
Collaborate	Yearly Monthly Weekly	Monthly Weekly	Monthly Weekly	Monthly Weekly	Yearly Monthly Weekly	Monthly Weekly	Monthly Weekly	Monthly Weekly	Monthly Weekly
Schedule	Develop and implement	Implement	Revise if needed and implement	Implement	Revise if needed and implement	Implement	Implement	Write teacher description of schedule use	Implement
Plan, monitor, self-evaluate (student forms)	Develop sheets (as generic as possible)	Implement for daily/weekly activities/instruction	Revise if needed and implement	Implement	Revise if needed and implement	Implement	Implement	Implement	Implement
Data	Baseline	Collect and chart/graph	Collect and chart/graph	Collect and chart/graph	Collect and chart/graph	Collect and chart/graph	Collect and chart/graph	Collect and chart/graph	Collect and chart/graph
Portfolio	Devise system for collection and storage of student work; Develop entry plans	Collect student work	Collect student work	Collect student work and "weed out" extra "stuff"	Revise entry development charts; Check to find "holes" in evidence of student work	Collect student work; Check state alternate assessment web page	Collect, check for "holes"; "weed out" extra; organize into entries; Get letters from peers, teachers; Write student letter to reviewer; Develop job resume—12th grade	Fill out entry cover sheets; Get parent validation letter; Write table of contents; Number portfolio pages; Submit portfolio	Score portfolios

(CBI) might supplement ongoing instruction across environments for *all* students.

The individualized student schedule should be a part of daily instruction and should serve to facilitate independence for the student. Math concepts and communication skills can easily be included as components of schedule use (see Chapter 6 for an extended discussion of individualized student schedules). The collection of data to assess these skills documents effective teaching and should be a part of instruction for those students who have communication deficits significant enough to require an object/symbol schedule.

Planning, monitoring, and self-evaluating should also be a part of daily instruction, focusing on the targeted IEP goal(s)/objective(s). Involving the student in ways that have a significant impact on his or her own learning will enhance student involvement and ownership of that performance.

Data collection on a regular basis will help instructional teams make good decisions regarding programming. Flat-line (or decreasing performance) data indicate a need to change programming, implement adaptations, or revise goal(s)/objective(s). Charting and graphing of student performance can be done by the teacher and/or the student. The latter option serves to involve the student in increasingly meaningful ways. Since these data reflect student performance on targeted IEP goal(s)/objective(s), a closer connection between the portfolio and the IEP is realized.

Portfolio development is an ongoing process. By making these activities a part of daily instruction, teachers can improve student achievement on the learning standards and collect the necessary evidence for the alternate assessment. As with any accountability year, there is a certain amount of extra work for both the student and the teacher. Following a timeline such as the one suggested above should keep the "extra" to a minimum.

REFERENCES

Browder, D., & Bambara, L. (2000). Home and community. In M. Snell & F. Brown (Eds.), *Instruction of students with severe disabilities* (5th ed., pp. 543–589). Columbus, OH: Charles E. Merrill.

Ezell, D., Klein, C., & Ezell-Powell, S. (1999). Empowering students with mental retardation through portfolio assessment: A tool for fostering self-determination skills. *Education and Training in Mental Retardation and Developmental Disabilities, 34*(4), 453–463.

Fickel, K., Schuster, J., & Collins, B. (1998). Teaching different tasks using different stimuli in a heterogeneous small group. *Journal of Behaviorial Education, 8,* 219–244.

Heward, W. (2000). *Exceptional children: An introduction to special education* (6th ed.). Columbus, OH: Merrill Prentice-Hall.

Individuals with Disabilities Education Act (IDEA) Amendments of 1997, PL 105-17, 20 U.S.C. §§ 1400 *et seq.*

Kampfer, S., Horvath, L., Kleinert, H., & Kearns, J. (In press). Teachers' perceptions of one state's alternate assessment portfolio program: Implications for practice and teacher preparation. *Exceptional Children.*

Kentucky Statewide Alternate Assessment Project. (1999). *Kentucky alternate portfolio teacher's guide.* Lexington: University of Kentucky, Interdisciplinary Human Development Institute.

Kleinert, H., & Kearns, J. (1999). A validation study of the performance indicators and learner outcomes of Kentucky's alternate assessment for students with significant disabilities. *Journal of The Association for Persons with Severe Handicaps, 24*(2), 100–110.

Kleinert, H.L., Kearns, J.F., & Kennedy, S. (1997). Accountability for all students: Kentucky's Alternate Portfolio assessment for students with moderate and severe cognitive disabilities. *Journal of The Association for Persons with Severe Handicaps, 22*(2), 88–101.

Kleinert, H., Kennedy, S., & Kearns, J. (1999). Impact of alternate assessments: A statewide teacher survey. *Journal of Special Education, 33*(2), 93–102.

Parker, M. (2000). *The effectiveness of simultaneous prompting on the acquisition of observational and instructive feedback stimuli when teaching a heterogeneous group of high school students.* Unpublished master's thesis, University of Kentucky, Lexington.

Snell, M., & Brown, F. (2000). Developing and implementing instructional programs. In M. Snell & F. Brown (Eds.), *Instruction of students with severe disabilities* (5th ed., pp. 115–172). Columbus, OH: Charles E. Merrill.

Special educators share their thoughts on special education teaching conditions (1999). *CEC Today, 5*(9), 1, 5, 15.

Wolery, M., Ault, M., & Doyle, P. (1992). *Teaching students with moderate and severe disabilities: Use of response prompting strategies.* Reading, MA: Addison Wesley Longman.

chapter 6

*How important is it for
students to make their own choices?*

SYSTEMATICALLY
TEACHING THE
COMPONENTS OF
SELF-DETERMINATION

Harold L. Kleinert, Anne Denham, Vanessa Burke Groneck,
Jean Clayton, Mike Burdge, Jacqui Farmer Kearns, and Meada Hall

Certainly, one of the greatest potential benefits to including students with significant disabilities in large-scale educational assessments is the opportunity that this presents for students to take part in the development of their own assessments. This is especially true in the context of portfolio assessment, which assesses collections of student work. Student involvement can extend from choosing one's own entries and the content that will be included within each entry, monitoring one's own performance and evaluating overall progress, and setting new goals based on that performance. Not only does such student involvement in the process help to make assessment a part of daily instruction but it also provides opportunities to build the component skills necessary for *self-determination*. As this chapter discusses, self-determination is itself an essential educational outcome for students.

SELF-DETERMINATION: AN IMPORTANT
OUTCOME FOR STUDENTS WITH SIGNIFICANT DISABILITIES

Self-determination has emerged as a critical outcome for all learners and as an underlying principle of public policy. Self-determination—the ability to control the basic decisions and directions of one's life—is especially important for students with significant disabilities. Historically, most of these individuals have not been given opportunities to make choices for themselves; their choices have been made by parents, guardians, teachers, and service providers. This is not merely a matter of lack of opportunity. Many students with significant disabilities do not have the skills and behaviors to assume control over their lives, and few educators and service providers know how to teach the components of self-determination. This chapter explores the specific component skills of self-determination and, through several examples of student work, shows how the systematic teaching of self-determination can be incorporated into alternate assessment practice.

What Is Self-Determination?

Holub, Lamb, and Bang (1998) defined self-determination as the process of choosing one's goals and taking the initiative to reach those goals. Martin and Marshall offered this description of self-determined individuals:

> They know how to choose—they know what they want and how to get it. From an awareness of personal needs, self-determined individuals choose goals and they doggedly pursue them. This involves asserting an individual's presence, making his or her concerns known, evaluating progress toward meeting goals, adjusting performance, and creating unique approaches to solve problems. (1995, p. 147)

Wehmeyer (1998) further described such an individual as someone who determines his or her own fate without undue constraints or external influences. Self-determination thus represents a fundamental approach to one's own life; it can rightly be called a culminating outcome of education and preparation for adulthood. As such, the development of self-determination skills should be reflected as an integral outcome within the alternate assessment.

Components of Self-Determination

A number of leading authorities have given consideration to the component skills of self-determination. Their work is very important for educators faced with the challenge of helping their students with significant disabilities to become self-determined. For example, Wehmeyer and Schwartz (1998) recognized the following components of self-determination: 1) choice-making skills, 2) decision-making skills, 3) problem-solving skills, 4) self-advocacy skills, 5) self-awareness skills, 6) self-management skills, 7) self-knowledge skills, 8) leadership skills, 9) goal-setting skills, 10) self-efficacy skills, and 11) internal locus of control.

Browder and Bambara noted that "self-determination is enhanced when students are involved in their own learning" (2000, p. 550) and that students are empowered through opportunities for choice, self-prompting, and self-management. Under the rubric of self-management, these authors included the multiple components of 1) goal setting (i.e., setting personal performance goals), 2) self-monitoring (i.e., recording progress toward goals), 3) self-evaluation (i.e., evaluating the acceptability of performance outcomes) and 4) self-reinforcement (i.e., rewarding oneself for a job well done).

Finally, Brown and Cohen (1996) identified the following skills that facilitate the development of self-determination for people with moderate and severe disabilities, including 1) making choices, 2) initiating activities without prompting,

3) using appropriate methods to gain the attention of someone, 4) asking questions, and 5) planning one's own schedule.

Although teachers may struggle with the difficulties associated with teaching such a broadly framed life outcome as self-determination, clearly they *are* able to teach many—if not all—of the component skills identified previously. Ezell, Klein, and Ezell-Powell described how students' involvement in the construction of their own portfolios provides those with cognitive disabilities opportunities to make choices, set goals, evaluate themselves, and take control of their own learning. For the secondary school students in their study, these researchers found that the skill of self-advocacy was the most "prominent and beneficial outcome of their students' involvement in the portfolio assessment process" (1999, p. 459).

This chapter presents several examples of how student choice-making, self-monitoring, self-evaluation, self-reinforcement, goal setting, self-initiation, and schedule planning can be built into performance-based assessment strategies for students with significant disabilities. Examples of student work that illustrate self-determination and its attendant skills are provided across all grade levels (elementary, middle, and high school) and major subject areas because we agree very much with Sands and Wehmeyer that self-determination, as a broad outcome, consists of component skills that can be developed systematically through "instruction, practice, and achievement" (1996, p. 268).

PLANNING, MONITORING, AND SELF-EVALUATION AS PART OF PERFORMANCE-BASED ASSESSMENT

According to Browder and Bambara (2000), the rubric of skills classified under self-management is essential to self-determination. Basic to acquiring self-management skills is learning the processes of planning, monitoring, and self-evaluating. All students should have opportunities to develop these skills. To illustrate our views, we include examples designed for students who are non-readers as well as readers (and in Chapter 7, we present similar examples that make use of computer and assistive technology for students with significant, multiple disabilities).

Designing Student Planning, Monitoring, and Self-Evaluation Formats

Student planning, monitoring, and self-evaluation formats should, of course, be directly related to the student's major learning goals. Figure 6.1 presents a blank teacher-made worksheet that can be especially helpful as a starting point in focusing on the student's targeted skills. Specifically, students can be given opportunities on this form to choose the skills they will practice (e.g., comprehension, basic addition and subtraction, independent task completion), as well as how they will work on various skills (e.g., highlighting the important parts of the sentence, working with a peer, practicing words/questions on the computer). Following is a short list of strategies and activities that a student can use to work on a specific skill:

- Working with a "buddy"
- Using visual/verbal cueing
- Working independently
- Using audiotapes/videotapes

Student name:_____ School year:_____

Target skill #1:_____
    Strategies/activities

      1. _____
      2. _____
      3. _____
      4. _____

Target skill #2:_____
    Strategies/activities

      1. _____
      2. _____
      3. _____
      4. _____

Target skill #3:_____
    Strategies/activities

      1. _____
      2. _____
      3. _____
      4. _____

Target skill #4:_____
    Strategies/activities

      1. _____
      2. _____
      3. _____
      4. _____

Target skill #5:_____
    Strategies/activities

      1. _____
      2. _____
      3. _____
      4. _____

Target skill #6:_____
    Strategies/activities

      1. _____
      2. _____
      3. _____
      4. _____

Figure 6.1.   Blank alternate assessment outline.

- Receiving hand-over-hand assistance
- Re-reading questions/passages
- Highlighting vocabulary/important parts of passages
- Using a calculator or some specific manipulative

Figure 6.2 presents a teacher's sample planning sheet for a high school student named Lester (a student with a moderate disability who is discussed in Chapter 4); the teacher's worksheet identifies Lester's targeted skills of comprehension, basic addition and subtraction, and independent task completion.

When creating planning and evaluation forms for student use, educators can start by giving the student the choice of what to work on (whenever feasible), and end with "Next time, I will work on ... " to enable the student to both gain and demonstrate more control over his or her own learning. Figure 6.3 presents Lester's planning, monitoring, and self-evaluation form that *he* uses across classes to plan and evaluate his performance for the skill of comprehension. (He would have additional planning, monitoring, and self-evaluation forms for basic addition/subtraction and for task completion.) The teacher has developed this form from the ideas generated in Figure 6.2. Lester chooses the strategy on which he wants to focus (e.g., reading each paragraph again, highlighting the important part of the sentence) to increase the percentage of study questions that he answers correctly. He also chooses *how* he will practice, and a peer or teacher initials his work. With the assistance of a classmate, he graphs the percentage of study questions answered correctly.

Elementary School Examples

Of course, there are as many ways to design student planning, monitoring, and self-evaluation forms as there are students! There are some components, however, that all such forms should have in common. The first is the targeted skill(s) on which the student is focusing.

Tim   For Tim, a student with multiple disabilities participating in fourth-grade social studies, his targeted skills for this class include "looking" and "choosing." Step 1 of Tim's plan, shown as Figure 6.4, enables him to choose by circling or pointing to which skill he most needs to emphasize. How he plans to practice that skill also is very important. Tim's physical therapist has indicated a range of positions in which Tim needs to be placed throughout the day. Tim's plan for practice, which will be indicated in Step 2 (see Figure 6.5), allows him to choose the position in which he practices the day's lesson. Each day, Tim could point to the picture of the position that he wants to use, and a teacher or peer could record his choice next to the correct day of the week on his planning sheet. (Of course, the teacher will ensure that Tim does use each of these positions, as prescribed by his physical therapist, throughout the week.)

The next part of Tim's form, shown in Figure 6.6 as Step 3, consists of the actual performance data collected on his targeted skill. These data may have been collected by a teacher or teacher's assistant, a peer, or by Tim himself. A visual representation of the data (bar graph) is included to allow Tim to more easily evaluate his progress. Tim or a peer could shade in the correct percentage on the bar graph each day at the bottom of the data chart/graph. Then, Tim could note the overall trend in his performance: Did he improve, stay the same, or do worse than he did in his previous try? Tim could circle or point to his response. (For

Student name: _Lester White_   School year: _2000—2001_

Target skill #1: _Comprehension_
    Strategies/activities
    1. _Highlight important parts of sentence_
    2. _Work with a peer_
    3. _Read the question over_
    4. _Practice the words/questions on the computer_

Target skill #2: _Basic addition and subtraction_
    Strategies/activities
    1. _Use a calculator_
    2. _Work with a buddy_
    3. _Use grid paper to align_
    4. _Highlight numbers to add/subtract_

Target skill #3: _Completing tasks independently_
    Strategies/activities
    1. _Use a checklist/on my own_
    2. _Work with a buddy_
    3. _Check with teacher after each part of task_
    4. _____

Target skill #4: _____
    Strategies/activities
    1. _____
    2. _____
    3. _____
    4. _____

Target skill #5: _____
    Strategies/activities
    1. _____
    2. _____
    3. _____
    4. _____

Target skill #6: _____
    Strategies/activities
    1. _____
    2. _____
    3. _____
    4. _____

Figure 6.2.   Sample of an alternate assessment outline for Lester.

Subject/class: <u>Language Arts</u>

Name: <u>Lester White</u>

Date: <u>4/18</u>

I need to work on (circle all that apply):

1. Looking at the question again (reading each question twice)

2. Reading each paragraph again ⟵*(circled)*

3. Highlighting the important part of the sentence

Today I will work on reading comprehension in (pick one):

Health   Social Studies   (Humanities)   Language Arts   Science

I will practice by (circle all that apply):

1. Studying with a friend ⟵*(circled)*

2. Working on the computer

3. Doing homework

4. Other

Day	Teacher/peer initials
Monday	MF
Tuesday	JD
Wednesday	JD
Thursday	MF
Friday	MF

100	100
90	90
80	80
70	70
60	60
50	50
40	40
30	30
20	20
10	10
% of study questions correct last time	% of study questions correct today

How did I do today (circle one):

(I improved)

I stayed the same

I did worse

Compare the percentage of study questions correct today with last time by shading in blocks above.

Next time I will work on (circle one):

1. Looking at the question again

2. Reading each paragraph again

3. Highlighting the important part of the sentence ⟵*(circled)*

Figure 6.3.   Student planning, monitoring, and self-evaluation form.

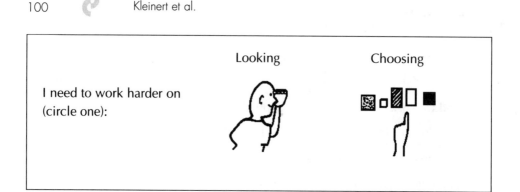

Figure 6.4. Step 1 of Tim's planning, monitoring, and self-evaluation form: Identifying targeted skills. (Picture Communication Symbols © 1981–2000, Mayer-Johnson, Inc., Solana Beach, CA, used with permission.)

example, Figure 6.8 shows that on 10/30 Tim looked up 60% of the time he needed to, but by the end of the week he looked up 90% of the time. Therefore, Tim has circled that during this particular week he improved on this activity.)

Step 4, the final portion of Tim's planning, monitoring, and self-evaluation sheet, provides him with the opportunity to indicate the skill on which he most needs to focus during his next instructional session (see Figure 6.7). This is the culminating step in having him take more ownership for his success and allows him to gain greater insight into his own learning needs. Figure 6.8 illustrates Tim's planning, monitoring, and self-evaluation form in its entirety, with sample data for the week recorded.

Isabella   Figure 6.9 presents a math monitoring sheet for Isabella, who is learning to use a calculator. The monitoring form includes a place for her to

	On the wedge	In chair	In stander
My plan to practice (check one each day):			
Monday	____	____	____
Tuesday	____	____	____
Wednesday	____	____	____
Thursday	____	____	____
Friday	____	____	____

Figure 6.5. Step 2 of Tim's planning, monitoring, and self-evaluation form: Identifying a plan for practice. (Picture Communication Symbols © 1981–2000, Mayer-Johnson, Inc., Solana Beach, CA, used with permission.)

% of correct responses						Date	Setting/activity
100							
90							
80							
70							
60							
50							
40							
30							
20							
10							
Date							

I improved   I stayed the same   I did worse

Figure 6.6.   Step 3 of Tim's planning, monitoring, and self-evaluation form: Monitoring and self-evaluating perform-ance. (Picture Communication Symbols © 1981–2000, Mayer-Johnson, Inc., Solana Beach, CA, used with permission.)

indicate the component skill on which she most needs to focus (e.g., looking at the numbers more carefully, being careful where the calculator is touched, writing the numbers more carefully), the operations in which she will work (e.g., two-column addition, two-column subtraction, multiplication, division), and how she plans to practice these operations (e.g., at a store, with newspaper ads, with a math workbook, with a friend). As on Tim's monitoring form, there is a

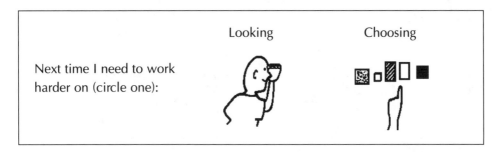

Figure 6.7.   Step 4 of Tim's planning, monitoring, and self-evaluation form: Refocusing for the next time. (Picture Communication Symbols © 1981–2000, Mayer-Johnson, Inc., Solana Beach, CA, used with permission.)

	Looking	Choosing

I need to work harder on
(circle one):

	On the wedge	In chair	In stander

My plan to practice
(check one each day):

	On the wedge	In chair	In stander
Monday	✓		
Tuesday			✓
Wednesday		✓	
Thursday			✓
Friday		✓	

% of correct responses						Date	Setting/activity
100						10/30	General class/reading
90					▓	10/31	General class/cooperative group
80		▓		▓	▓	11/1	Library/computer research
70		▓	▓	▓	▓	11/2	General class/reading
60	▓	▓	▓	▓	▓	11/3	General class/journal
50	▓	▓	▓	▓	▓		
40	▓	▓	▓	▓	▓		
30	▓	▓	▓	▓	▓		
20	▓	▓	▓	▓	▓		
10	▓	▓	▓	▓	▓		
Date	10/30	10/31	11/1	11/2	11/3		

I improved	I stayed the same	I did worse

	Looking	Choosing

Next time, I need to work harder on
(circle one):

Figure 6.8. Sample planning, monitoring, and self-evaluation form for Tim, incorporating all steps. (Picture Communication Symbols © 1981–2000, Mayer-Johnson, Inc., Solana Beach, CA, used with permission.)

I need to work harder on (circle all that apply):

number   write

Look at number   Be careful   Be careful
more carefully   where I touch   what I write

My goal for this week in math is using a calculator to (circle all that apply):

Multiply   Divide   Two-column addition   Two-column subtraction

How I will learn (circle all that apply):

money   math   friend

At the store   Store ads   Math book   Study with a friend

% of correct responses						Date	Setting/activity
100							
90							
80							
70							
60							
50							
40							
30							
20							
10							
Date							

(Circle one.)

I improved   I stayed the same   I did not improve

Next time, I need to work harder on (circle all that apply):

number   write

Look at number   Be careful   Be careful
more carefully   where I touch   what I write

Figure 6.9. Student math planning, monitoring, and self-evaluation form for Isabella. (Picture Communication Symbols © 1981–2000, Mayer-Johnson, Inc., Solana Beach, CA, used with permission.)

place for Isabella to indicate how she did and on what she needs to work next time. Many of the same planning and evaluation features are built into this form, as well.

Marcie   Figure 6.10 presents the planning, monitoring, and evaluation form for Marcie, the fourth-grade science student discussed in Chapter 4. You will recall that Marcie is working on identifying sight words and writing simple sentences using capital letters and ending punctuation. Her monitoring sheet provides a place for her to indicate how she will improve her studying and attending (e.g., listening) skills in science, as well as a place for her to chart and graph her correct use of capital letters in the context of her science writing (i.e., by filling in or coloring on the chart the number of times that she capitalized correctly).

Jerome   Figure 6.11 presents a self-monitoring job checklist form for Jerome, an elementary-age student with a disability who is learning a vocational activity (i.e., school job) in partnership with Stephen, a peer who does not have a disability. Jerome completes this form using a rubber stamp and help from Stephen. This form also can be completed on the computer using a custom overlay and text-to-speech software instead of graphics (see Chapter 7 for a more complete description of this software). The "Documentation" column of this form relates the student's reply to each question to one or more of the criteria (e.g., student use of daily schedule, peer participation, applicability to multiple environments) within the scoring rubric of that state's alternate assessment. For the reviewer of the student's portfolio, this makes it easy to see how each aspect of the student's self-evaluation relates to the assessment scoring rubric.

Middle and High School Examples

Figure 6.12 presents an example of a blank book journal and report format for a middle or high school student with more advanced academic skills in language arts. This evaluation sheet includes questions about the main characters and the story's ending, as well as a question about the new vocabulary that the student has learned from the book. An added feature of this planning and evaluation form is the question that asks the student what he or she found to be the most effective learning strategy on this task (e.g., reading with a buddy, listening to an audiotaped version, reading on one's own). As students gain more control over their own learning, being able to identify the most effective learning strategies for themselves is an important skill.

Peter   Figure 6.13 is an example of a form designed for a middle school student, Peter, who is taking a keyboarding class. Peter selects the priority objective on which he will focus for that day, as well as the strategies he will use to maintain that focus. There also is a place for him or the teacher (or both) to indicate the number of teacher cues that he required for that day and to visually compare that day's performance with the previous day's lesson. Again, there are places for Peter to evaluate his overall performance for the day and to indicate the target skill(s) for the next lesson. An important feature of this planning, monitoring, and self-evaluation form is a place for comments by the teacher and/or a peer with whom the student practiced.

Finally, Figure 6.14 is designed as a generic—or universal—planning, monitoring, and self-evaluation sheet, which can be supplemented with a student's own pictures, photographs, or line drawings. Mayer-Johnson (Johnson, 1994)

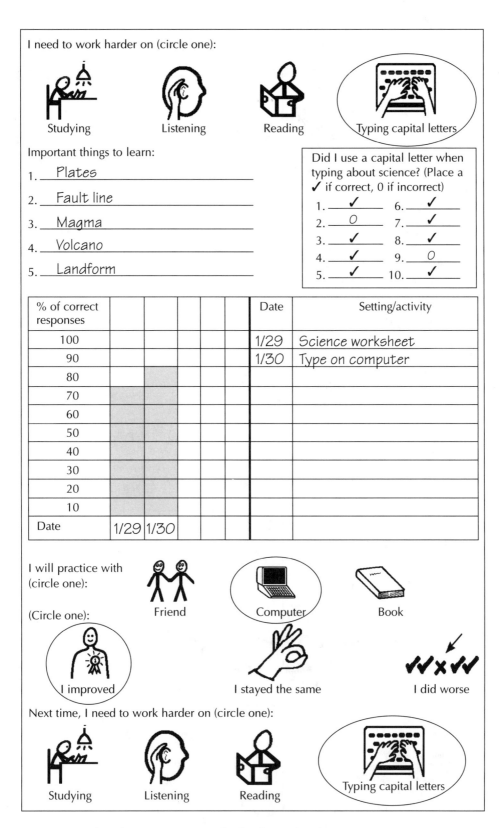

I need to work harder on (circle one):

Studying Listening Reading (Typing capital letters)

Important things to learn:

1. Plates
2. Fault line
3. Magma
4. Volcano
5. Landform

Did I use a capital letter when typing about science? (Place a ✓ if correct, 0 if incorrect)

1. ✓   6. ✓
2. 0   7. ✓
3. ✓   8. ✓
4. ✓   9. 0
5. ✓   10. ✓

% of correct responses					Date	Setting/activity
100					1/29	Science worksheet
90					1/30	Type on computer
80						
70						
60						
50						
40						
30						
20						
10						
Date	1/29	1/30				

I will practice with (circle one):

Friend (Computer) Book

(Circle one):

(I improved) I stayed the same I did worse

Next time, I need to work harder on (circle one):

Studying Listening Reading (Typing capital letters)

Figure 6.10. Student planning, monitoring, and self-evaluation form for Marcie: Writing in science. (Picture Communication Symbols © 1981–2000, Mayer-Johnson, Inc., Solana Beach, CA, used with permission.)

Date	10/24	10/25	10/26	Documentation to demonstrate . . .
I am working on . . .				Planned focus for instruction
Did I use my schedule?	Yes	No	Yes	Use of schedule
Did I find out if the newspapers were delivered?	Yes	Yes	No	Solving a problem
Where did I go?	Office Other classes	Office Other classes	Office Other classes	Environment
Did I get what I needed— stamp, ink, etc?	Yes	No	Yes	Preparation
Did I help count the newspapers?	Yes	Yes	Yes	Math skills
What will I do first?				Planning, choice
Did I use my words?	Yes	No	Yes	Evidence of targeted skill

Figure 6.11. Sample elementary level job checklist for Jerome. (Picture Communication Symbols (c) 1981–2000, Mayer-Johnson, Inc., Solana Beach, CA, used with permission.)

Did I put my things away?	Yes	Yes	Yes	Management of belongings
Did I do a good job?	Yes	Yes	Yes	Evaluation
Did I try harder at . . . ?				Self-evaluation
Did I get paid	No	No	Yes	
Next time I will do better at . . .				Planning for improved performance (graphics represent targeted skills).
Which friend helped me today?	Tim	Sarah	Brooke	Peer participation
What did my friend do?	Help count	Help put things away	Help get supplies	Peer activity

graphics make excellent resources for this purpose, and several of our examples from this chapter incorporate Mayer-Johnson symbols.

MAKING CHOICES DURING NORMAL ROUTINES: ANOTHER KEY TO SELF-DETERMINATION

Bambara and Koger (1996) and Falvey (1995) discussed the importance of helping people with significant disabilities learn to make their own choices. As Falvey noted, "The freedom to have choices and personally make decisions is cherished by people in all stages of life, yet it is a freedom that is typically denied to persons

Name: _____

Dates: Start _____ Finish _____

Title: _____

Author: _____

Main characters (two or more): _____

_____

How I chose to complete this book (circle one):

    Read with buddy   Listen to audiotaped version   Read on my own

New vocabulary I learned from book (five or more words):

_____

The book's ending was (circle one or both):

    Happy   Sad

The book was (circle one):

    Great!   Good   Okay   Poor (not so good)

    ****   ***   **   *

What worked well and helped you do well while reading this story?
(Circle all that apply.)

    Reading with a buddy   Audiotaped version   Reading on my own

What will work well for you when reading your next selection? (Circle one.)

    The same strategy   I would like to try something different

Figure 6.12.   Blank book journal/report form.

Name: _Peter Smith_____ Date: _9/26_____

I will work on (circle one):

(Placing my fingers correctly in home key position)

Following directions

Completing tasks

Speeding up my work pace

I will work on this by (circle one):

Practicing with a peer before starting

(Asking teacher to repeat/explain directions (say, "I don't understand"))

Not looking at my neighbors in class while typing

10	10
9	9
8	8
7	7
6	6
5	5
4	4
3	3
2	2
1	1
Number of teacher cues last time	Number of teacher cues today

Teacher/peer comments

Peter needs to learn to feel comfortable with asking me to repeat directions.
   —LB

How did I do today? (Circle one.)

I improved (I stayed the same) I did worse

Next time I will work on (circle one):

Placing my fingers correctly in home key position

(Following directions)

Completing tasks

Speeding up my work pace

Figure 6.13. Sample planning, monitoring, self-evaluation form for Peter: Keyboarding class.

with disabilities" (1995, p. 229). Bambara and Koger noted at least four reasons for the importance of choice in the lives of children and youth with significant disabilities: 1) Choice enhances personal satisfaction and the quality of one's life, 2) choice-making is an important preparation for independence, 3) choices increase student motivation, and 4) choices can prevent problem behaviors. These authors have noted that choice-making produces two important educational outcomes: the expression of one's personal preferences and a sense of control and self-efficacy over one's life. Giangreco, Cloninger, and Iverson included "having choice and control that match one's age and culture" (1998, p. 18) as one of the five essential life outcomes that families and students are asked to consider in prioritizing IEP objectives through the COACH (*Choosing Outcomes and Accommodations for Children: A Guide to Educational Planning for Students with Disabilities, Second Edition*) process. Giangreco et al. noted that not having choices has "perpetuated an unproductive cycle of limited expectations and opportunities for persons with disabilities" (1998, p. 18).

Choice-making also is closely related to self-management. As Giangreco et al. commented, "A common theme that cuts across cultures is that children are given increasing choice and control, along with corresponding responsibilities, as they are prepared for adulthood" (1998, p.18). Because choice-making does represent both an important educational outcome in itself as well as a necessary step to self-management and self-determination, Kleinert, Kearns, and Kennedy (1997) argued that *opportunities* for choice making, as well as direct evidence of students making meaningful choices, should be included in the process of alternate assessment. In a national survey of 44 content experts in the field of moderate and severe disabilities, Kleinert and Kearns (1999) reported that these experts rated opportunities for choice-making highly as an essential performance indicator for these students (mean rating of 4.8 on a 5-point scale, with 1 meaning *lowest importance* and 5 meaning *highest importance*).

The Context and Format of Choices

Bambara and Koger (1996) identified strategies both for teaching choice-making and for embedding student choices across daily routines and classes. For a more complete description of how to teach choice-making, we refer the reader to their work. In embedding choices across daily routines, Bambara and Koger noted that once daily routines are identified for the student, educators need to consider both *between-activities* choices (e.g., choosing between a math and science assignment, choosing between two extracurricular activities) and *within-activity* choices (e.g., choosing which book to read for a book report, choosing which set of materials to use). Both types of choices are important, and performance-based assessment strategies (especially portfolio assessment) allow students to demonstrate multiple instances of making choices to direct their own learning or to express their personal preferences.

Once between- and within-activity opportunities for choices have been identified, teachers need to consider a choice *format*. As Bambara and Koger (1996) noted, a closed-ended question format (giving the student a choice among a limited number of explicit choices, such as, "Would you like to use oil paint or water paint?") may be most appropriate for a student with a limited communication system or for a student who is just learning to make choices. For

I need to work harder on:
(Teacher: Place two or three symbols representing subskills of targeted skill.)

My plan to practice:
(Teacher: Place two or three symbols representing instructional activities or ways to practice. Circle plan and then check off as completed.)

% of correct responses						Date	Setting/activity
100							
90							
80							
70							
60							
50							
40							
30							
20							
10							
Date							
Activity							

(Circle one:)

I improved   I did not improve

Next time, I need to work harder on:
(Place same symbols from the top and circle here.)

Figure 6.14. Generalized planning, monitoring, and self-evaluation form. (Picture Communication Symbols © 1981–2000, Mayer-Johnson, Inc., Solana Beach, CA, used with permission.)

a student with more experience in making choices, an open-ended question format may be more appropriate (e.g., "Which CD do you want to play during your lunch break?").

High- and Low-Impact Choices

Choice making may be described not only in terms of the context of the choice (between- and within-activity choices) and the format of the choice (closed- and open-ended choices) but also in terms of the long-term, potential impact on the student's life. Smull and Danehey (1994) described two levels of choices: *boundary* choices (high-impact choices) and *everyday* choices (low-impact choices).

Boundary choices can be depicted as those choices that have direct and long-term effects on a person's lifestyle, education, and/or vocation. These may include choices such as "Where do I want to live?," "What is something I would like to learn?," and "What type of job would I like to have?" Conversely, everyday choices usually have an immediate impact on a situation but rarely have long-term effects. These may include decisions such as "What television program do I want to watch?," What color marker do I want to use?," and "What do I want for lunch?"

Students with disabilities often are restricted in their opportunities for choice-making, especially in opportunities for making potentially high-impact choices. For most students with moderate to severe disabilities, if choices are provided at all, they are primarily low-impact choices. As expectations are continually raised for all students, however, we are beginning to understand just how important both opportunities and instruction involving high-impact choices are for everyone!

In establishing opportunities for high-impact choices, it helps to delineate the types of choices that students might be expected to make. These high-impact choices, which can be available throughout the school day, fall into four main categories:

1. Learning or practicing a skill

   - Deciding which materials to use
   - Deciding with whom to practice/learn

2. Goal setting

   - Deciding how much to learn
   - Deciding what to learn

3. Scheduling

   - Adjusting one's schedule
   - Scheduling practice time

4. Demonstrating acquisition of skill/information

   - Deciding which method to use
   - Deciding which materials to use
   - Deciding which position to work in

The following example illustrates the principle of embedding high-impact choices into student learning.

Christine   Christine is a primary-level student who uses a voice output communication device and who requires daily positioning in a prone stander, an adapted desk chair for group tables, and additional positioning (prone over wedge and side-lying). Her IEP objectives of improving her reach and grasp and use of communication device will be targeted during math time. Each day before math, Christine chooses her strategy for learning, which includes helping to decide how she will be positioned while working on math; and she helps to set her own goals (i.e., what to learn). To do this, she is presented with icons of an adapted desk chair, prone stander, wedge, and side-lyer; which are placed on an eye-gaze board. Once she looks at her choice of working positions, she is asked, "Do you want to work in the _____?" (e.g., stander, wedge, side-lyer). She then answers "yes" or "no" using her communication device. With physical assistance, she pulls off the corresponding preprinted sticker (made from mailing labels; they indicate the position that she has chosen) and places the sticker on her math calendar. This calendar demonstrates her choice-making abilities and can be used as part of her alternate assessment evidence. Christine then uses her communication device to choose math counters she can use to work on counting or colored cubes to work on recognition of patterns. During the lesson, performance data are collected on her targeted skills of reach and grasp and her use of her communication device. Of course, Christine also is receiving instruction in counting and patterns (along with all of the other children), and she is benefiting from the increased motor control that results from working in her required positioning.

Teach Choice-Making Systematically   Simply presenting choices, however, such as those described previously, does not mean that students will be able to make effective decisions. Choice-making must be taught systematically. This is especially true for high-impact choices, for which the consequences of our choices might not always be immediately apparent. Here are some effective strategies:

- **Provide regular opportunities for making choices.** First, the opportunity to make those choices must be made available on a regular basis. Throughout this chapter, we suggest several ways these opportunities might be incorporated into a student's school day, especially in the context of planning, monitoring, and evaluating one's own performance.
- **Make choices meaningful.** The choices must be presented in a way that is meaningful for the student. This can be quite challenging, considering the communication modes of some students and the messages they will be expected to understand and convey. The importance of a consistent mode of communication cannot be overestimated in this learning process. Some students may need only the written word to indicate their preference among the choices available, while others may need verbal input, real objects, symbolic objects/textures, and so forth.
- **Provide guidance as needed.** Students need guidance in understanding the consequences of their choices. This should include not only a discussion of "Did I get what I wanted/needed?" but also, "Was this the best choice I could have made?" For example, talking with students about how their choice of a *strategy for learning* influences their achievement is completely appropriate and necessary if they are expected to choose the strategy that will have the most positive impact on their performance. If

the performance was better than the preceding time, the choice was probably a good one. If the performance was not as good, then a student should be directed to make a more effective choice the next time. The evaluation of the effectiveness of choices is critical to the development of good choice-making skills.

DOCUMENTING STUDENT CHOICE MAKING: AN INTEGRAL ASPECT OF PERFORMANCE ASSESSMENT

Within the context of alternate assessment, documentation of student choices certainly can be noted through the use of student planning, monitoring, and self-evaluation forms. The principle of choice-making is incorporated in the forms throughout this chapter. For example, choice-making is embedded into the monitoring sheet depicted in Figure 6.3, in that the student must choose on what he or she needs to improve (e.g., looking at the questions again, reading the paragraph again, highlighting the important part of the sentence), as well as the plan for practice (e.g., studying with a friend, working on the computer, doing homework exercises). As a second example, the monitoring sheet depicted in Figure 6.13 for keyboarding class presents a student choice for working on the following skills: 1) placing fingers in the home position, 2) following directions, 3) completing tasks, and 4) increasing work pace. This figure also presents students with choices to help them develop a practice plan in class while typing, including 1) practicing with a peer before starting, 2) asking the teacher to repeat or explain directions, and 3) keeping one's eyes to oneself (not looking at one's neighbors).

Peer reflections also can be included as additional evidence of a student's choice-making. For example, several states require that the student's alternate assessment be introduced by a letter to the reviewer, which is to be written by the student and/or his peers. Here is an excerpt from one such letter written by a peer of a student with a disability:

> Together we picked out his portfolio entries. When I asked Sam if he wanted to put his English entry first (where we cooked the chicken pastries), he smiled and shook his head yes. When I showed him his vocational entry—apple crafts—and his humanities entry—decorating—Sam looked at his apple crafts, and I knew that he wanted [the vocational entry for] number two. So that made the decorating number three. We talked about how important it is to use math skills, so we chose his vending machines, elevator use, and name stamp activities as his fourth entry. Because Sam feels so much better, we talked about a health and physical education entry. He smiled when we asked him if he wanted to include this, and he clapped his hands. He loves line dancing with the LOUD music and the [girls]. We hope you like Sam's portfolio. It has been hard work and fun to be a part of his high school life. —A peer

Of course, student choices should be both age-appropriate and reflective of family cultural and religious beliefs (Giangreco et al., 1998). The point is *not* that children and youth with significant disabilities should be given greater latitude "to do what they want" than are typically developing children, but that students with significant disabilities, who have long been denied an appropriate voice in even trivial decisions in their daily routines, should have systematic opportunities and instruction to begin to assume an age-appropriate level of control and self-direction over their lives in preparation for adulthood.

TEACHING STUDENTS TO
MANAGE THEIR OWN DAILY SCHEDULES

Self-management is a crucial skill for all students, and for students with significant disabilities it not only increases independence but also fosters generalization
(Heward, 2000). A crucial part of teaching self-management is instructing students to manage their time and to take responsibility for getting themselves
where they are supposed to be, that is, to independently follow their own daily
schedule! Indeed, learning to schedule one's day and to carry through with that
schedule provides opportunities for acquiring many related skills. As Bambara
and Koger noted, "Self-scheduling moves beyond simple choice-making and
encourages self-determination by giving people a strategy for identifying what to
do and how and when to do it" (1996, p. 34). The primary mechanisms for
teaching self-scheduling are student calendars or daily schedule systems. As
Mirenda noted, student calendar or schedule systems can be very valuable teaching tools:

> Calendar or schedule systems can be excellent communication aids. They provide an
> overview of upcoming activities, so that students know exactly what will happen next.
> They are a vehicle for introducing new symbols that represent activities or classes dur-
> ing the school day. They also can provide a means for students to respond to direct ques-
> tions (e.g., "What's next?") and can be used expressively to request desired activities
> (e.g., Is it lunchtime yet?"). Finally, they can help students who engage in behavior
> problems during transitions to move from one activity or class to the next with fewer
> problems by making upcoming activities more predictable. (1999, pp. 130–131)

Individualized student schedules, designed so that students can learn to use
them, are excellent tools for teaching students to make choices, initiate interactions, plan activities, and develop time concepts. Finally, an individualized student schedule provides a wealth of information about the student's day (e.g., time
spent in general education class activities; scheduled community-based instruction; opportunities to learn across a range of school environments, including
extracurricular activities).

For all of these reasons, a number of states are designing requirements for
individualized student schedules as well as evidence of students learning to follow their own daily schedules into their respective alternate assessments. This
section presents strategies for teaching students to manage their daily schedules
and for indicating how this important skill can be incorporated into the students'
assessment portfolios.

Designing the Format for an Individualized Schedule[1]

The student's individualized schedule should reflect his or her primary mode of
communication. Students who can read, for example, typically use printed word
schedules, perhaps with the printed time noted or a clock face stamped by each
activity or class. Students who are learning to communicate through pictures may
use pictorial or line-drawn symbols (such as Mayer-Johnson line drawings—see

---

[1]This section is adapted in part with permission from Kentucky Systems Change Project. (1993,
Winter). *Designing individualized student schedules*. Lexington: University of Kentucky, Interdisciplinary
Human Development Institute.

Johnson, 1994) or actual photographs to denote each activity in their day. Again, printed times (written digitally) or actual clock faces with the correct time may accompany each picture, and the printed name of the activity should be included along with the picture or line drawing.

Early communicators or students with significant visual impairments may use actual objects, miniature objects, *tangible symbols*, or *textured symbols*. Tangible symbols are similar to real objects, except that they are "objects, or parts of objects, that feel or sound like what they represent" (Mirenda, 1999, p. 123). For example, a heavy sock for gym class or chain links to indicate a swing for recess would be tangible symbols. Textured symbols could include a piece of film for camera club, a stretchy piece of bathing suit for swimming, or a paper napkin for lunch. As Mirenda noted, the symbols chosen should take into account the student's communicative ability, the student's own preferences (which type of symbol the *student* most prefers), and the fact that other people will need to understand the student's messages.

On-Line Clip Art for Planning, Monitoring, and Self-Evaluation Forms

A number of web sites include free, downloadable* symbols that are useful when designing assessment forms. For a virtual tour, visit these sites on the Internet:

Technology (computers, audio/video, overhead)

http://www.aaaclipart.com (click on office, computers, or technology)

TVs, VCRs, cameras

http://www.clipartgallery.com (click on electronics)

Team/group work (people at tables)

http://www.coolarchive.com (click on clipart)
(click on office)

Domestics/food

http://www.barrysclipart.com
(click on clipart)
(click on agricultural or assorted black & white)
(fruit–click on Images by Jacci)

Science/math

http://www.iband.com/clip (click on clipart)
http://www.barrysclipart.com (find: chemistry)

*Check each site carefully for copyright and usage guidelines.

Once the symbol system has been chosen, it is time to consider the display format for the schedule, the method of highlighting the activity, and a strategy for indicating activity completion. For example, a student learning to use a written schedule may write or print out his or her own schedule, highlight the current or next activity by circling it, and indicate that the activity is completed by placing a check by it. For a student using a picture or photograph symbol, the pictures can be placed in plastic pockets (similar to those found in photography albums) and arranged horizontally from left to right. A student might highlight the activity by removing it from the pocket (to initiate the activity) and carrying it on a ring during the activity. To indicate completion, the student can replace the picture face down in its original slot. Students who are using objects or tangible symbols will need a compartmentalized box or series of boxes—one compartment for each symbol—typically arranged in a left-to-right sequence. To highlight the current activity, the student might uncover the current box and take the symbol with her as she performs that activity. A separate box (perhaps arranged at the end of the series of compartments) could be used in which to place the objects or symbols for the completed activities. Should the student place each object or symbol into the completed box as she finishes that activity, she would just need to go to the next remaining object in the left-to-right sequence to know what activity comes next. See Mirenda (1999) for a more detailed description of calendar and schedule systems.

Of course, students should be taught, as much as possible, to generate their own daily schedules (a further step in self-management). For example, using Mayer-Johnson symbols and the accompanying software program (*Boardmaker for Windows*, Mayer-Johnson, 1998), the student can format his schedule for each day while simultaneously taking note of any special events or changes in that daily schedule.

Collecting Data on Schedule Management

At least one state, Kentucky, also requires that instructional data be included in the alternate assessment on how the student has learned to follow his or her schedule. These data give additional evidence that the student has learned this important self-management skill. Evidence of students learning to manage their own daily schedules can be collected in a number of ways:

- **A description of activity completion.** For a student who is totally independent and is able to use a monthly pocket calendar and/or assignment book, teachers could include a description of how the student indicates activity or assignment completion, with several duplicated pages from the calendar or assignment book across the year. The completed pages should indicate how the student has made notations and checked off completed items, with instructional programming data (e.g., number of daily prompts) included as appropriate. See Figure 6.15 for an example of this type of student schedule.
- **Samples of the student schedule.** For a student using a picture or line-drawing schedule, teachers could include samples of the actual student schedule from several points across the school year that also indicate how the student uses the schedule. This evidence should include how the student denotes completed activities, as well as what opportunities for student choice-making and planning were provided. Instructional programming data (e.g., percentage of activities initiated independently and correctly checked off) should be included as appropriate. See Figures 6.16 and 6.17 for examples of pictorial schedules. The

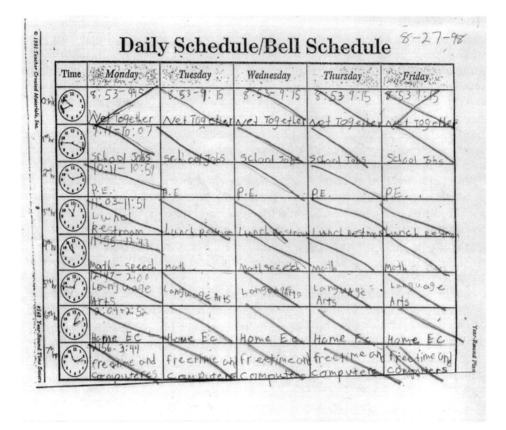

Figure 6.15.　Individualized student schedule: Student marks off response. (From Kentucky Statewide Alternate Portfolio Project. [1999]. *Kentucky alternate portfolio assessment teacher's guide.* Lexington: Kentucky Department of Education; reprinted by permission.)

student who uses the individualized schedule depicted in Figure 6.16 uses a stamp to indicate each completed activity. The student who uses the schedule depicted in Figure 6.17 indicates activity completion by a printed *yes* or *no*. In order to assist this student in relating digital time to clock-face configurations (an instructional objective), both are included in the schedule.

- **Mixed data.** For a student using an object/tangible symbol system, the evidence should include a photograph of the student's system, a description of how the student uses the system, and instructional programming data (taken from teacher and/or peer data sheets) that indicate student progress in managing his or her own schedule.

Individualized student schedules and calendars present numerous opportunities for embedding choice-making (Bambara & Koger, 1996). Student schedules can be built to reflect the activities for one day, or can be expanded to a broader time frame (e.g., weekly chart). As these authors have noted, students can learn to identify and include preferred activities during those discrete times that they have free, and this strategy can be used for written, pictorial, or object schedules or calendars. For students who may be assuming greater control over their day, they can be taught to first identify those activities that they need to do followed by those activities they would like to do and to develop a schedule that allows for both.

Finally, individualized student schedules also can be very readily combined with planning, monitoring, and self-evaluation forms. Figure 6.18 presents an

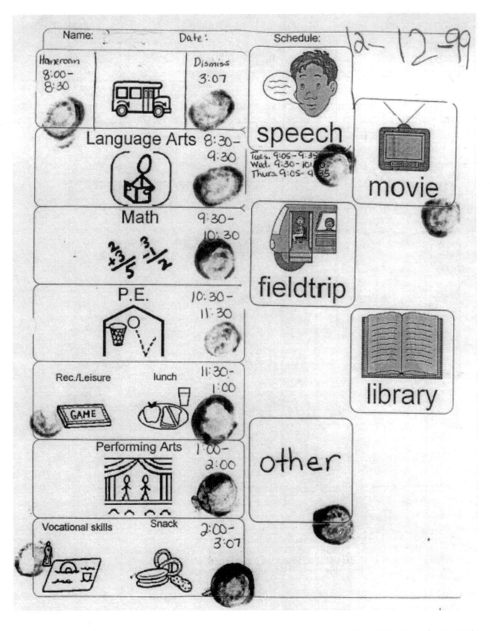

Figure 6.16. Sample individualized student pictorial schedule: Student stamps response. (From Kentucky Statewide Alternate Portfolio Project. [1999]. *Kentucky alternate portfolio assessment teacher's guide.* Lexington: Kentucky Department of Education, reprinted by permission. Picture Communication Symbols © 1981–2000, Mayer-Johnson, Inc., Solana Beach, CA, used with permission.)

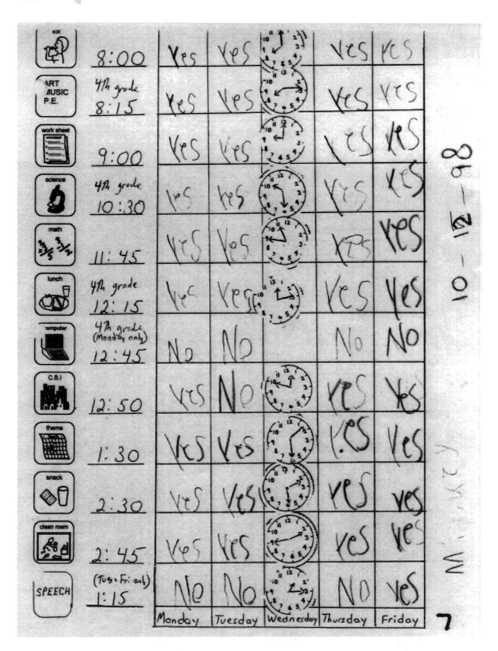

Figure 6.17.   Individualized student pictorial schedule: The student indicates what activity comes next, draws the correct starting time on the clock face that corresponds to the printed digital time, and indicates when the activity is completed. (From Kentucky Statewide Alternate Portfolio Project. [1999]. *Kentucky alternate portfolio assessment teacher's guide.* Lexington: Kentucky Department of Education, reprinted by permission. Picture Communication Symbols © 1981–2000, Mayer-Johnson, Inc., Solana Beach, CA, used with permission.)

individualized student schedule, developed by Amanda Kinder, a teacher from Maysville, Kentucky, for just that purpose.

___

Teaching Students to Follow Their Own Daily Schedules: An Example from the Field

Sandra, one of my students who has a significant disability, prepares her schedule daily with the use of a metal tray (cookie sheet), a paper overlay with activities pictured, matching activity cards with magnets on the back, and two small plastic bags. Sandra has a different overlay for each morning and afternoon. When Sandra arrives at school in the morning, her schedule is waiting for her on her desk, with a small plastic bag full of activity cards. She places her activity cards on the overlay by matching her activity cards to the correct pictures. As Sandra begins each activity, she removes the magnetic card from her tray and places it on a magnetic surface in front of her. This denotes the activity in which she is presently working. After the activity is completed, Sandra places the card in the second plastic bag hanging on the board beside her; this denotes completion. After lunch, the second tray of activities is used.

In the fall, Sandra required hand-over-hand assistance to use her schedule. She now recognizes the picture cards as representing activities and can name them by using one word for identification. At the completion of many activities, Sandra now removes her card independently and places it in the bag denoting completion. She even sets up her afternoon activities without needing a cue. At times, with one of her favorite activities, she will try and place the card on the board to tell me, her teacher, it is time for that particular activity and to bypass the others! At that point, she is gently reminded that she must complete the activities in order!

Putting It All Together: A Step-by-Step Process for Alternate Assessment

Alternate educational assessment should reflect best practice; it should serve not just as another paperwork requirement for teachers, but as a framework for improving instruction for the student and teacher. At the beginning of the school year, I look at the requirements for a distinguished portfolio (the highest rating in the alternate assessment in my state), in relation to the strengths and interests of each student and his or her individual goals as outlined by the IEP. I consider each goal within the context of the content areas required by my state's alternate assessment, and decide where those goals may best be implemented. Some goals may be easily addressed across many environments, as might be the case with an embedded skill objective for a student with more significant disabilities. For example, a student who is working on motor skills of reach and grasp may work on this skill within all content areas (e.g., reaching for a block for a counting activity in math, reaching for art supplies in arts and human-

Time	Activity	Activity	What do I plan to take?	X	How did I do?
8:00		bathroom			great / OK / Not good
8:10		breakfast	Library 100		great / OK / Not good
8:30	P.E. music library computer class art class	Activity period	coat		great / OK / Not good
9:00		calendar			great / OK / Not good
9:20		weather			great / OK / Not good
9:45		playground	coat		great / OK / Not good
10:00		book			great / OK / Not good
10:15		brush teeth			great / OK / Not good
10:30		math class			great / OK / Not good

Figure 6.18. Student schedule and daily planning, monitoring, and self-evaluation form for Sandra. (Courtesy of A. Kinder. Picture Communication Symbols © 1981–2000, Mayer-Johnson, Inc., Solana Beach, CA, used with permission.)

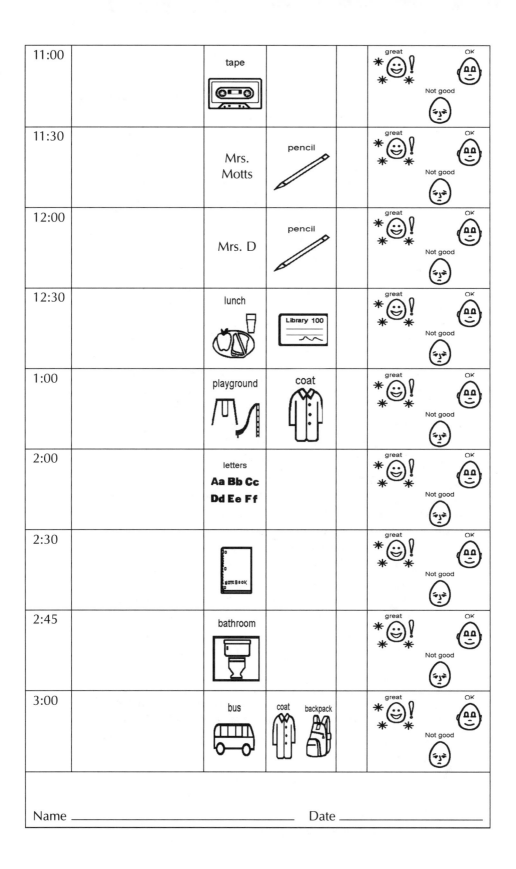

11:00		tape			great ✱☺! ✱✱ OK 😐 Not good 😔
11:30		Mrs. Motts	pencil		great ✱☺! ✱✱ OK 😐 Not good 😔
12:00		Mrs. D	pencil		great ✱☺! OK 😐 Not good 😔
12:30		lunch	Library 100		great ✱☺! ✱✱ OK 😐 Not good 😔
1:00		playground	coat		great ✱☺! ✱✱ OK 😐 Not good 😔
2:00		letters **Aa Bb Cc Dd Ee Ff**			great ✱☺! ✱✱ OK 😐 Not good 😔
2:30		NOTE BOOK			great ✱☺! ✱✱ OK 😐 Not good 😔
2:45		bathroom			great ✱☺! ✱✱ OK 😐 Not good 😔
3:00		bus	coat backpack		great ✱☺! ✱✱ OK 😐 Not good 😔

Name _____   Date _____

ities, reaching to hand a library card to the librarian in language arts). A more specific goal of learning math facts may be focused most within the math content area. I then make a chart (see Table 6.1) illustrating objectives and entry/content areas for each student.

Next, I look at some of the activities in which the student participates, and I add those activities to the chart by targeting those that will best illustrate the requirements of our state's alternate assessment (see Table 6.2). Varied activities, especially in the context of general education classes, allow my students to demonstrate the academic expectations required of all students.

After listing possible activities, I must ensure that students are receiving instruction in each objective across environments, as well. Four inclusive environments must be present for the highest rating in the "multiple environments" rubric of our state's alternate assessment. It is now clear that there may be gaps in the *environments* column, which means there are weaknesses in the student's program. I determine where these gaps are and how I need to fill them. If I can demonstrate a variety of activities in integrated environments within each content area, then I feel comfortable that the program I am offering is rich and varied (see Table 6.3).

Implementing a variety of activities, including general education classes and community environments, renders it likely that I am covering the academic expectations required of all students, as well as those rated most essential for students completing the alternate assessment. I list the academic expectations on my chart to be sure that I am covering all the required ones (see Table 6.4). Once again, it is clear where the gaps are; I can target these within an additional activity or be sure to link the "missing" expectation to an activity already established.

Having established my chart for each student, I then start to think about the performance evidence that I will need to develop my monitoring forms. I consider the kinds of evidence that will be most appropriate for each activity. I concentrate on the use of multiple kinds of evidence, including teacher data forms; peer notes and reflections; student planning, monitoring, and self-evaluation forms; student schedules; and so forth (see Table 6.5).

These charts are designed to help the student plan, monitor, and evaluate his or her own performance, but the results also have benefited me as a teacher. The work at the beginning of the school year is heavy in preparation time, but student planning and evaluation forms are guides for all

Table 6.1.   IEP objectives paired with content areas

Entries	Potential student objectives
Vocational	Using a switch
Math	Reaching
Language arts	Making a request

Table 6.2. Relating specific activities to each objective and entry type

Entries	Activities	Objectives
Vocational	1. Deliver newspapers	Using a switch
	2. Sort and deliver mail	
	3. Recyle (outside)	
	4. Record class attendance and take it to the office	
	5. Help with tutoring in Power Hour	
Math	1. General education math class	Reaching
	2. Collect box tops for school box tops collection	
	3. Purchase items at the store	
	4. Use math facts	
Language Arts	1. Library class	Making a request
	2. Library, open session	
	3. Bookmobile	
	4. Journal	
	5. Menu	
	6. Check-in, name and number	

those assisting students in completing their work (see Figure 6.19). It does not matter who is working with the student, the student's skill level, or what class he or she is in; the monitoring form remains a guide that shows if all areas are targeted—planning, monitoring, evaluating, multiple environments, academic expectations, natural support, and so forth. It helps all those working with the student to focus on the essential tasks that must be evidenced. All of my charts are computer-generated so that they are easy to change and edit. I can also include an explanation on the bottom of the sheet to indicate the process for those scoring the portfolio.

Students can complete this form in a variety of ways, corresponding to the student's level of performance and method of communication. Graphics assist the nonreader in monitoring his or her performance, while a general education peer reads the prompts. This also provides an opportunity for students to spend time together—a prerequisite for developing friendships. A student who is unable to write may complete the sheet using a stamp—perhaps a smiley face and sad face for younger students, or a more age appropriate graphic or *yes/no* words for an older student. Scented ink or paper with raised lines may be used for students with visual impairments. These charts may also be completed on the computer with the use of an adaptive keyboard, switches, and text-to-speech software (see Chapter 7 for a more detailed description).

Data collection is an important consideration in teaching, and documenting improved performance clearly is a requirement within the alter-

Table 6.3.   Relating settings to activities

Entries	Activities	Environments	Objectives
Vocational	1. Deliver newspapers	Mail room Classrooms Hallway	Using a switch
	2. Sort and deliver mail	Office Mail room	
	3. Recyle	Outside	
	4. Record class attendance and take it to the office	Classrooms Office	
	5. Help with tutoring in Power Hour	Boys Club	
Math	1. General education math class	Classrooms Hall Office Library	Reaching
	2. Collect box tops for school box tops collection	Classroom	
	3. Purchase items at the store	Store	
	4. Use math facts	Boys Club	
Language Arts	1. Library class	School library	Making a request
	2. Library, open session	City library	
	3. Bookmobile	Bookmobile Outside	
	4. Journal	Classrooms	
	5. Menu	Classrooms	
	6. Check-in, name and number	Boys Club	

nate assessments of several states. Ideally, data should be collected in all environments in which the targeted skill is performed. There are many different data collection methods and forms available; Figures 6.20 and 6.21 are two that I have found useful over the years.

Figure 6.20 provides a visual representation or graph of the data. Each level of participation (e.g., independent, verbal, gesture, partial physical or full physical prompt) is assigned a number of points, which are averaged across activities and presented as a daily functioning level. For example, Figure 6.20 shows a chart that was filled out for a student named Christine.

The sheet is printed out and completed by the supervising adult in each environment as appropriate. Figure 6.21 is a more universal data sheet that relates the student's targeted objectives to general education content areas.

With monitoring sheets in place and data collection methods established, I outline when data will be collected and who is responsible. All people collecting data must be trained on how to complete the forms. My

Table 6.4. Aligning academic expectations with the student's program

Entries	Activities	Environments	Required academic expectations	Objectives
Vocational	1. Deliver newspapers	Mail room Classrooms Hallway	Speaking	Using a switch
	2. Sort and deliver mail	Office Mail room	Career path	
	3. Recyle	Outside	Postsecondary employability	
	4. Record class attendance and take it to the office	Classroom Office		
	5. Help with tutoring in Power Hour	Boys Club		
Math	1. Collect box tops for school box tops collection	Classrooms Hall Office Library	Quantifying Classifying	Reaching
	2. General education math class	Classroom		
	3. Purchase items at the store	Store	Structure and function of numbers	
	4. Use math facts	Boys Club		
Language Arts	1. Library class	School library City library	Accessing information Reading	Making a request
	2. Library, open session	Library	Writing	
	3. Bookmobile	Bookmobile Outside	Speaking Using electronic technology	
	4. Journal	Classroom		
	5. Menu	Classroom		
	6. Check-in, name and number	Boys Club		
Science	1. Science class	Bryant's class	Scientific activity	Asking a question
	2. Aluminum can drive	Recycling center Warehouse Office Bus	Patterns constancy	
	3. Pet care	Classroom Bryant's class Wal-Mart		
	4. Weather bulletin board	Hallway Outside Library		
Arts/ Humanities	1. Music	Music class		
	2. Art	Art room		
	3. Woodworking	Art room Student's classroom		
	4. Dance	Cafeteria		
	5. Art activity	Boys club		

data forms are detailed, but I have found that they can really help me document progress and make timely instructional modifications in working with students with significant disabilities. Data formats such as these not only provide a measure of performance over time but they also serve as a record of the many activities in which the student has participated. Parents often are surprised at the different activities in which their children can participate with the appropriate supports!

Table 6.5.   Indicating types of performance data for each activity

Entries	Evidence	Activities	Environments	Required academic expectations	Objectives
Vocational	Monitoring sheet Site evaluation Peer notes Data sheet	1. Deliver newspapers	Mail room Classrooms Hallway	Speaking Career path Postsecondary employability	Using a switch
	Monitoring sheet Site evaluation Peer notes	2. Sort and deliver mail	Office Mail room		
	Monitoring sheet Site evaluation Peer notes	3. Recyle	Outside		
	Attendance sheet Note from attendance clerk	4. Record class attendance and take it to the office	Classroom Office		
	Community site evaluation	5. Help with tutoring in Power Hour	Boys Club		
Math	Monitoring sheet Peer assistance with graphing own work Data sheet	6. Collect box tops for school box tops collection	Hallway Classrooms Office Library	Quantifying Classifying Structure and function of numbers	Reaching
	Monitoring sheet Peer work	7. Help with general education math class	Classroom		
	Monitoring sheet Shopping list receipts	8. Purchase items at the store	Store		

Date				
I am working on . . .	(switch/head symbol)	(switch/head symbol)	(switch/head symbol)	(switch/head symbol)
Did I use my schedule basket? (Schedule symbol)				
Where did I go?	$\left(+\frac{2}{3}\ \frac{3}{5}-\frac{1}{2}\right)$ Math class	$\left(+\frac{2}{3}\ \frac{3}{5}-\frac{1}{2}\right)$ Math class	$\left(+\frac{2}{3}\ \frac{3}{5}-\frac{1}{2}\right)$ Math class	$\left(+\frac{2}{3}\ \frac{3}{5}-\frac{1}{2}\right)$ Math class
Did I get what I needed?				
Did I use my switch? (switch symbol)				
What did I use my switch for?	Overhead projector Information Quiz			
Did I hold my head up? (head symbol)				
Did I try harder at . . . ?	(switch/head symbol)	(switch/head symbol)	(switch/head symbol)	(switch/head symbol)

(continued)

Figure 6.19. Sample of student planning, monitoring, and self-evaluation form for Amanda. Amanda completes this activity sheet with the help of a peer in a general education math class. She participates by using her switch to give information/question the class, operating the overhead projector through an environmental control, and operating a dial scan with a switch to enter her response to quizzes and to make choices with the class. Amanda makes choices that affect her learning with the use of the Discover Switch, which is set up for auditory scanning of two choices. She makes her selection with a switch accessed by head movement. (Picture Communication Symbols © 1981–2000, Mayer-Johnson, Inc., Solana Beach, CA, used with permission.)

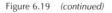

Figure 6.19 *(continued)*

Did I do a good job?				
Next time I will do better at . . . (choice determined with Discover switch)				
Which friend helped me today?				
What did the class do/learn?				

"I Did My Best Work"—A Concept that Applies to All Students!

Each student in my program completes a monitoring and evaluation sheet for most activities he or she does throughout the day. Within this format, the student must respond to questions regarding his or her level of performance. One of the questions is designed to promote self-assessment and planning for improvement on targeted skills. I have always prompted my students to reflect on their performance wherever possible and to make a commitment to perform better.

Tina, a student in my program who has a significant cognitive disability, was getting ready for her next activity. She looked at her monitoring sheet and announced emphatically that she was working on "looking," represented by a pair of eyes highlighted in yellow. The pair of eyes denote visual attending, one of her IEP goals. Tina's monitoring sheet had two pictures (see Figure 6.22), each representing a targeted skill, and Tina used the pictures to choose the skill on which she wanted to focus the next time that she did the activity. Her choice was then recorded at the top of the column for the next day to remind her of the skill she had chosen.

I had always prompted Tina to make a choice determining an instructional focus for the next activity, but I did not dream she had internalized the concept. Was I wrong! Now, when she goes with a peer to participate in a class or activity, she always tells the peer what she is working on or has them check her sheet to see what that skill is. Without the guidelines of our alternate assessment, I would not have included this more abstract skill as part of this student's daily program. It proves that a student with significant cognitive disabilities is capable of internalizing such a higher order concept.

—Anne Denham, Teacher

Activity			Calendar	Attendance	Baking	Math	Language arts	Calendar	Attendance	Baking	Math	Language arts	Calendar	Attendance	Baking	Math	Language arts
Prompt	Independent	5			▓						▓						
	Verbal	4	▓	▓		▓	▓	▓	▓	▓		▓					
	Gesture	3	▓	▓	▓	▓	▓	▓	▓	▓	▓	▓					
	Partial physical	2	▓	▓	▓	▓	▓	▓	▓	▓	▓	▓					
	Full physical	1	▓	▓	▓	▓	▓	▓	▓	▓	▓	▓					
	Date		9/2	9/2	9/2	9/2	9/2	9/3	9/3	9/3	9/3	9/3					
	Daily average prompt level				4.0					4.2							
					—												

Figure 6.20. Level of prompts data form across activities. Objective: Christine will fully participate in an activity as directed, for periods of 5 minutes, in ___ out of 5 trials daily, for 3 consecutive trial days, as recorded by the special education teacher. Full participation is defined as eyes and hands focused on the activity and following each task direction with no instances of noncompliance. (At least three opportunities for following task directions should be given per activity.) Specially designed instruction: Student is to be given expectations verbally before the activity begins (e.g., remain stationary in wheelchair, participate as modeled). Activities should be short in duration. System of reward includes points toward free time. Activities include those involving daily living and fine motor tasks.

Dates: 5/99–1/00   Student: CJ   Objective number: 2.4

Date	Content	Prompt	+/-	Activity	Date	Content	Prompt	+/-	Activity

Content area		Prompts	
Math	M	Independent	I
Science	S	Verbal	V
Language arts	LA	Gesture	G
PE	PE	Partial physical	P
		Full physical	F

Figure 6.21.   Generalized data form.

132

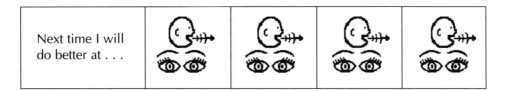

| Next time I will do better at . . . | | | | |

Figure 6.22.   Sample of a monitoring form for Tina. (Picture Communication Symbols © 1981–2000, Mayer-Johnson, Inc., Solana Beach, CA, used with permission.)

SUMMARY

Chapters 4 through 6 present many ways teachers can construct alternate assessments that

- Reflect state learning standards for all students
- Are embedded into general education classes and activities with peers without disabilities
- Are a part of ongoing instruction
- Include opportunities for teaching students the basic components of self-determination

The process of incorporating these practices may seem a bit daunting, but it is possible to put it all together, as evidenced by Anne Denham's teacher-created framework. Ms. Denham's process for designing portfolio entries systematically relates the student's IEP objectives to required alternate assessment content areas, possible student activities and environments within each content area, the state's required academic expectations or content standards for all students, and potential portfolio evidence for each of these dimensions. Finally, Ms. Denham illustrates how she constructs her students' planning, monitoring, and self-evaluation forms; and her own data collection sheets, as the culminating step of this systematic process.

REFERENCES

Bambara, L., & Koger, F. (1996). *Innovations: Opportunities for daily choice making.* Washington, DC: American Association on Mental Retardation.

Browder, D., & Bambara, L. (2000). Home and community. In M. Snell & F. Brown (Eds.), *Instruction of students with severe disabilities* (5th ed., pp. 543–589). Columbus, OH: Charles E. Merrill.

Brown, E., & Cohen, S. (1996). Self-determination and young children. *The Journal of The Association for Persons with Severe Handicaps, 21*(1), 22–30.

Ezell, D., Klein, C., & Ezell-Powell, S. (1999). Empowering students with mental retardation through portfolio assessment: A tool for fostering self-determination skills. *Education and Training in Mental Retardation and Developmental Disabilities, 34*(4), 453–463.

Falvey, M. (1995). *Inclusive and heterogeneous schooling: Assessment, curriculum and instruction.* Baltimore: Paul H. Brookes Publishing Co.

Giangreco, M.F., Cloninger, C.J., & Iverson, V.S. (1998). *Choosing outcomes and accommodations for children (COACH): A guide to educational planning for students with disabilities* (2nd ed.). Baltimore: Paul H. Brookes Publishing Co.

Heward, W. (2000). *Exceptional children: An introduction to special education* (6th ed.). Columbus, OH: Charles E. Merrill.

Holub, T., Lamb, P., & Bang, M.Y. (1998). Empowering all students through self-determination. In C.M. Jorgensen, (Ed.), *Restructuring high schools for all students: Taking inclusion to the next level* (pp. 183–208). Baltimore: Paul H. Brookes Publishing Co.

Johnson, R. (1994). *The picture communications symbol combination book.* Solano Beach, CA: Mayer-Johnson.

Kentucky Statewide Alternate Portfolio Project. (1999). *Kentucky alternate portfolio teacher's guide.* Lexington: University of Kentucky, Interdisciplinary Human Development Institute.

Kentucky Systems Change Project. (1993, Winter). *Designing individualized student schedules.* Lexington: University of Kentucky, Interdisciplinary Human Development Institute.

Kleinert, H., & Kearns, J. (1999). A validation study of the performance indicators and learner outcomes of Kentucky's alternate assessment for students with significant disabilities. *Journal of The Association for Persons with Severe Handicaps, 24*(2), 100–110.

Kleinert, H., Kearns, J., & Kennedy, S. (1997). Accountability for all students: Kentucky's alternate portfolio assessment for students with moderate and severe cognitive disabilities. *Journal of The Association for Persons with Severe Handicaps, 22*(2), 88–101.

Martin, J., & Marshall, L. (1995). ChoiceMaker: A comprehensive self-determination transition program. *Intervention in School and Clinic, 30*(3), 147–156.

Mayer-Johnson, Inc. (1998). *Boardmaker for Windows* (Version 4.0). [Computer software]. Solana Beach, CA: Author.

Mirenda, P. (1999). Augmentative and alternative communication techniques. In J. Downing (Ed.), *Teaching communication skills to students with severe disabilities* (pp. 119–138). Baltimore: Paul H. Brookes Publishing Co.

Sands, D., & Wehmeyer, M. (1996). *Self-determination across the lifespan: Independence and choice for people with disabilities.* Baltimore: Paul H. Brookes Publishing Co.

Smull, M., & Danehey, A. (1994). Increasing quality while reducing costs: The challenge of the 1990s. In V. Bradley, J. Ashbaugh, & B. Blaney (Eds.), *Creating individual supports for people with developmental disabilities* (pp. 59–78). Baltimore: Paul H. Brookes Publishing Co.

Wehmeyer, M. (1998). Self-determination and individuals with significant disabilities: Examining meanings and misinterpretations. *Journal of The Association for Persons with Severe Handicaps, 23*(1), 5–16.

Wehmeyer, M., & Schwartz, M. (1998). The relationship between self-determination and quality of life for adults with mental retardation. *Education and Training in Mental Retardation and Developmental Disabilities, 33*(1), 3–12.

chapter 7

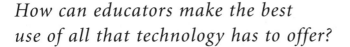

How can educators make the best
use of all that technology has to offer?

IMPLEMENTING TECHNOLOGY TO DEMONSTRATE HIGHER LEVELS OF LEARNING

Anne Denham, Deborah E. Bennett,
Dave L. Edyburn, Elizabeth A. Lahm, and Harold L. Kleinert

This chapter discusses the power of educational technology, both as a means for students with significant disabilities to achieve levels of learning previously not thought possible and as a means for organizing and documenting student performance across environments in a way that can easily be implemented by teachers, parents, and students themselves. In the first section, educators Anne Denham and Elizabeth Lahm describe the technology that has enabled students with significant cognitive and communication disabilities to monitor and evaluate their own work and develop their own plans for improving their performance. This technology, based on IntelliKeys (IntelliTools, 2000a) and BoardMaker (Mayer-Johnson, 1998), has enabled students who previously had not shown either reading or writing skills to develop written products summarizing their own performance in their state's alternate educational assessment, and to take far greater control for their own learning than they had previously been able to demonstrate. Moreover, the use of this technology has increased these students' interactions with typical peers and increased their peers' perceptions of the students' abilities to perform complex tasks. Instructional assistants working with these students also reported increased expectations, based on the students' use of this technology.

The authors thank Dr. Barney Fleming for his helpful suggestions in preparing this chapter for publication.

Educational technology has enabled students with significant disabilities to go beyond our expectations of what is possible. The same technology also has increased educators' capacity to collect and organize student learning, though the uses of electronic portfolios are just now beginning to be understood. In the second section of this chapter, Dave Edyburn, editor of *Teaching Exceptional Children*, discusses his thoughts about the value of electronic portfolios in capturing student learning and in enabling teachers and students to demonstrate a wider range of student products over time. Not only do electronic portfolios increase our capacity to store, link, and organize a wide range of videotape, audiotape, and print materials related to student performance, electronic portfolios also can increase students' motivation and self-evaluation because of their capacity for enabling students to review and rate their own work. Dr. Edyburn provides a valuable set of resources for teachers in developing their own electronic portfolios, including several Internet sites with much to offer. He also discusses teacher issues in implementing electronic portfolios, as well as the essential need to link the electronic collection of performance data to intervention strategies to improve student learning.

The third section brings this discussion of electronic portfolios into even sharper focus for students with significant disabilities, with Deb Bennett's description of the *Indiana Assessment System of Educational Proficiencies* (IASEP), an electronically based alternate education assessment. Dr. Bennett discusses the philosophical principles on which the Indiana assessment is based, the steps in developing an electronically based alternate assessment, and the basic structure and functions of that assessment. She describes the technological capabilities that the system has given to classroom teachers in using multiple methods to demonstrate student performance, as well as some of the benefits that she and her research team are finding for teachers, students, and families through the use of this electronic assessment.

HOW ASSISTIVE TECHNOLOGY CAN HELP
STUDENTS WITH SIGNIFICANT COGNITIVE DISABILITIES
PLAN, MONITOR, AND EVALUATE THEIR OWN PERFORMANCE

Throughout this book, and especially in Chapter 6, we have taken the position that students with significant disabilities should be directly involved in planning, monitoring, and evaluating their own learning and that such higher order skills should be an integral part of the alternate assessment for these students. Many teachers, however, have questioned the appropriateness of planning, monitoring, and self-evaluation strategies for students with significant cognitive disabilities. The purpose of this section is to describe one system, an alternative keyboard with custom overlays, which uses assistive technology to facilitate student participation and control within both learning and assessment. This technology is one way of providing a means for students with significant physical and cognitive disabilities to show how they are able to plan, monitor, and evaluate their own performance.

As Male suggested, "The computer can assist with providing experiences to enhance and supplement strengths and skills, or compensate and accommodate for limitations and disabilities" (1994, p. 29). The use of a computer is one way an individual with significant disabilities can produce written work. It also can facilitate participation in the general education classroom, an environment that has, historically, excluded individuals with disabilities (U.S. Department of Education, 1992). Both of these factors are important within the development of an alternate assessment, which should encourage active participation from the student and participation in inclusive environments.

Male stated, "Designed to fit each child's meaning system and reality, the computer explodes physical limitations and perceived limitations" (1994, p. 29). This reflects the essence of what an alternate assessment should be—one that is designed to demonstrate what the student with significant disabilities *can* do, not to inventory what the student cannot do. In a naturally inhibitive world, the student's performance hinges on this very premise—that there is a way the student can outperform expectations—and the computer can provide the means.

Alternative or Expanded Keyboards

An alternative keyboard simplifies input and output of information from individuals with disabilities (Demchak & Weber, 1996). Alternative keyboards are used by people who have trouble accurately striking the keys of a standard keyboard and who may require larger target areas. These keyboards can be customized to meet the individual needs of people with physical, cognitive, and learning disabilities. Such custom setups can simplify the user's interaction with almost any application software and increase the speed and accuracy of input or application control.

An alternative keyboard has definable key actions, sizes, and configurations that are programmed to perform computer functions. Most alternative keyboards can be programmed to perform standard keyboard operations, mouse functions, and custom key actions. The more recent models of these keyboards plug directly into the keyboard connector on personal computers and allow access to standard software. These keyboards often are used with predesigned or custom keyboard layouts called *overlays*, which define keyboard function. Predesigned layouts may include 1) QWERTY key arrangement, as found on standard computer keyboards and typewriters; 2) alphabet (ABC) key arrangement, which may be appropriate for younger children; and 3) frequency-of-use arrangement of keys, which minimizes the movement required for striking keys (Heiner, 1991). Examples of alternative keyboards can be found at http://www.abledata.com/Site_2/project.htm.

Settings, such as key latching (StickyKeys), so that a person does not have to press two keys simultaneously to perform the shift or control function, and auto-repeat rate, so that a key is not unnecessarily repeated because a user cannot quickly release that key, can be adjusted to meet the needs of an individual user. For people who have visual impairments, overlays may be created with special software programs to provide increased visibility of keys and to allow symbols, pictures, or even real objects to be used as custom-programmed key actions. All of these adjustable features make the keyboard more accessible for students with significant disabilities.

IntelliKeys from IntelliTools (2000a) is an example of an alternative keyboard. It is a flat membrane (i.e., the keys are not raised), programmable keyboard that plugs into the standard keyboard port of any PC or Macintosh computer. Holzberg (1993) described the many advantages of IntelliKeys in her hardware picks review for *Technology and Learning*. She depicted it as slightly larger than a standard keyboard and connected by a "Y" connector to the standard keyboard port. This allows the standard keyboard and mouse to function in addition to the IntelliKeys, which is particularly useful in an inclusive environment. As many as five units can be daisy-chained (i.e., linked) successfully to operate in the classroom. The keyboard can be adjusted to an angle of 35 degrees from the work surface in order to minimize fatigue, and it has two switch jacks on the left side to allow those individuals who are more physically restricted to access the computer through a switch. These can be programmed with 11 built-in settings but can be redefined to identify a selection of key commands.

IntelliKeys runs any software that responds to keyboard commands. It comes with six laminated plastic overlays with pictures of arrows, letters of the alphabet, basic writing, numbers, and standard computer keyboard (PC and Macintosh) symbols. When one of the overlays is placed on the keyboard, a magnetic strip on the back enables the keyboard to instantly recognize it, and it automatically reconfigures. A setup overlay allows users to adjust keyboard sensitivity, repeat rate, and many additional options. Figure 7.1 provides an image of the IntelliKeys keyboard with one of the standard overlays in place, and illustrates the switch capabilities of IntelliKeys (IntelliTools, 2000a).

Overlay Maker (IntelliTools, 2000b) is an IntelliTools software program that can be used with IntelliKeys to build custom overlays designed to meet individual needs. It works like a drawing program to design custom keys or to add letters, phrases, mouse movements, or special IntelliKeys settings. There are a variety of fonts from which to choose, customizing both color and size. A custom overlay may look very different from a regular keyboard because the keys may be colored and enlarged, and placed to allow the maximum function by the student. Switch access may also be used to further customize application and can be used simultaneously with IntelliKeys and the standard keyboard.

Custom Overlays Using IntelliKeys

Sandra and Christine are two elementary-age students, both of whom have recently participated in their state's alternate assessment. Both Sandra and

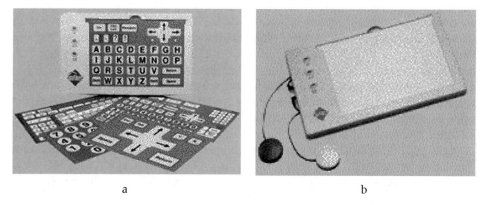

a   b

Figure 7.1.   a) IntelliKeys keyboard and accompanying standard overlays; b) IntelliKeys Illustrating Switch Access. (Picture source: IntelliTools web site, http://www.intellitools.com/index.html. Copyright © IntelliTools 2000; reprinted by permission.)

Christine have multiple disabilities. Each is enrolled in a self-contained classroom with daily participation in the general education program. Table 7.1 provides additional information about Christine and Sandra and identifies one targeted skill and two associated activities that were included in each of these students' respective alternate assessments.

Using a table format as a framework for the students to record their own participation in class activities, the teacher developed custom activity sheets on the computer. The students used these to plan, monitor, and evaluate their performance within the activity and to demonstrate one or more targeted skills, a variety of academic expectations, and the five dimensions of the Alternate Portfolio as follows: 1) student performance, 2) support utilized by the student (e.g., assistive technology, peers, other personnel), 3) environments, 4) social relationships, and 5) contexts (e.g., choice making and decision making) within a specific content area (Kentucky Statewide Alternate Portfolio Project, 1998). The students, with the help of peers or support personnel, read the questions on the activity sheet using textHELP! text reading software (textHELP!, 1998) and a standard mouse, trackball, or switch access through the use of IntelliKeys. The students then responded to the questions using the choices available on the custom overlay constructed for that activity. The response was audible because of the text-to-speech properties of the software. Each student completed the activity sheets in a manner that met her needs and allowed the greatest level of independence.

Christine   Because of physical limitations, Christine is unable to write and presently lacks the cognitive skills to construct a written sentence, though she is able to respond verbally. Christine also has a visual impairment requiring special materials. Her targeted goal was to improve visual scanning. When not using the computer, Christine uses a rubber stamp to indicate a yes/no response to questions on the activity forms, or she marks on available pictures. Both of these methods require significant physical assistance from a peer or adult.

Christine's overlays were constructed to make a simple user display. Each large key was outlined in black to aid in contrast, and arranged by color and loca-

Table 7.1.   Characteristics of individual students and activities illustrated within the Alternate Portfolio

Student	Physical characteristics	Cognitive characteristics	Disability	Targeted skill	Activity
Sandra Age 9	Hearing impairment, diagnosis of hyperactivity, impaired speech and language	Approximate cognitive function: 2- to 3-year-old level	Multiple: Hearing impairment and moderate to severe cognitive disability	Requesting assistance	General education art class Purchase of art supplies in the community
Christine Age 9	Student has low to fluctuating tone; is nonambulatory; is verbal, though not clearly understood by anyone other than parent	Approximate cognitive function: 3- to 4-year-old level	Multiple: Moderate to severe physical and cognitive disabilities; visual impairment	Visual scanning	Cooking with general education peers Shopping for ingredients in the community

tion to facilitate correct response choices (Figures 7.2 and 7.3). The overlays were designed to facilitate ease of use by placement of the most frequently used keys to her dominant left side. The inclusion of graphics on each key was a necessity because Christine is a nonreader, though she does demonstrate interest in the written word. All output was audible using the text-reading features of the software. Directional arrows were added to the overlays to allow her to move independently among the cells on the activity sheet (though that concept proved too difficult for her, and consequently was not used).

Christine enjoyed working with her general education peers. They used the mouse to navigate the cells within the activity sheet so that she could use the switch easily to read the text. It was less tiring for her and more enjoyable. By using the IntelliKeys utility for switch access, two switches were set up (direct select) with the key content designed to highlight a cell and read the highlighted text, respectively. All keys included the "nonrepeat" function, minimizing errors due to extended activation of the key. Christine's store overlay is illustrated in Figure 7.2, and her cooking overlay is shown in Figure 7.3.

The keys on both overlays directly addressed her IEP objectives—to visually scan pictures or objects from left to right or from top to bottom. Keys on each overlay, in conjunction with the activity sheet (Figure 7.4), allowed Christine to monitor and evaluate her performance during the activity and to plan for those areas needing improvement. Cooking and purchasing items from the store were selected activities for this content area.

Sandra   Because of Sandra's inadequate motor skills, her inability to attend to a task for more than a short period of time, and her limited cognitive

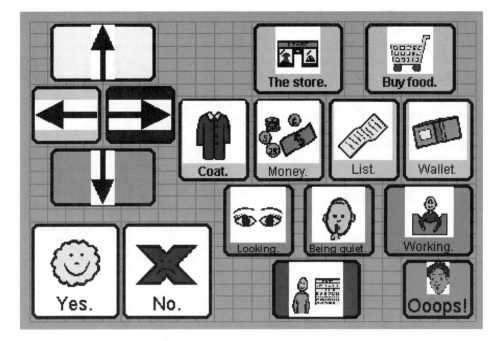

Figure 7.2.   Christine's store overlay used with IntelliKeys (copyright Intellitools 2000). This overlay is reproduced in grayscale and reduced in size for the purposes of illustration. Christine uses this overlay to enter text to respond to questions on her corresponding activity sheet. [Produced with the aid of BoardMaker for Windows, Mayer-Johnson, Inc., Solana Beach, CA; used with permission.]

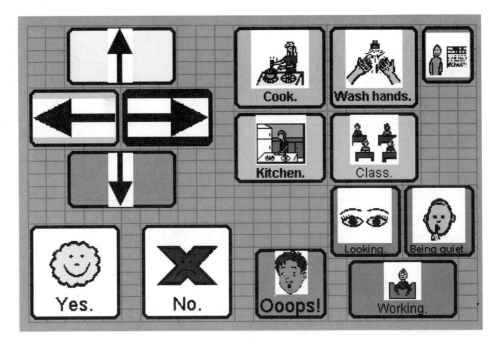

Figure 7.3.   Christine's cooking overlay used with IntelliKeys (copyright Intellitools 2000). This overlay is reproduced in grayscale and reduced in size for the purposes of illustration. Christine uses this overlay to enter text to respond to questions on her corresponding activity sheet (see Figure 7.4). [Produced with the aid of BoardMaker for Windows, Mayer-Johnson, Inc., Solana Beach, CA, used with permission.]

skills, she found writing a stressful activity! Without the use of the IntelliKeys, she was limited to using a rubber stamp or tracing letters for a written response onto the activity sheets. Her limited ability to attend to a task was addressed through the use of the textHELP! program (1998), which read out loud the contents of her activity sheet and her responses as she keyed in text on her art activity sheet (Figure 7.5). As a text-reading software program, textHELP! is very helpful for enabling nonreaders to hear what they have typed with the aid of a customized keyboard. Sandra used a switch to highlight and read the text. By limiting her use of the switch her teachers had one way to restrict her access to the entire keyboard, which Sandra often found distracting, without creating conflict.

The overlays required to meet Sandra's needs were similar in most respects to those used by Christine, though the underlying justification was different. Sandra's overlay, depicted in Figure 7.6, required a simple design. Choices were grouped by color and position to facilitate cueing and ease of use. The keys were made large, but key size was not a concern as it was for Christine, who has a visual impairment. The nonrepeat key feature was essential for Sandra, however, because of her occasional noncompliance and lack of fine motor control.

For both of these students, the use of IntelliKeys with its versatile keyboard and supporting software provided the opportunity for increased independence. A peer assisted Christine and Sandra in the completion of their activity sheets after cooking and art class. The peer controlled the cursor by placing it in the correct cell of the table and utilizing the text-reading software so that the students could easily highlight and read the text with the use of the switch. Through peer cues,

Prompt	Response			
Date				
I am working on				
Did I use my schedule?				
What am I making?				
Did I say I was ready?				
What will I do first?				
Did I wash my hands?				
Where did I go?				
Did I use pictures to read the recipe?				
Did I help?				
Did I make a choice?				
Did I scan my pictures/objects?				
Did I try harder at				
Did I do a good job?				
Next time I will do better at				
What friend cooked with me today?				
What did my friend do?				
Next time we will make				

Figure 7.4.   Christine's cooking activity sheet. On the student activity sheet, the prompt was in black, the type size was 20-point, the student response entered by IntelliKeys was in blue, and the peer text was in red for easy indentification. This form was used within Christine's language arts entry for the Alternate Portfolio.

Prompt	Response			
Date				
I am working on ….				
Where am I going?				
Did I get what I needed?				
What am I going to make?				
What do I need?				
Do I know what to do?				
Did I ask for help if I needed it?				
Did I have good manners in class?				
Did I ask for help correctly?				
Did I follow directions?				
Did I try my hardest?				
Did I make a choice?				
Did I put my things away?				
Did I try harder with ….				
Did I do a good job?				
Next time I will try harder with ….				
Who did I sit with today?				
What did my friends do?				

Figure 7.5.   Sandra's art activity sheet. On the student activity sheet, the prompt was in black, the type size was 20-point, the student response was in blue, and the peer response was in red for easy identification.

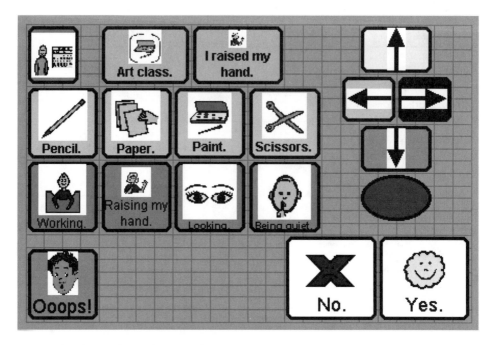

Figure 7.6.   Sandra's art class overlay used with IntelliKeys (copyright Intellitools 2000). This overlay is reproduced in grayscale and reduced in size for purposes of illustration. Sandra used this overlay to enter text in response to questions on her corresponding activity sheet (see Figure 7.5). [Produced with the aid of BoardMaker for Windows, Mayer-Johnson, Inc., Solana Beach, CA, used with permission.]

both students learned the correct switch sequence—one switch to highlight the activity sheet cell followed by a second switch to read it. These students' level of independent response was considerably above expectations as compared with their other activities in the classroom, and increased over time.

Christine was very accurate in her response with the yes/no keys. She consistently focused on the small text of the word beneath the enlarged graphic, and she attended to the auditory rather than the visual output. Figure 7.7 illustrates examples of her responses during the cooking activity.

Christine responded positively to the use of IntelliKeys when documenting activities to be included in the language arts entry for her Alternate Portfolio. She enjoyed computer tasks, which give her an avenue for written expression, and she liked to take things home to show to her family. On several occasions,

	Response			
Prompt	Day 1	Day 2	Day 3	Day 4
Did I wash my hands?	Yes	Yes	Yes	Yes
Where did I go?	Kitchen Class	Class	Class	Kitchen Class

Figure 7.7.   Christine's responses, with IntelliKeys and her custom overlay, to two questions from her cooking activity sheet (see Figure 7.4). These questions and responses document settings and academic expectations within the language arts entry and represent 2 of the 16 questions posed from her cooking activity sheet presented in Figure 7.4.

Christine's mother came into the classroom when she was completing the activity sheets, and Christine demanded that her mother watch what she was doing!

By utilizing the IntelliKeys in the documentation process, Christine was provided with many opportunities to work with peers. For example, one peer controlled the mouse and, consequently, the cursor. This allowed Christine to concentrate on her key choice from the overlay rather than on technical aspects of the placement of the cursor within the table format. Christine experienced success on her first trial and repeatedly showed interest in the keys; she also exercised control over her own work. This aspect of student control should be an important dimension of any alternate assessment.

Sandra also demonstrated a keen interest in the computer, and appeared to enjoy the IntelliKeys. She was generally happy to work on the computer and remained seated and focused for periods as long as 7 minutes, far longer than she would remain at her desk. Obviously pleased as each entry was keyed into the cell, she read with the text-to-speech software as she typed.

Although many responses required cueing, Sandra's independence increased and she was able to *write* on her own. She had been restricted in the past to copying over handwriting and was unable to read at all. She reacted positively to the graphics representing familiar objects or actions used for the custom overlays, and exercised better control over her behavior when utilizing the IntelliKeys. She responded positively to the help from peers, as long as they allowed *her* to use the IntelliKeys, while they worked with the standard keyboard. Figure 7.8 shows Sandra's participation in art class.

Changing Perceptions

The consensus of the peers working with Sandra and Christine was that they liked helping these individuals with their use of the IntelliKeys for the alternate assessment, primarily because doing so enhanced student levels of performance and increased their independence. Sometimes peers were amazed at how well Sandra and Christine could do and admitted that it elevated their opinion of the students' abilities. Spending time with one another also provided the opportunity for relationships to develop, an important element within the social relationships dimension of that state's alternate assessment. Most important, of course, friendships are valuable by themselves.

Prompt	Student response			
	Day 1	Day 2	Day 3	Day 4
What do I need?	Pencil Pencil	Pencil Paper	Paper	Pencil Paper
Did I ask for help if I needed it?	Yes	Yes Paper	Yes Raising my hand	I raised my hand

Figure 7.8.   Sandra's responses, with IntelliKeys and her custom overlay to two questions from the art class monitoring form (see Figure 7.5). These questions and responses document planning and academic expectations.

The instructional assistants involved with these students reported a similarly favorable response to this technology. One instructional assistant remarked that "it ... opened up a way for students with disabilities to communicate and come closer to realizing their potential" (Denham, 1999, p. 59). Even after this initial success, instructional assistants found themselves intimidated by the technology, however, and they identified training as a key issue. Instructional assistants noted that IntelliKeys enabled students to write, had graphics included on the overlay to help students find what they want to say, was simple to use, had individually designed overlays with infinite possibilities, and increased student independence.

As noted, the individual needs of the students were easily met through the utilization of customizing features such as key size, key and background color, graphic, and key content. One piece of assistive technology, then, provided the versatility to meet a great variety of student needs and reduced the need for further equipment. The IntelliKeys was relatively easy for students to use who had some basic computer skills and produced reliable and consistent results. The combination of IntelliKeys, custom overlays, and text-to-speech and text reading software facilitated a move toward independent performance for each student.

The final portfolios submitted by these two students demonstrated accomplishments in all areas required by their state's alternate assessment guidelines. Table 7.2 shows the relationship between the activities performed by these two students to demonstrate accomplishments in five dimensions. Both students received a "distinguished" rating, the highest rating possible.

Realities and Issues Faced

Almost any type of innovation takes some getting used to. Issues surrounding training, equipment, and design do arise as assistive technology is implemented

Table 7.2.   Use of IntelliKeys with custom overlays in one state's alternate asessment requirements

Dimension	Criteria	Evidence
Performance	Student work indicates progress on specifically targeted skills that are meaningful in current and future environments. Planning, monitoring, and evaluating progress are clearly evident. Evaluation is used to extend performance. Extensive evidence of Academic Expectations in all entries	Completion of activity sheet
Support	Support is natural. Use of adaptations, modifications, and/or assistive technology demonstrates independence	Use of IntelliKeys, custom overlays, text-to-speech software; general education peer participation
Environments	Student performance occurs in an extensive variety of integrated environments, within and across all entries	Reported as part of activity sheet, entered by student or peer using IntelliKeys and custom overlays
Social relationships	The student has clearly established mutual friendship(s) with peers without disabilities	Time with general education peers
Context	Student choice and control in age-appropriate portfolio products is clearly evident within and across all entries	Options of quality choices presented as keys on the custom overlay (e.g., targeted skills, areas for improvement)

in classrooms. Some level of expertise is required of peers and staff to operate the computer workstation and the IntelliKeys, and in prompting students. Training of both staff and peers in basic computer operations, troubleshooting, and use of assistive technology is essential to maximize the potential of this approach, as well as to provide effective support for students. Time to prepare materials also is critical. Although creating overlays and activity sheets are not difficult tasks, they are time consuming.

The availability of technology in the classroom also can be a challenge. Only one computer was available in Sandra's and Christine's classroom, and they sometimes had to wait to practice student monitoring of an activity while other students used the computer. Though more computers were available in the school, they were not equipped with the devices required for students to complete these tasks. For any student, but especially for students with significant cognitive disabilities, student performance and interest drop if too much time elapses between the activity and the completion of the activity sheet. For students to complete their work in the general education classroom, access to the assistive technology must be at that site. Although the software is designed to be installed on other computers so that access is possible, a laptop computer would be consistently accessible in all environments.

The design of the custom overlays also is a significant issue. Sandra's and Christine's overlays were originally designed for efficiency within one activity, but as more overlays were used we found that consistency across overlays was an important consideration. Key location, graphics, color, and shape are issues that need to be addressed across activities to take advantage of student skills and the development of more normalized motor patterns, as well as student needs.

Implications for Teachers

For Christine and Sandra, the opportunity to use the IntelliKeys alternative keyboard and custom overlays within the development of their respective alternate assessments allowed them to demonstrate both increased involvement in the process and highly successful outcomes. Clearly, this technology should be viewed as a potential means for a student with a significant disability to demonstrate his or her learning and to be actively involved in the planning, performance monitoring, and self-evaluation of that learning. As we note throughout this text, student planning, performance monitoring, and self-evaluation are key building blocks to self-determination. Assistive technology can enable students with significant disabilities to show they have the needed foundation to attain these important educational goals.

The use of IntelliKeys represents, of course, just one potential application of assistive technology to alternate educational assessments, but it is an important application of how technology can enable students to demonstrate higher order outcomes. We now turn to another important use of technology in the creation of alternate assessments—the use of electronic portfolios. As you will find in the next section, electronic portfolios are providing an increasingly powerful means for organizing student performance data, and for providing a broad range of documentation—including videotape and audiotape clips, scanned documents and other products—of important student learning.

ELECTRONIC PORTFOLIOS: TOOLS TO
ORGANIZE AND EVALUATE STUDENT PERFORMANCE

Federal educational reform initiatives require states to define educational standards, create statewide assessments to measure student achievement in meeting the standards, and develop accountability systems that make performance data available to the public. These reforms were prompted by Congress and linked to the Individuals with Disabilities Education Act (IDEA) Amendments of 1997 (PL 105-17). As a result, interest in the issues surrounding educational assessment has been elevated because students with disabilities must be included in educational accountability systems (Erickson, Ysseldyke, Thurlow, & Elliott, 1998). Whereas many students with disabilities are expected to participate in the typical district and statewide assessment procedures (Thurlow & Thompson, 1999), others can only do so with appropriate accommodations (Elliott, Kratochwill, & Schulte, 1998; Tindal, Helwig, & Hollenbeck, 1999). Because of the special needs of a small percentage of students, however, school districts are required to create alternate assessments to document the educational progress of students with disabilities (Ysseldyke & Olsen, 1999).

When someone tries to evaluate student learning, they must resolve some fundamental questions:

- How do I know what the student knows?
- What is the student's current level of performance?
- Given that current level of performance, is satisfactory progress being made?

Typical classroom assessment strategies that require children to recite a fact, complete a short-answer test, or construct a project are not generally appropriate for students with significant disabilities. Likewise, high-stakes assessment procedures (e.g., statewide testing) utilize presentation and response modes that do not yield an accurate profile of what an individual with significant disabilities knows and is able to do. As a result of the shortcomings of traditional assessment methods, there has been increased interest in the use of portfolios as a form of alternate assessment for students with disabilities (Poteet, Choate, & Stewart, 1996).

Paulson, Paulson, and Meyer defined a portfolio as "... a purposeful collection of student work that exhibits the student's efforts, progress, and achievements in one or more areas. The collection must include student participation in selecting contents, the criteria for selection, the criteria for judging merit, and evidence of student self-reflection" (1991, p. 60). Gelfer and Perkins offered a related perspective when they described a portfolio as "... a meaningful collection of student work that exemplifies the student's interests, attitudes, ranges of skills, and development over a period of time" (1998, p. 44). Thus, a portfolio illustrates a representative collection of the processes and outcomes of the child's interaction in an educational program.

The use of portfolios as an assessment strategy has gained considerable acceptance at all levels of education. A number of attributes associated with portfolios suggest their value as an assessment strategy (Pike & Salend, 1995; Swicewood, 1994; Wesson & King, 1996). First, portfolios clearly demonstrate the connection between instruction and assessment. Second, portfolios serve as a formative assessment tool, which means that the information gained from a portfolio review can inform changes in instructional practice. Third, as part of the process that requires students to select items for inclusion in a portfolio, students are required to reflect on their progress and growth, which promotes ownership and responsibility for learning. Finally, a portfolio provides a broader perspective on the outcomes of learning than can easily be measured through a test.

According to Powers, Thomson, and Metcalf (1999), in their summary of relevant literature, portfolio-based assessment is valuable and beneficial because it

- Encourages a "sense of ownership" and empowerment (Wesson & King, 1996)
- Emphasizes the development of products that are functional and have legitimacy outside of the classroom environment (Valencia, 1990)
- Establishes a clearer and more meaningful relationship between learning and the assessment of learning (Paulson, Paulson, & Meyer, 1991)
- Examines the process of learning (Pike, Compain, & Mumper, 1994)
- Values input from both student and teacher regarding progress toward instructional goals (Anthony, Johnson, Mickelson, & Preece, 1991)
- Has particular value when used with students from culturally and linguistically diverse backgrounds (Pike & Salend, 1995)
- Joins quantitative and qualitative data together to produce a richer reflection of learning (Keefe, 1995)
- Invites learners to participate as active knowledge seekers and users (Tancock & Ford, 1996)
- Encourages reflective thinking and self-reflection (Tancock & Ford, 1996)

Increased Feasibility

Concurrent with the expanding popularity of portfolios in education have been developments in the marketplace that have reduced the cost of computer memory, storage media, and computer peripherals. The convergence of these two trends has increased the viability of electronic portfolios in education.

In many respects, electronic portfolios are similar to traditional paper-based portfolios. A number of factors contribute to an obvious attraction to electronic portfolios; electronic portfolios offer fingertip access to a treasure trove of artifacts illustrating academic performance, rapid retrieval of source documents to review and discuss in planning meetings and parent–teacher conferences, comprehensive multimedia representation of a child's current level of performance and development, unparalleled "proof" or evidence of a child's performance because everyone present can view the artifacts, significant opportunities for advocacy on behalf of a child, a convenient "container" for obtaining a longitudinal perspective on a child's performance, and a significant savings in the space requirements compared with the storage of a paper-based portfolio.

The technological possibilities for electronic portfolios have generated much enthusiasm for their development and use. Interested readers are encouraged to visit the web sites listed here to experience a type of virtual field trip as a method to learn more about current applications of electronic portfolios.

General Web Sites on Portfolio Assessment

The Kalamazoo Portfolio: http://www.kzoo.edu/pfolio/index.html

Multimedia Electronic Portfolios: http://jarl.cs.uop.edu/~cpiper/
portfol.html

University of New Orleans, College of Education, Portfolios:
http://www.uno.edu/~edci/portfoli.htm

Electronic Portfolios: Enhancing Interactions Between Students and
Teachers: http://www.oac.uci.edu/~franklin/doc/mfried/portfol.html

K–12 Web Sites on Portfolio Assessment

Electronic Portfolio Assessment Project:
http://watson2.cs.binghamton.edu/~loland/index.html

Kent School District:
http://www.kent.wednet.edu/toolbox/portfolio.html

Ligon Middle School, Electronic Portfolios:
http://schools.wcpss.net/Ligon/dept/tech/technology.htm

Discovery Middle School: http://longwood.cs.ucf.edu/~MidLink/port-
folios.dms.html

University Web Sites on Portfolio Assessment:

Computers and writing course:
http://www.cwrl.utexas.edu/~tonya/309m/port/port.html

Portland State University, School of Education, Going Electronic:
Modeling a "Paperless" Classroom: http://cssjournal.com/bullock.html

Options for Creating Electronic Portfolios

Special educators are encouraged to become well versed in key concepts of alternate assessment, performance assessment, and portfolio assessment prior to undertaking an electronic portfolio project (Pike & Salend, 1995; Poteet, Choate, & Stewart, 1996; Swicewood, 1994; Valencia, 1990; Wesson & King, 1996). Having a conceptual framework regarding portfolio assessment enhances the ability to develop, implement, and use electronic portfolios.

Special education teachers have four options to consider when planning and designing electronic portfolios. One option is simply to purchase a software-based portfolio product. As of this writing, several products are available. *The Grady Profile* (Aurbach & Associates, Inc.) is available for both Macintosh and Windows and has been around the longest. Each student record is composed of a series of cards that allow users to enter contact information, health records, performance data, and so forth. In addition, work samples can be scanned and linked to the program, along with sound files for recording oral reading, and QuickTime movies to view student performances. Figure 7.9 depicts a sample screen from

The Grady Profile. Evaluation rubrics are provided for the student, teacher, and family to rate the child's performance on a variety of indicators that can be modified. Other common software-based portfolio products are *The Electronic Portfolio* (Scholastic), a Macintosh product, and *Portfolio Assessment Toolkit* (Forest Technologies), a HyperStudio-based product for both Windows and Macintosh. The chief advantage of using a commercially available software-based portfolio is that you simply install the product and begin filling in the templates. Each product offers extensive opportunities to modify the templates as needed.

Another option is to purchase a handheld data collection system along with software. This option reached its peak with the introduction of the *Newton* (Apple Computer, Inc.) in the mid-1990s. Now, several products are being converted to work on the Palm Pilot (3Com). Two leading tools in this category are *Learner Profile* (Wings for Learning) and *The Grady Profile* (Aurbach & Associates, Inc.). The primary advantage of these systems is that they allow the teacher to move about the classroom and collect student performance data by entering his or her observations and evaluations into a handheld device. At the end of the day, the information is uploaded to the computer and automatically integrated into software containing the students' records.

A third option is to build one's own electronic portfolio. A vast number of generic tools make it possible for schools to create a custom design and format for their portfolios. In addition, the generic nature of these tools (e.g., HyperStudio, FileMaker Pro, Adobe Acrobat, digital cameras, microphones, scanners) make it very cost-effective to equip a computer lab with the necessary equipment for creating portfolios. Because the portfolio essentially is a computer file, there is no

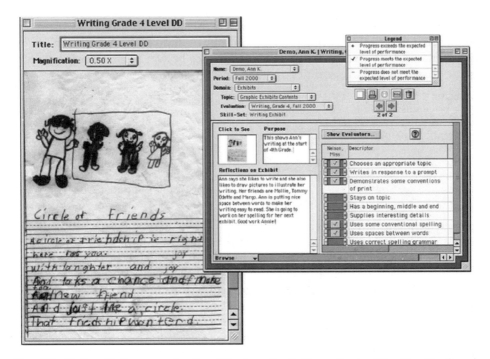

Figure 7.9.   *The Grady Profile* stores multimedia exhibits along with reflections and teacher-defined descriptors for evaluating the exhibit. (From Aurbach, R., & Aurbach, L. [2000]. *The Grady Profile.* St. Louis, MO: Aurbach & Associates, Inc.; reprinted by permission.)

cost involved in making multiple copies of the template of the portfolio. (In order for users to enter information into the portfolio, however, they will need a copy of the software on their computer.) Although this option certainly appears to offer the most flexibility, there is a considerable start-up cost in designing the template and making it easy to use. Portfolios developed using this option are often stored on Zip disks (or a similar mass storage media) or CD-ROMs (CD-W or CD-RW).

A final option for creating electronic portfolios is to create a web-based portfolio. Many generic tools are available to support the task of creating a web page: HyperStudio (Roger Wagner), Digital Chisel (Persian Software), Microsoft Publisher (Microsoft), Claris HomePage (Apple), and PageMill (Aldus). The primary advantage of a web-based electronic portfolio is that it can be accessed for any computer using a web browser. This possibility offers individuals the opportunity to work on the portfolio both at school and at home as well as to showcase work at school or to a potential employer, admissions counselor, and so forth. One drawback to this approach is that it fails to protect the privacy of the individual.

Readers interested in the practical considerations involved in purchasing or creating one of the four options for developing electronic portfolios will find the guidelines and suggestions offered by Barrett (1998), Duckworth and Taylor (1995), and Haufland (1999) to be extremely helpful.

Critical Issues Surrounding the Use of Electronic Portfolios

At the beginning of the 21st century, it is difficult to ascertain the true extent of electronic portfolio implementation. It also is difficult to summarize the current state of affairs concerning electronic portfolios in special education and particularly their application for students with significant disabilities. A close reading of the literature, however, reveals a clear discrepancy between the potential of electronic portfolios and the realities associated with making them work:

> During the first semester of project implementation, it became clear that the initial project proposal rested on overly optimistic assumptions about [initially licensed teachers] and intern entry-level technology skills and portfolio knowledge. (Powers, Thomson, & Metcalf, 1999, p. 83)

> Generally, however, most [teachers] were overwhelmed by the multistage processes required to create files, develop categories of storage within files, link text to icons, and retrieve data. The teachers left the second session with more questions than answers. (Holbein, & Jackson, 1999, p. 209)

Although the attributes of electronic portfolios have already been described, it is important also to highlight the realities associated with capturing their potential.

A Serious Commitment of Resources and Time   First, electronic portfolios require a considerable infrastructure to develop, produce, and maintain. Some schools have found that, in order to create an electronic portfolio for each student, they needed to purchase an additional file server and/or additional memory (RAM) for some computers. Second, unless users already are familiar with a given set of technology tools, considerable time and effort are required to train educators and students on how to copy and paste text and graphics, to store files in an appropriate file format, to scan, to record audio files, and to create multimedia movies. Although some of these tasks have potentially valuable applications in other contexts, for some individuals, these responsibilities represent an additional burden beyond the essence of the learning activity. Finally, it is important to understand that the electronic portfolio is simply a container. Given the massive storage space (e.g., file server, CD-ROM, Zip disk), is the electronic portfolio like a well-maintained file drawer or more like the family junk drawer?

Effect on Accountability and Decision Making   There is little doubt that technology can be used to create electronic portfolios that reflect student learning (Duckworth & Taylor, 1995; Edyburn, 1994) or teacher professional development (Holbein & Jackson, 1999; Powers, Thomson, & Metcalf, 1999; Tancock & Ford, 1996). The essential question, however, is how to use electronic portfolios to enhance teaching and learning while providing accountability assurances.

A study by Rueda and Garcia (1997) sought to identify whether the use of portfolios would influence educational decision-making differently from the traditional use of standardized assessment measures among special education teachers, bilingual teachers, and school psychologists. A repeated-measures design was used so that the 63 participants reviewed student performance data in both traditional and portfolio formats. The findings suggested that portfolio assessment data yielded more specific and detailed instructional recommendations, enhanced communication with parents, produced less negative judgments about student academic competence, and influenced the decision-making. Such results are encouraging and provide an emerging basis of empirical support for the value of portfolio assessment. Similar studies have yet to appear, however, in the literature documenting the value of electronic portfolios.

Questions Regarding Improvement and Quality   Whereas the educational reform movement has created a context for linking instruction, assessment, and accountability, there is a lingering need to ensure that assessment does indeed improve student performance (Jamentz, 1994; Wiggins, 1993):

> How do we know what's good? The Digital Portfolio, like most multimedia endeavors, can be very glitzy. Readers who first see a student's compilation of work are often impressed by how this information can be organized around a few button clicks and are thrilled to see student work containing video and audio clips. At this early stage, the actual completion of a Digital Portfolio is a significant achievement. As the novelty wears off, we are left with the question of quality. (Niguidula, 1998, p. 192)

Indeed, the issue of quality can be masked by the glitziness of the electronic portfolio. As a result, given current explorations with portfolios for students with significant disabilities, additional attention is needed in two components of the accountability system: decision-making frameworks and reporting formats.

Assuming that the student, parents, and teachers have developed a portfolio to document the learning activities in which the student has engaged during the past year, there are few guidelines for evaluating portfolios (electronic or traditional) relative to growth, progress, and expectancy. Of course, when achievement is obvious, the records will clearly indicate the accomplishments and provide links to the corresponding artifacts. However, for many students receiving special education services, achievement levels tend to be depressed and academic progress tends to be difficult. Therefore, the portfolio for a student with a disability is more likely to provide evidence about the *lack* of achievement. Portfolio reviewers are likely to find that when achievement is flat (i.e., learning is not occurring), the portfolio system does not have a mechanism for suggesting when and what kind of changes in instruction should be made to enhance achievement or for prompting the need to introduce assistive technology as a strategy for enhancing performance. Likewise, when achievement is negative (i.e., students regress or are unable to maintain skills previously taught), the portfolio provides no mechanism for intervention. Hence, although portfolios can offer concrete evidence about learning and learning difficulties, accountability requirements will be meaningless if educators are allowed to simply document low performance rather than use it to introduce valid interventions to help students learn what they need to know and be able to do. Although the electronic portfolio can be a convenient container, clearly, much more work is needed in the area of educational decision making for students with disabilities, relative to using academic performance data.

A Need for New Measurement Tools   Finally, the need to collect and report student performance data has created an urgent need for new tools to measure and report learning outcomes. Without a doubt, grades are an inadequate measure of student achievement; however, what types of rubrics clearly differentiate levels of performance? Likewise, what types of systems communicate the academic, behavioral, and social growth of a student?

Important new options and alternatives are being advanced. Alternatives to paper-and-pencil tests as the *de facto* standard of what students know and are able to do enable students with disabilities to offer evidence of their learning (Marzano, Pickering, & McTighe, 1993; Wiggins & McTighe, 1998). In addition, innovations in reporting on measures of student learning have the potential to make the investments in assessment more valuable for understanding the rate and level of student growth (Azwell & Schmar, 1995; Guskey, 1996). If electronic portfolios are going to contribute to enhanced educational accountability for students with disabilities, it is essential that issues of evaluation of student learning and growth be intrinsic to the design and development of electronic portfolios. Failure to do so will result in CD-based electronic portfolios that are "glitzy," but of little value in the educational planning process. Thus, the key question concerning electronic portfolios is not whether they *can* be made but, rather, how they will they *enhance* educational performance.

To examine how these questions are being addressed in a statewide, electronic alternate assessment, we now turn to a description of the Indiana Assessment System of Educational Proficiencies (IASEP).

A STATEWIDE ELECTRONIC PORTFOLIO ASSESSMENT: THE INDIANA ASSESSMENT SYSTEM OF EDUCATIONAL PROFICIENCIES

IASEP was first considered in the fall of 1997, as states were starting to acknowledge the challenges of systematically assessing and reporting the progress of students with the most significant disabilities in compliance with IDEA '97. A group of stakeholders representing general educators, special educators, parents, administrators, and university researchers met to discuss how best to capture the performance of students who may be making smaller gains, principally in functional and preacademic areas.

The Development of a Computer-Based Rating and Documentation System

With the intention of extending technology accessibility to teachers of students with moderate to severe disabilities, the stakeholders elected to create an assessment system that was technology-based. The group envisioned that software could be loaded on a laptop computer for portability and flexibility in capturing performance events, and multimedia technology could be used to support the system.

Since those initial discussions, the IASEP software has been provided to more than 1,000 Indiana teachers who are using the system to document the progress of their students. Plans are underway for extending the system to additional states, with extensions being planned for preschool assessment, assessment of students with mild disabilities, and assessment of students in alternative school environments. This section describes the development of IASEP and illustrates some of the unique components of the system.

The Stakeholder Process

As stakeholders began the initial deliberations about the nature and structure of Indiana's alternate assessment, key documents from the National Center on Educational Outcomes (NCEO, 1993a, 1993b) and other relevant state sources were consulted. Because little work had been done in the implementation of alternate assessment systems at that point, the translation of the IDEA '97 amendments was open to a variety of competing interpretations. The image of "finding one's way in the dark" was certainly applicable at the inception of IASEP development. The unique opportunity for creating a best practice assessment system coexisted, however, with participants' initial uncertainty. The stakeholders were convinced that system development should start with a core set of beliefs or guiding principles that could inform all subsequent work. These principles should reflect the strong commitment of the group to positive educational outcomes for the children who would be included in the alternate assessment, the group believed. The guiding principles that were established from these early discussions are included in Table 7.3.

From this foundation, the stakeholders continued discussion of the nature and structure of the alternate assessment. It was decided, fairly early on, that the system would be based on both functional skills and state academic standards. Although the belief that "what is important for one student is important for all children" was commonly held, it was also recognized that the curriculum for students with the most significant disabilities would be focused on the acquisition of functional skills for independent living and learning. As such, both academic and functional outcomes were important in the education of this population of students and should be adequately reflected in the alternate assessment system. The IASEP domain and subdomain structure is reflected in Table 7.4.

The second critical decision of the group was whether to create a technology-based assessment. It was reasoned that, because of the increasing availability of inexpensive and efficient technology, computer-based systems would soon be a routine component of all classroom assessment and instruction. Although it was understood that the provision of laptop computers to every teacher implementing IASEP would be a challenge for administrators, the stakeholders held the vision of developing an assessment prototype that would carry school systems into the next decade and beyond. The following is a description of the system that was developed from these forward-thinking discussions.

Table 7.3. Indiana Assessment System of Educational Proficiencies, guiding principles

- Honor the belief that all children have value, can learn with appropriate supports, and can be expected to make measurable gains
- Reflect high standards for attaining proficiencies relevant to independent living and learning in the school and community
- Promote a coordinated and inclusive educational system (including parents, general educators, special educators, administrators, and school boards)
- Be used to improve the content and quality of education
- Clearly reflect an accurate picture of a student's attainment of proficiencies and be relevant to a student's education
- Reflect shared responsibility for the accomplishments of all students within accountability systems
- Provide meaningful assessment results that are easily communicated and understood
- Include continuous documentation of student performance from multiple sources, environments, and domains
- Measure the progress of students whose needs focus on functional and life skills as extensions of the general course of study

The Indiana Assessment System of Educational Proficiencies

As noted previously, IASEP is based on teacher ratings of essential skills deemed important for students' independent living and learning. Unlike traditional portfolios, which focus on the collection of evidence and the subsequent rating of the evidence by trained judges using established rubrics, IASEP begins with the rating of skills by teachers most familiar with the performance of the student. The rubric that is used in the rating provides guidance for the teacher in evaluating the student's level of skill attainment. The rubric dimensions include generalization, accuracy, level of teacher support, and frequency of performance (see Table 7.5). Figure 7.10 illustrates a sample rating screen at the subdomain level, while Figure 7.11 illustrates a screen for rating essential skills.

After the rating of all the skills is completed, teachers identify the knowledge or skills that are included in the student's current curriculum. The rating of these skills is then substantiated with performance documentation in the form of videotape clips, audiotape clips, scanned documents, digital photos, and text entries. As such, the system is based on an "inverted portfolio" in the traditional sense. Teacher ratings are anchored with electronic documentation, rather than anchoring documentation with teacher ratings.

Of great importance in this process is the collection of high-quality evidence to support the ratings. Careful attention has been paid to articulating the characteristics of quality documentation, with an emphasis on exhibits that reflect 1) process (e.g., a videotape clip of the student performing the task or creating a product), 2) product (e.g., a scanned image of a student's work, such as would be included in a traditional paper portfolio), and 3) teacher verification (e.g., teacher notes, observations, feedback to student, editorial comments). The multimedia

Table 7.4.   IASEP academic domain and subdomain structure

  I. Academic domain (information acquisition and use)
      A.   Language arts
      B.   Mathematics
      C.   Social studies
      D.   Science
 II. Social adjustment
      A.   Social communication
      B.   Participation in group settings
      C.   Relationships with others
      D.   Contributions
III. Personal adjustment
      A.   Personal care
      B.   Domestic living
      C.   Responsibility
 IV. Recreation and leisure
      A.   Leisure time activities
      B.   Safety
      C.   Physical fitness
  V. Vocational experience
      A.   Preparing-for-work activities
      B.   Work skills
      C.   Work behaviors
      D.   Self-appraisal

technology allows considerably more flexibility in capturing process evidence than traditional paper portfolios have allowed. Videotape clips, especially, provide a rich multidimensional view of student performances. Audiotape clips also can be used very successfully in documenting the learning process.

Teacher verification is an important component in documenting student performance because often it is difficult to determine the level of teacher support or the generalization of the skill without some commentary from the rater. These entries are critical when one attempts to understand products that are created by students with more significant disabilities. Was teacher or peer support provided to the student in the creation of this product? How was that support provided? In what context was the product created and for what purpose? These and other questions can be answered through teacher text entries, scanned observation notes, or audiotaped commentary that is linked to the portfolio entry. These entries also assist the teacher in understanding the instructional accommodations, adaptations, and modifications that are most effective for a particular student.

Table 7.6 illustrates guidelines for the collection of high-quality documentation to support teacher ratings. Although not exhaustive, these suggestions provide teachers with strategies for ensuring that the electronic evidence is used most efficiently and effectively in demonstrating educational progress.

In 2000, the IASEP software included more than 1,000 skills representing five domains: 1) social adjustment, 2) personal adjustment, 3) vocational experience, 4) recreation and leisure, and 5) academic skills. Teachers begin by rating

20 core essential skills chosen to best represent each domain of interest (100 skills total). The total rating on the 20 core items in each domain is then used to create a tailored assessment for that student. The 1,000 items are divided into three difficulty levels. Based on the initial 20-item score, the software will recommend the student for one of the three levels of items. Consequently, a student with uneven skill development could have an assessment that would include skills

Table 7.5.　IASEP rating rubric

Teachers use rubrics based on four skill parameters: frequency or amount, amount of support, generalizability, and quality of performance.

- **Frequency or amount [of demonstrated skills]:** More generally is a positive indicator of development.

- **Amount of support:** Less support (e.g., instructional, physical) is generally an indication of more independence and greater skill acquisition.

- **Generalizability of skill:** The more situations (e.g., environments, situations within environments) in which a student can exhibit a skill, the more likely it is that the student has acquired the skill and related concepts concerning its use.

- **Quality of performance:** The more accurately and promptly the skill is exhibited, the more likely it is that the skill is well developed.

Subdomains are given global ratings on or between four basic levels according to the rubrics described below.

- **Independence:** A subdomain is at the Independence Level if the student shows the ability to apply the knowledge or perform the skill accurately in several contexts without instructional support.

- **Functional independence:** A subdomain is at the Functional Independence Level if the student frequently shows the ability to apply the knowledge or perform the skill in more than one context with little instructional support. The student performs the skill accurately in most instances but makes occasional errors.

- **Supported independence:** A subdomain is at the Supported Independence Level if the student occasionally shows understanding or use of the knowledge or skill in one or more contexts with moderate instructional support. The student makes errors but occasionally performs one or more portions of the skill. The student has difficulty integrating all task components to arrive at a solution, even with extensive instructional support.

- **Emergent:** A subdomain is at the Emergent Level if the student is just beginning to show understanding or use of the knowledge or skill in one context with extensive instructional support. The student is unable to perform the skill without teacher assistance.

Essential skills are rated individually using the rubrics described above as well as the additional rubrics described below.

Participation: An essential skill is at the Participation Level if the student participates in instructional activities that utilize this essential skill, but demonstrates no measurable understanding of the skill. If participation is selected, the teacher indicates level of participation.

- **Full participation:** The student clearly demonstrates awareness of participation in an activity or skill. This may include, but is not limited to, verbal expressions, physical reactions, or forms of nonverbal communication (e.g., gestures, facial expressions). The student may be receiving maximal instructional support including assistance from educational personnel and/or technology, but the skill is not considered to be emerging.

- **Partial participation:** The student demonstrates some awareness of participation in an activity or skill. The student may be receiving some instructional support to enhance participation.

- **Inclusive participation:** The student demonstrates little or no awareness of participation in an activity or skill. The student is physically included in an activity or skill as part of the individual educational programming.

- **No opportunity:** The teacher had no opportunity to observe this essential skill.

- **Not applicable:** This essential skill is currently not applicable to the student's educational program.

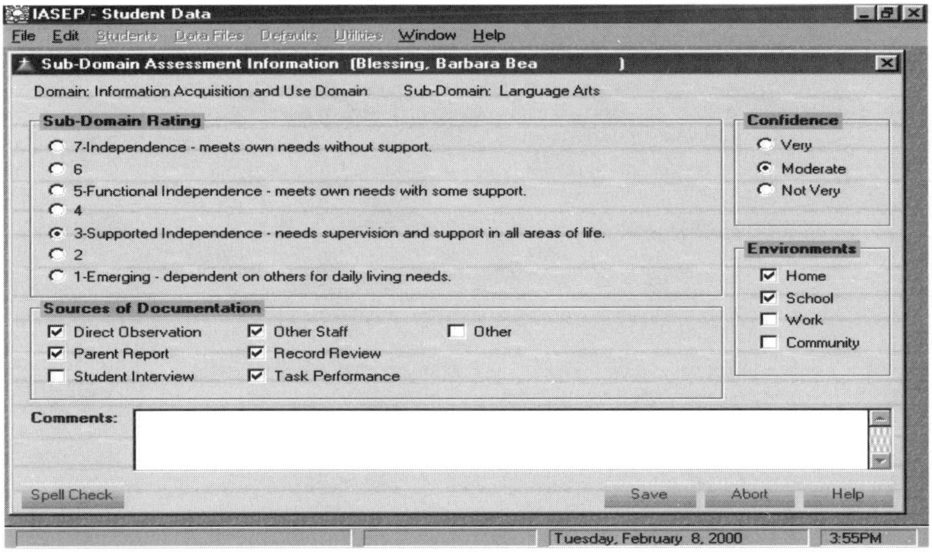

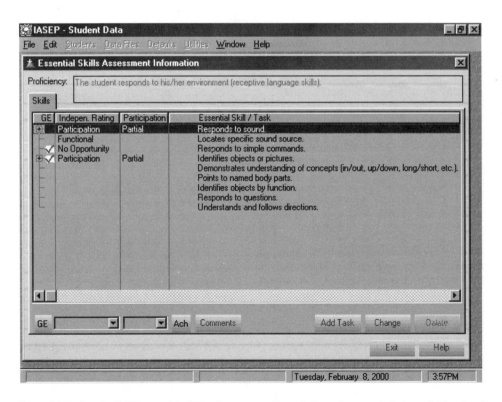

Figure 7.10. Sample IASEP subdomain rating screen. (From Indiana Assessment System of Educational Proficiencies–Computer Based Rating and Documentation Systems [IASEP; Ref. No. C-99049]. West Lafayette, IN: © Purdue Research Foundation; reprinted by permission. All rights reserved.)

Figure 7.11. Sample IASEP essential skill rating screen. (From Indiana Assessment System of Educational Proficiencies–Computer Based Rating and Documentation Systems [IASEP; Ref. No. C-99049]. West Lafayette, IN: © Purdue Research Foundation; reprinted by permission. All rights reserved.)

Table 7.6.   IASEP documentation guidelines

- Keep video and audio clips short and focused on the target skill.

- Determine whether information that you are collecting is necessary in order to document the attainment of a skill, knowledge, or disposition.

- Scan documents to demonstrate degree of student accuracy in performing written work.

- Include process evidence (e.g., videotape), product evidence (e.g., scanned document), and teacher verification (e.g., text entry) for comprehensive documentation of skill.

- Ensure clarity with audiotape clips. Play back clip to check audibility.

- Supplement clips and scanned documents with text files: teacher or parent observations, notes, and comments.

- Be concise as to exact purpose of documentation.

- Collect rich samples of student performance that demonstrate problem solving and the integration of skills. Then, link evidence to multiple skills.

- Collect data in a manner that is conducive to student's use in a portfolio. Allow for self-evaluation of documentation and individual goal setting.

- Encourage students to become proficient in the collection of their own documents.

- Encourage the student to engage in "cooperative assessment," helping a peer with the documentation process.

- Label and date each piece of data, referencing specific instructional objectives.

- Show student mastery in multiple settings.

- Use multiple formats (e.g., scan documents, journals, diagrams; videotape student; include explanations of work programs, community-based activities)

- Document degree of reliance on supportive devices.

- Capture ability of student to teach skill to another student.

- Include scans of student's technical certificates.

- Document instructional accommodations utilized.

from Level A (easiest difficulty) in the academic domain; Level B (moderately difficult) in the vocational experience, personal adjustment, and recreation and leisure domains; and Level C (most difficult) in the social adjustment domain.

As teachers engage in instruction, they are encouraged to consider collecting performance evidence in a continuous fashion. That is, by having the documentation tools available in the classroom at all times, it becomes possible to capture student development as it occurs. The handheld video camera, about the size of a computer mouse, can be used easily and directly from the laptop (see Figure 7.12). It is unobtrusive, and students quickly become accustomed to its presence. Likewise, the digital camera can be used to capture events both within the classroom and within the community, and the scanner can be used to regularly capture any work that would be appropriate for a paper portfolio. Audiotape clips

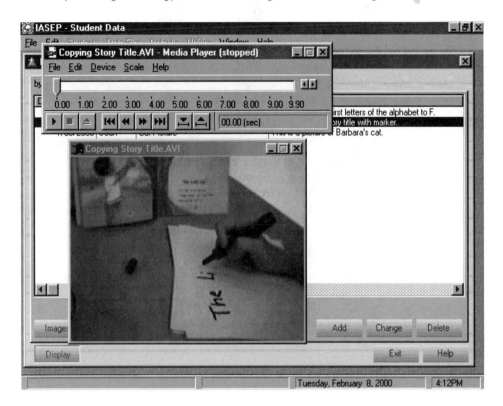

Figure 7.12. Sample IASEP video recording screen. (From Indiana Assessment System of Educational Proficiencies–Computer Based Rating and Documentation Systems [IASEP; Ref. No. C-99049]. West Lafayette, IN: © Purdue Research Foundation; reprinted by permission. All rights reserved.)

can be gathered directly from the Windows sound recorder included on the laptop or augmented with the external microphone. As the teacher gathers this documentation, it is stored in the student's electronic portfolio and linked directly to the skill being documented. It is recommended that the evidence gathered should be as focused as possible with a clear relationship to the skills of interest. Unlike the typical electronic portfolio, which may include videotapes of entire lessons or performances, the videotape clips that are included in IASEP tend to be short and focused. Multiple fields are available for teachers to enter observations, supportive comments, and other descriptive text information.

The performance ratings can be archived to provide a snapshot of the student at any point in time, and the archived ratings and evidence can be compared from one period of time to the next. A teacher may be able to view a student's performance at the beginning of the year, compare it to a midyear sample, and finally compare the performance to an end-of-year sample. The teacher thereby is able to document not only the student's progress over time but also the effectiveness of the curriculum and instructional strategies for this particular child. A charting function also is available to provide a visual representation of student growth over time. Figure 7.13 illustrates a sample graph of subdomain ratings. Other features of IASEP include screens to document demographic information, special education programming, medical information, and assistive technology use (see Figure 7.14 for sample screens).

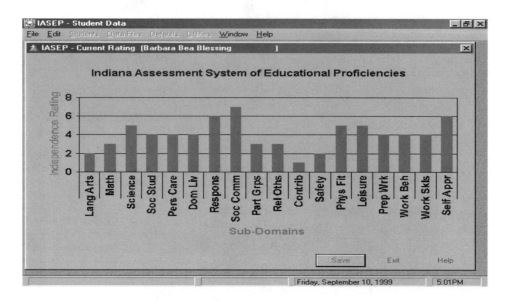

Figure 7.13. Sample IASEP graph of student ratings. (From Indiana Assessment System of Educational Proficiencies–Computer Based Rating and Documentation Systems [IASEP; Ref. No. C-99049]. West Lafayette, IN: © Purdue Research Foundation; reprinted by permission. All rights reserved.)

An optional electronic IEP also is available for teachers to use for each student. As the system was developed, teachers clearly articulated a desire for a comprehensive instructional management system that would serve not only assessment needs but also as a vehicle for more in-depth documentation of instructional activities. The system, as such, effectively links instruction to assessment and the curriculum in a seamless and efficient manner.

Training Issues   Some teachers have been introduced to IASEP with little or no computer experience. Fortunately, the IASEP training package was designed for the novice user. Many teachers engaged in the piloting of this system had never used a computer for more than word processing, and some had never turned on a computer. After using the system for less than a year, novice users are now working as teacher-trainers. Although this testimonial may seem "system serving," it does speak to the strength of this type of technology to empower teachers who may have been viewed as little more than caregivers by the broader educational community. Parents also have been highly supportive, noting that for the first time, they are able to witness what their child *can* do rather than hearing once again what their child *can't* do. A sampling of these comments is available on a system overview videotape that was constructed with the help of teachers, parents, and administrators (Bennett, Davis, Arvidson, & Cunningham, 1999).

A Powerful Motivator   Finally, it should be noted that the documentation capability of IASEP has been a powerful motivator for students, as well. Although the stakeholders evaluated evidence from goal theory, motivational research, and effective teaching when constructing the system (Bennett & Davis, in press, 2000), the full impact of the documentation on students was not realized until the system was introduced into the classroom. Students have been motivated by listening to their performance through audiotape documentation and especially by viewing their performance through video clips.

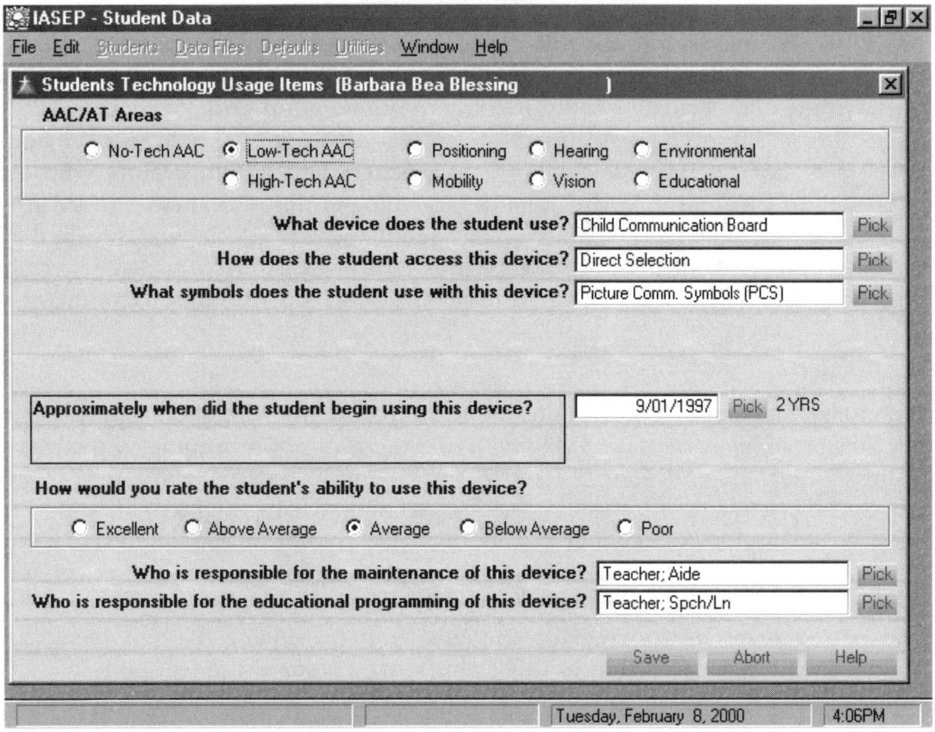

Figure 7.14. Sample IASEP augmentative and alternative communication and assistive technology screen. (From Indiana Assessment System of Educational Proficiencies–Computer Based Rating and Documentation Systems [IASEP; Ref. No. C-99049]. West Lafayette, IN: © Purdue Research Foundation; reprinted by permission. All rights reserved.)

Compelling examples of the impact of the videotape capabilities of the system on student motivation and task persistence have been seen during the pilot year. When viewing a performance on the laptop as it is occurring, students are able to engage in active self-evaluation. Feedback is proximal, tied to instructional materials, and unique to the individual needs of the students. One need only review the research on motivation and goal theory (Ames, 1992; Ames & Archer, 1987; Blumenfeld, 1992; Blumenfeld & Marx, 1997; Dweck, 1986; Maehr, 1984; Nicholls, 1989) to understand why this type of feedback is such a powerful component of effective instruction.

Future Directions

Although IASEP has been used effectively by teachers of students with more significant disabilities, the potential applications of the assessment and instructional management technology are far-reaching. As noted, pilots were underway in 2000 to adapt IASEP to the assessment of the preschool population and the assessment of students who are in the "gray area" (i.e., students who do not perform well on standardized group assessments but may have attained academic proficiencies that can be measured in other ways) (Bennett, 1999a). The technology also is being adapted to existing portfolio assessment systems in several states by inserting the state academic standards and component skills in place of the domains and essential skills included in IASEP. Initial studies of the reliability and validity of the system have been encouraging (Bennett & Davis, in press; Davis, 1999), suggesting that this approach to assessment can be both instructionally useful and technically sound. Finally, IASEP has prompted a closer look at electronic data security in educational environments (Bennett & Miller, 2000; Miller, 1999). Prototype security architecture and educational policies have been developed that can provide guidance to teachers and administrators who are interested in incorporating this type of technology into assessment and instructional practices. For further information about these and related extensions of this system, visit http://www.soe.purdue.edu/projects/iasep/AltAssessSystem .htm or http://www.soe.purdue.edu/projects/iasep/Security/DataControl.htm.

SUMMARY

Technology is creating exciting possibilities for students with significant disabilities. In this chapter, we have explored two dimensions of technology directly relevant to alternate educational assessments for these students: assistive technology and electronic portfolios. In the first section, we highlighted the value of assistive technology in enabling students with significant disabilities to plan, monitor, and evaluate their work and, in the process, to take greater control over their own learning. Assistive technology can provide an important avenue for unexpected levels of literacy for students who previously did not have that option. In the second section of this chapter, we explored the feasibility of electronic portfolios as a strategy for organizing and evaluating performance data for students with significant disabilities. We discussed both the advantages and limitations of electronic portfolios and provided a set of resources for teachers who wish to further explore this option in their own program. In the final section of the chapter, we described IASEP, one state's application of electronic portfolios in response to IDEA '97. IASEP has provided teachers and students with a powerful vehicle for capturing and organizing student performance data. IASEP also has shown that electronic portfolios can provide parents with valuable insights into their children's achievements as well as serve as powerful motivators for students who, for the first time, can fully view and appreciate their own work.

REFERENCES

Anthony, R.J., Johnson, T.D., Mickelson, N., & Preece, A. (1991). *Evaluating literacy: A perspective for change.* Portsmouth, NH: Heinemann.

Aurbach, R., & Aurbach, L. *The Grady Profile* [Computer software] (2000). St. Louis, MO: Aurbach & Associates, Inc.

Azwell, T., & Schmar, E. (1995). *Report card on report cards: Alternatives to consider.* Portsmouth, NH: Heinemann.

Barrett, H.C. (1998). Strategic questions: What to consider when planning for electronic portfolios. *Learning and Leading with Technology, 26*(2), 6–13.

Bennett, D.E. (1999). *The development of a comprehensive accountability system for the state of Indiana.* (Project report submitted to the Indiana Department of Education, Division of Special Education). West Lafayette, IN: Purdue University Department of Educational Studies.

Bennett, D.E., & Davis, M.A. (2000). Integrating computer-based performance assessment systems in the instruction of assessment techniques for preservice special education teachers. Unpublished manuscript, Purdue University, West Lafayette, IN.

Bennett, D.E., & Davis, M.A. (in press). The development of an alternate assessment system for students with significant disabilities. *Diagnostique.*

Bennett, D.E., Davis, M.A., Arvidson, H., & Cunningham, J. (1999). *Meaningful assessment of successful educational outcomes: Training video # 1*. South Bend, IN: Golden Dome Productions.

Bennett, D.E., & Miller, S. (2000). Electronic educational data security: System analysis and teacher training. *Journal of Educational Technology Systems*.

Davis, M. A. (1999). *The concurrent validity of the Indiana Assessment System of Educational Proficiencies*. Unpublished doctoral dissertation. West Lafayette, IN.: Purdue University.

Demchak, M., & Weber, D. (1996). Using assistive technology with individuals with severe disabilities. *Computers in the Schools, 12*(3), 43–56.

Denham, A. (1999). Using the IntelliKeys alternate keyboard to develop alternate portfolios of students with moderate and severe disabilties. Unpublished specialists thesis. Lexington: University of Kentucky.

Duckworth, S., & Taylor, R. (1995). Creating and assessing literacy in at-risk students through hypermedia portfolios. *Reading Improvement, 32*(1), 26–31.

Edyburn, D.L. (1994). An equation to consider: The portfolio assessment knowledge base + technology = The Grady Profile. *LD Forum, 19*(4), 35–37.

Elliott, S.N., Kratochwill, T.R., & Schulte, A.G. (1998). The assessment accommodation checklist. *Teaching Exceptional Children, 31*(2), 10–14.

Erickson, R., Ysseldyke, J., Thurlow, M., & Elliott, J. (1998). Inclusive assessments and accountability systems. *Teaching Exceptional Children, 31*(2), 4–9.

Gelfer, J.I., & Perkins, P.G. (1998). Portfolios: Focus on young children. *Teaching Exceptional Children, 31*(2), 44–47.

Guskey, T.R. (1996). *Communicating student learning*. Alexandria, VA: Association for Supervision and Curriculum Development.

Hanfland, P. (1999). Electronic portfolios. *Learning and Leading with Technology, 26*(6), 54–57.

Heiner, D. (1991). Alternate keyboards: Technology user in the classroom (ERIC Document Reproduction Service No. ED 339 145). Reston, VA: Council for Exceptional Children.

Holbein, M.F., & Jackson, K. (1999). Study groups and electronic portfolios: A professional development school inservice project. *Journal of Technology and Teacher Education, 7*(3), 205–217.

Holzberg, C. (1993, February). IntelliKeys: The smart keyboard. *Technology and Learning, 13*(5), 12–15.

Individuals with Disabilities Education Act (IDEA) Amendments of 1997, PL 105-17, 20 U.S.C. §§ 1400 *et seq.*

IntelliTools. (1996a). *IntelliTalk* (Version 1.0) [Computer software]. Novato, CA: Author.

IntelliTools. (1996b). *Overlay Maker* (Version 1.0) [Computer software]. Novato, CA: Author.

IntelliTools. (2000a). *IntelliKeys*. [Online]. Available: http://www.intellitools.com/index.html

IntelliTools. (2000b). *Overlay Maker*. [Online]. Available: http://www.intellitools.com/index.html

Jamentz, K. (1994, March). Making sure that assessment improves performance. *Educational Leadership*, 55–57.

Keefe, C.H. (1995). Portfolios: Mirrors of learning. *Teaching Exceptional Children, 27*(2), 66–67.

Kentucky Statewide Alternate Portfolio Project. (1998). *Kentucky Alternate Portfolio Assessment teacher's guide* (Rev. ed.). Lexington: University of Kentucky, Interdisciplinary Human Development Institute.

Male, M. (1994). *Technology for inclusion: Meeting the special needs of all students* (2nd ed.). Needham Heights, MA: Allyn & Bacon.

Marzano, R.J., Pickering, D., & McTighe, J. (1993). *Assessing student outcomes: Performance assessment using the dimensions of learning model*. Alexandria, VA: Association for Supervision and Curriculum Development.

Mayer-Johnson Co. (1998). *BoardMaker for Windows*. (Version 4.0) [Computer software]. Solana Beach, CA: Author.

Microsoft Corporation. (1997). *Microsoft Word '97*. [Computer software]. Redmond, WA: Author.

Miller, S.A. (1999). *Using the techniques of a security assessment to guide technology development in education (Technical Report 99–12)*. West Lafayette, IN: Purdue University, Center for Education and Research in Information Assurance and Security.

National Center on Educational Outcomes, University of Minnesota. (1993a). *IEPs and standards: What they say for students with disabilities?* (Technical Report 5). Minneapolis: Author.

National Center on Educational Outcomes, University of Minnesota. (1993b). *State accountability reports: What do they say about students with disabilities?* Minneapolis: Author.

Niguidula, D. (1998). A richer picture of student work: The student portfolio. In D. Allen, (Ed.), *Assessing student learning: From grading to understanding* (pp. 183–198). New York: Teachers College Press.

Paulson, F.L., Paulson, P.R., & Meyer, C.A. (1991). What makes a portfolio a portfolio? *Educational Leadership, 48*(5), 60–63.

Pike, K., Compain, R., & Mumper, J. (1994). *New connections: An integrated approach to literacy*. New York: HarperCollins.

Pike, K., & Salend, S.J. (1995). Authentic assessment strategies: Alternatives to norm-referenced testing. *Teaching Exceptional Children, 28*(1), 15–20.

Poteet, J.A., Choate, J.S., & Stewart, S.C. (1996). Performance assessment and special education: Practices and prospects. In E.L. Meyen, G.A. Vergason, & R.J. Whelan (Eds.), *Strategies for teaching exceptional children in inclusive settings* (pp. 209–242). Denver, CO: Love Publishing.

Powers, D.A., Thomson, W.S., & Metcalf, D. (1999). *Electronic vs. traditional portfolios: A comparison of portfolio quality, technology comfort level, and technology skill development with interns and initially licensed teachers*. Excellence Through Partnerships: Research in Action. Greenville, NC: East Carolina University School of Education.

Rueda, R., & Garcia, E. (1997). Do portfolios make a difference for diverse students? The influence of type of data on making instructional decisions. *Learning Disabilities Research and Practice, 12*(2), 114–122.

Swicewood, P. (1994). Portfolio-based assessment practices. *Intervention in School and Clinic, 30*(1), 6–15.

Tancock, S.M., & Ford, K.L. (1996). Facilitating reflective thinking: Technology-based portfolios in teacher education. *Journal of Technology and Teacher Education, 4*(3/4), 281–295.

textHELP! (1998). *Read and Write* (Version 2.0) [Computer software]. Antrim, N. Ireland: Author.

Thurlow, M.L., & Thompson, S.J. (1999). District and state standards and assessments: Building an inclusive accountability system. *Journal of Special Education Leadership, 12*(2), 3–10.

Tindal, G., Helwig, R., & Hollenbeck, K. (1999). An update on test accommodations: Perspectives of practice to policy. *Journal of Special Education Leadership, 12*(2), 11–20.

U.S. Department of Education. (1992). *To assure the free appropriate public education of all children with disabilties: Fourteenth annual report to Congress on the implementaion of the Individuals with Disabilities Education Act*. Washington, DC: Author.

Valencia, S. (1990). A portfolio approach to classroom reading assessment: The whys, whats and hows. *The Reading Teacher, 43*(4), 338–340.

Wesson, C.L., & King, R.P. (1996). Portfolio assessment and special education students. *Teaching Exceptional Children, 28*(2), 44–48.

Wiggins, G. (1993). Assessment: Authenticity, context, and validity. *Phi Delta Kappan, 75*(3), 200–214.

Wiggins, G., & McTighe, J. (1998). Understanding by design. Alexandria, VA: Association for Supervision and Curriculum Development.

Ysseldyke, J., & Olsen, K. (1999). Putting alternative assessments into practice: What to measure and possible sources of data. *Exceptional Children, 65*, 175–185.

chapter 8

Are friendships an
important educational outcome?

THE ROLE OF
SOCIAL RELATIONSHIPS
IN ALTERNATE ASSESSMENT

Harold L. Kleinert, Anne Denham, Colleen Bracke,
Anthony Bracke, Mary Reeves Calie, Mike Burdge, and Vanessa Burke Groneck

Planning a birthday party is always important to a child. Ryan was especially interested in planning this one. Not only would he be turning 13, but he was finally going to have kids from school over for the festivities. Ryan has Down syndrome, and it can be hard to understand him when he speaks. He has always been fully included in a general classroom at school, but we were nervous about how far that extended beyond the school walls. So, while Ryan has had a birthday party every year, all of the prior ones had been attended primarily by family members and other kids with disabilities we knew from a support group. We were reluctant to push Ryan's social skills by thrusting him into circumstances in which he might feel inadequate.

Ryan was having none of it this year, however. Family and old friends were fine, but he talked for months about inviting his "new friends" from school to his big party. Reluctantly, we finally told him that he could bring home the names and telephone numbers of some friends from school. The next day he came home with 20 kids' names, all of whom just had to be invited. Now the fun began for us. He had 20 names; we had lots more than 20 questions: Where do we have it? How many of these "new friends" do we invite? How many would come? Would they enjoy themselves doing the kind of things that Ryan enjoyed? We weren't crazy about being old enough to have a teenager in the first place. Was there any chance that we could call off the party (and the birthday) and just hold him at 12 for another year?

We talked to Ryan and decided to have the party at a local place where the guests could play basketball and all of the video games they wanted. I called and invited everyone on his list. Within a week we had kids who weren't even on the list calling our house saying that Ryan had invited them to the party also and asking where it was. Evidently, attendance wasn't going to be a problem.

The big day had finally arrived. Ryan's level of excitement was winning out over our level of concern, but concern was definitely a close second. We were surprised on arriving at the party site to find some of the "new friends" already there anxiously awaiting the guest of honor. Ryan happily sped off with them without even a glance back at us. You could actually watch him fade into the group and forget about us for the moment. All we could do was watch and hand out food, drinks, and game tokens to the participants.

It was amazing to see how excited his friends were to be with Ryan and how happy he was with them. It would have been easy for the other kids to show up and just use the occasion as an opportunity to play games and get a free meal without any real interaction with Ryan. But that didn't happen. Every one of the guests spent substantial time with Ryan. The other kids rotated in and out of the basketball game, but Ryan stayed on the court until he was ready for something else. Everyone played video games with Ryan and helped him win tickets for prizes. We actually had to call Ryan three times to get him to come to the table for the pizza and cake. You won't understand how unusual that was unless you realize that Ryan has occasionally asked if he can have a snack while in the middle of dinner. Not only did he manage to forget about food (unbelievable), and his parents (uncomfortable), but he even forgot about the presents (unthinkable)!

The whole issue of presents was particularly mysterious to us. Presents have a way of telling you what the giver thinks about the recipient. We really wondered about the kind of items his guests would bring. Many age-appropriate things fascinate Ryan, but others hold no interest for him. How did his friends see him? Was he a peer or more of a mascot? Did they even know what he liked? The wisdom of the gifts surprised us as much as everything else. Ryan is a very vocal fan of the Kentucky Wildcats and Cincinnati Reds. He was ecstatic to get several team shirts and hats. The guests also knew that Ryan's favorite singer was Shania Twain, so they got him one of her CDs (it was even one that he didn't already have). They even knew about his newfound desire to own "real tools" and got him tools real enough to make a handyman proud.

This is how we always hoped a birthday party would be. However, those thoughts were far away when we first learned of Ryan's disability. Inclusion in school has always been wonderful for Ryan, but carryover outside of school is a larger (and much more frightening) question. This party helped begin to answer it and could never have happened if Ryan had not been included with his peers at school. They would never have even known Ryan, much less cared about him and supported him that much. His new friends saw him as one of their own and made it clear that he belonged with them. "My new friends" wasn't just a phrase that Ryan used. It was a true statement.

—Colleen Bracke, Parent

FRIENDSHIPS AS AN EDUCATIONAL OUTCOME

There can be no doubt that the presence of friendships—and a strong fabric of supporting and affirming relationships in our lives—is a universal need, a fundamental dimension of human experience. Whether a person has a significant disability does nothing to change this truth. Yet as Giangreco, Cloninger, and Iverson noted in the introduction to *Choosing Outcomes and Accommodations for Children (COACH): A Guide to Educational Planning for Students with Disabilities, Second Edition,* "Too many people with disabilities have not been given the opportunities to develop a full range and network of relationships, which sometimes puts undue pressure on the smaller existing network of families and friends" (1998, p. 12). For this reason, these authors have included "Having Meaningful Relationships" as one of the five valued outcomes central to the educational planning process.

Friendships are essential educational outcomes in themselves, as well as an important context for learning new skills. Friendships provide frequent opportunities for individuals to model and practice social interaction and communication skills (Falvey, 1995); to develop age-appropriate patterns of behavior; to try out emerging roles on the path to adulthood (Perske, 1989); to problem-solve real-life situations; and to teach basic values of dependability, truthfulness, and faithfulness. Friendships are commonplace while also mysterious—sometimes inexplicable, and certainly not reducible to a set of easy-to-follow steps (Perske, 1989). If that were the case, how many families, witnessing the isolation and loneliness of their child or adolescent with a significant disability, would have used that recipe again and again?

The Value of Friendships: A Conceptual Framework

Staub, Peck, Galluci, and Schwartz (2000) developed an outcomes framework that provides a conceptual basis for understanding the role of relationships and skill acquisition in the lives of children with significant disabilities. These researchers described three broad outcome domains for children in inclusive classrooms; each of these domains strongly influences the other two:

1. **Skill acquisition**: Children with significant disabilities in inclusive classroom learn skills the same as other children with significant disabilities in less inclusive environments.
2. **Membership**: Membership consists of belonging to a group and sharing both the symbols and rituals that imply that one is a part of that group. The importance of membership and belonging in the school lives of all children is well documented (Schnorr, 1990, 1997).
3. **Relationships**: Relationships in the sense of being an outcome domain are described as personal and dynamic patterns of interaction between two individuals. Friendship is among the most important forms of relationships, but other significant relationships for learning (which may or may not lead to friendship) include play companion, helper and helped, and conflictual (antagonist) relationships.

Together, these three outcome domains support an even broader and more essential outcome, which Staub et al. described in terms of "increased participation in valued roles, activities, and settings" (2000, p. 385). The importance of this outcome model lies in the fundamental supposition, supported by Staub et al.'s research, that skill acquisition and relationships, along with membership, are all important, and that each outcome supports the others. Skill acquisition thus facilitates membership and relationships, and membership and relationships facilitate skill acquisition.

Are relationships and membership, then, critical educational outcomes in themselves, and are they related, in turn, to skill acquisition and academic outcomes? Staub et al. described it this way:

> Our observations suggest that the social aspects of a child's life in school (which we have defined in terms of membership and relationships) constitute the motivational contexts in which many fundamental life skills are learned. The false dichotomization of social and academic or other skill outcomes may in fact lead teachers away from creating functional and meaningful instructional contexts for learners with severe disabilities. Teachers who are falsely led by this dichotomization may focus solely on teaching skills or working on relationships. (2000, pp. 386–387)

THE ART OF MAKING FRIENDS: A MATTER OF OPPORTUNITY

What does Staub et al.'s outcome framework have to do with Ryan's story? As his mother and father stated, Ryan's school experience has been one of full inclusion. The increased expectations resulting from his total participation in the general education curriculum have not only positively influenced his academic performance but also have given him opportunities to learn the kinds of social behavior and interpersonal skills one needs in order to work, play, and live with other people. This is especially illustrated by the fact that none of the friends who came to his party were friends from his elementary school. In the 5 months that Ryan had been in middle school, he had made a whole new group of friends. Obviously, he not only understands the concepts and reciprocal nature of friendship but also he has developed the lifelong skills of friendship building.

Special educators understand the importance of friendships for children with disabilities and often invest their time and energies into developing relationships between children that they hope will continue into adulthood. But, in reality, we know that people move, personalities change, and friends come and go. Ryan teaches us that developing the skills needed to make and be a friend wherever life takes us is more critical than developing one special relationship.

His parents' and teachers' push to make sure Ryan had access to the general curriculum led to his full inclusion in general classes. His inclusion in general classes led to his sharing of time and space with peers without disabilities. Shared time and space led to familiarity, acceptance, and membership for both Ryan and his peers. In this case, Ryan's membership in the group has led to friendships and the development of his social network.

Finally, while most childhood friendships usually do not carry over into adulthood, the *capacity* to develop friendships is critical to the development of long-term relationships characteristic of adult life. As Falvey (1995) noted, relationships with other people provide individuals with a network of opportunities to engage in shared activities and to fill valued roles in community life. As one parent we know has so eloquently noted, the best protection for many people with significant disabilities against loneliness, exploitation, and abuse are the sustained connections of caring and reciprocal relationships they form with others as students during the process of growing into adulthood.

What can educators do to ensure that students have opportunities to develop friendships and to engage in a rich and full range of relationships that support academic and other forms of learning? How can they increase the likelihood that real friendships will occur (with the understanding that they cannot *make* them happen) that will support their students' increased participation in valued roles, activities, and settings, as described by Staub et al.?

As a special educator with years of experience, I have learned and believe this: There is *no* service I can provide for my students with significant disabilities (and their peers without disabilities) that is more important than promoting the development of social relationships. Functional programming is important and necessary. However, consider that when my students leave school, they become the co-workers and customers of their peers without disabilities; they belong to the same neighborhoods and civic associations; they worship and play together; and they are affected by the same issues in their community. Knowing how to interact effectively with and get to know one another (personally), both in school and outside of school, is going to mean more to *all* of our students than whether or not those with disabilities can do laundry and dishes independently.

—Vanessa Burke Groneck, Special Education Teacher

The Role of Teachers in Facilitating Friendships

A number of educators have written about the necessary conditions for the development of friendships and the role of teachers in ensuring the presence of these conditions. An important part of educators' role is to provide these necessary conditions. Moreover, as much as is feasible, the presence of these conditions should be documented in the alternate assessment process for students with significant disabilities, as a measure of the effectiveness to which educators provide those supports.

Falvey (1995) noted the importance of these conditions for fostering friendships: 1) *opportunity*, as defined by proximity and frequency; 2) *support* (e.g., instrumental supports such as transportation, educational supports such as a formal communication system), 3) *diversity* (i.e., embracing not only students with disabilities and typically developing students but also children from the spectrum of diverse cultures, backgrounds, and so forth, that make up our present society); 4) *continuity*, both across environments as defined by attending school with children from one's same neighborhood and community, and across time (i.e., a student moves through elementary, middle, and high school with the same peers); and 5) opportunities to develop relationships that are *freely given* and *chosen* (i.e., truly reciprocal, an essential element of friendship).

Seven Essential Conditions of Friendship

Martin, Jorgensen, and Klein (1998) noted the following seven essential conditions conducive to fostering friendships for students with disabilities. These conditions parallel, to a significant degree, those previously developed by Falvey:

1. Inclusion in all aspects of the school and community
2. The presence of a means of communication understood by both the students and their peers
3. The provision of supports, especially natural supports, which encourage independence, interdependence, and self-determination
4. Student involvement throughout the process, including problem-solving
5. Age-appropriate and respectful language; age-appropriate activities, materials, modifications, and expectations
6. Involvement of both family members and school personnel
7. The development of a schoolwide culture of acceptance and positive portrayals of diversity

Putting the Conditions into Practice

One obvious way friendships are fostered is by having students with varying abilities work together. For example, students can team up to complete portfolio entries, even when the requirements of their portfolios differ. Consider the following example.

Jenny   The students in a fourth-grade class are required to complete a writing portfolio as part of their state's regular assessment. One student in the class, Jenny, is participating in the state's alternate assessment. As an introduction to the writing assignment, the class reads a story about Uncle Joe, an adult with Down syndrome who must move from his group home to live with his sister and her family. After reading the story, each student in the class has to write a letter to Uncle Joe's sister, Amy, and express an opinion as to whether Uncle Joe should be required to live with the family or whether he should be allowed to move to an apartment of his own.

For most of the class, writing this piece addresses the writing skills of show-ing purpose, awareness of audience, use of language mechanics, and so forth. Jenny must also complete the writing piece, but she is addressing a different set of skills. She must demonstrate her communication and choice-making skills, and her ability to work with natural peer support.

Jenny uses her communication system to choose the things that she would like to include in her letter. She goes through the editing process by responding to yes/no questions about what she wants to say and how she wants to say it. A peer writes the final copy, and Jenny signs her name with a name stamp.

Even though she is targeting different skills, Jenny works cooperatively with other students on the same activity, which allows for several important things to occur. First, she is able to work with other students in partnership rather than in a tutor–learner relationship; this in itself enhances the likelihood of continuing natural supports and emerging friendships. Second, the opportunity to make choices—including those that could have a signficant impact on her own life—are provided throughout the writing process, especially as she explores her own opinion about where Uncle Joe, who has a disability similar to her own, should live. Finally, Jenny is provided with the opportunity to work on the same learn-ing standards as the rest of the class. This particular assignment also sets the stage for the class as a whole to look into the future social needs of people with dis-abilities.

Examples from the Field

As the example of Jenny shows, the conditions discussed previously are not just abstract principles that educators might implement if possible. They can be and are being implemented in classroom practices every day. Several states have actu-ally built many, if not all, of these conditions into their scoring rubrics or content requirements for their respective alternate assessments. For example, Kentucky states in its alternate portfolio content requirements that the "student mode of communication be consistently evidenced throughout" (*Kentucky Statewide Alternate Portfolio Project*, 1999, p. 21). Moreover, the state's scoring rubric requires evidence of

- *Support* that at the distinguished (highest) level is "natural (with students learning together). Use of adaptations, modifications, and/or assistive technology evidence progress towards independence" (p. 36).
- *Social relationships* that can be characterized as "diverse, sustained, appro-priate, and reciprocal within the context of established social contacts" (p. 38), and that at the highest level, evidence that "the student has sus-tained social relationships and is clearly a member of a social network of peers who choose to spend time together" (p. 38). One piece of evidence that can be used to support this highest rating is a student MAPs (Falvey, Forest, Pearpoint, & Rosenberg, 1992) that includes student, family, and peer involvement in a structured, problem-solving process.
- *Age-appropriate contexts*, defined as the "degree to which the skills taught, the activities and materials selected, and the language used reflect the chronological age of the student" (*Kentucky Statewide Alternate Portfolio Project*, 1999, p. 41).

Scoring rubrics from other states' alternate assessments also indicate the importance of social relationships as educational outcomes. For example, Tennessee has included in its pilot scoring rubric, "Student has social interactions with nondisabled peers in 4 out of 4 data points," for the entry to score at the highest level in the *Interactions Domain* (Tennessee Department of Education, 2000, p. 13). Delaware's portfolio entry score sheet from that state's alternate assessment notes that, at the highest level of performance, "opportunities for social relationships with typical peer(s) are sustained" (Delaware Department of Education, 1999, p. 20).

These rubrics do not reflect separate content standards for students with significant disabilities, but rather are taken from the learning standards identified for all students. For example, a Tennessee content standard states that all students must "understand the importance of a positive self-concept, interpersonal relationships, and the relationships of sound social, emotional, and mental health practices to wellness" (Tennessee Department of Education, 2000, p. 13). Other states (e.g., Kentucky, Delaware) have identified similar standards applicable to all students.

A WEEK IN THE LIFE OF ALTERNATE ASSESSMENT

The relationship between academic and social outcomes, and how both can be demonstrated in the context of alternate assessments, is illustrated by the example of Martha, as described by her mother, Mary.

Martha and an 11-year-old peer, Lauren, were working on their sixth-grade science project together. Their experimental question was "What is the effect of temperature on colloids (such as gelatin)?"

Day 1   The girls took over both the kitchen and the living room as they bounced back and forth between the science fair tri-fold board and the experiment itself. Both girls liked the variety of activities and the music blaring in the background. One girl was working on vocabulary such as *colloids, coagulate,* and *sol;* scientific methodology; and writing her report. Martha was working on a pincer grasp, switch activation of two light sources (the light sources are used to see the colloids and to measure the degree of diffraction, which is proportional to the concentration of colloids), and choosing colors for the poster board.

The girls clearly had a shared history with each other. As sixth graders, they spent third period together. As they worked, Lauren showed off her cosigns (hand-over-hand modified manual signs that she has learned to communicate with Martha), much to Martha's pleasure! Mid-afternoon, Martha leaned over and hooked her arm around Lauren's neck to give her a big, deliberate hug.

Day 2   The girls repeated their experiment. Talking through the results allowed Lauren to increase her knowledge. Martha felt cold gelatin, room temperature gelatin, and hot gelatin. Lauren paraphrased the music lyrics (not related at all to the science fair project!), while asking Martha questions that were just too middle school for our kitchen to have ever heard them before. Martha was delighted and patient while Lauren word-processed her report.

The two girls were working so well together on their project that I could go to the next room. As the visitor helped my daughter with the color choices for their project board, it became clear that she had learned every possible lesson that an 11-year-old was likely to absorb about communicating with her nonverbal friend. In between two color choice questions, she inquired, paraphrasing their music, "Martha, did you want yourself a Bad Boy?"

I stifled the impulse to interfere or even to look in. I did not see Martha's answer. I heard her friend respond to Martha in a knowing voice, "That's what I thought … ."

Day 3   I delivered the project to school for a sick Martha. She was really disappointed at not being able to go herself. In addition to Lauren, three older middle schoolers were waiting to see the project. Lauren showed up at the house after school with a note suggesting that Martha should really get well and show up on Tuesday. Maybe they would be able to present after all. …

Day 4   Martha delivered the procedure on the BigMack (her adapted switch) for her part in the presentation. Lauren answered all questions. Not having witnessed this event firsthand, I don't know a lot about what happened here.

Day 5   Lauren was waiting on Martha to arrive at school. "Shouldn't Martha and I spend the day in the gym to present the colloid information on Friday?" I quickly replied that Martha should do whatever the science teacher says.

I was approached by another girl. "Can Martha do her science fair project with me next year?" This student had done a project with Martha once before, so I have a comfort level that this student knows exactly what might occur.

Three Weeks Later   Three weeks later (a Sunday), Martha was wheeled from Mass early for excessive whistling (which is another story!); Martha found herself outside with two middle school girls who had just finished their performance of the gospel. However, you could hardly call it punishment when one of the girls, an eighth grader, said, "Martha, I just loved your science fair project!" The other girl, who attended a different school, asked, "What was it on?" and "What are colloids?" The first girl explained as Martha beamed. As they walked down the church driveway they began to discuss sandal weather and the resulting purple and blue toenail polish. The whistling was finished. These are two girls Martha definitely needs to get to know!

—Mary Reeves Calie, Parent

The power of Martha's learning in the context of her science fair entry could be illustrated by the following evidence presented in her alternate assessment: instructional programming data on her use of her switch to activate the light source and her use of a pincer grasp to manipulate the materials needed for the experiment; photographs of the final product, including the science fair poster that Lauren and Martha had constructed; Lauren's narrative description of what she and Martha had both learned from this experiment; and the teacher's evaluation summary of Martha's presentation to the class.

Martha's mother also reported that the two girls went to Wal-Mart to pick up the photos of their experiment; opportunities such as that outing provided additional instances to practice targeted skills in community settings in the context of the general curriculum (see Chapter 9 for further examples of this). Finally, there is a postscript to our science fair story as to how inclusion in school promotes inclusion in the community!

"ALL OF THIS SOUNDS WONDERFUL, BUT MY SCHOOL SYSTEM IS A LONG WAY FROM WHAT YOU DESCRIBE"

Schools vary greatly in their placement options for students with significant disabilities: Educational services range from self-contained programs in separate schools to inclusion in general education classes. Ideally, all teachers would find themselves in situations in which their students had full access to the general curriculum, ample opportunities for interactions with typical peers throughout school and extracurricular activities, and all of the conditions and supports for friendships readily available. Moreover, they would have all of this with the strong support from general educators and school administrators. Unfortunately, this is not always reality.

Clearly, alternate educational assessments for students with significant disabilities are predicated on access to the general curriculum and, for the most part, the general curriculum is best delivered in general education classes! Yet, even teachers working in more self-contained environments can increase learning opportunities and the possibilities of friendships for their students. Here is one teacher's perspective on how to make this journey from separate to more inclusive services and what to do if you're not there yet:

Encouraging Students To Be Mentors

As our program has moved further along the continuum toward inclusion, the role of peers has increased considerably. The interest of peers in their schoolmates with disabilities has made my job as a facilitator much easier.

When my class was fully self-contained, I had to make considerable effort to become a visible entity of the school, and a true part of the "system." As each new fourth-grade class entered our school (we are a fourth- and fifth-grade upper elementary school), I visited each new class and spoke to the students about what it meant to have a disability and what my job as a teacher of students with severe disabilities entailed. We discussed what it might be like to have fewer opportunities for choice or to talk with people, and we participated in short skits to illustrate a variety of situations. The students really enjoyed it and often had a story to tell. I set up some assistive technology in their rooms, and the students were always amazed at what they could do with technology; they wanted to try everything out.

After this, I talked to the students about the nature of friendship and how important it was for all of us to have friends. I then discussed how they might be able to get to know some of my students better and perhaps increase their own circle of friends.

I set up times when the students could come and visit my classroom. These times started as soon as they got to school, sometimes earlier than the bell, and we even used the time while the buses were arriving and students were having breakfast. Each peer would have a task, which I set up in the form of a tutoring responsibility (e.g., help set up a student's schedule for the day) or a task that both the peer and my student could work on together (e.g., going to the library, having breakfast together).

The first few weeks were always very busy. I had to schedule times for the peers to spend in my room, and I spent the first 30 minutes of the day modeling and training peers on ways to interact with my students. As the weeks progressed, the eager peers began to sort themselves out. There were some students who were no longer interested in visiting my classroom (perhaps the novelty wore off), and they stopped coming in. I always made it clear that no student ever had to *keep* coming, but when students made a commitment to visit on a certain day, I did expect them to show up at that time and to let me know if they no longer wanted to come in or if the time was no longer good for them. Coming to my room was not supposed to be a punishment! There were many students that considered this involvement important for themselves and they came in to help as peer tutors. These peers were great and helped me out in the classroom considerably with such things as getting ready for breakfast, getting books for the library, recording schedules and attendance, and so forth. I taught them how to follow the activity monitoring sheets that were set up for each of my students and for each classroom task. These monitoring sheets ensured that all aspects of the activity were addressed and that the peers knew what was expected of my students and what was expected of them. This format helped my students become more involved with peers and not as dependent on the teacher or instructional assistant. At times, it was hard for the instructional assistant to take the back seat.

The activities in which my students and their peers participated were carefully chosen to illustrate students working together. They completed many school jobs, such as taking attendance, recycling, sorting mail, and delivering newspapers—together. General education students often had responsibilities for these tasks in our school, and it was ideal for my students to work alongside them. For example, a peer would complete his class attendance and then assist my student with ours. Both would deliver the attendance sheets to the office.

Another example of shared learning programs has been our school fund-raisers. Our school has collected cereal box tops as a schoolwide fundraising activity. One general education class offered to keep data on the numbers of box tops collected and type (e.g., snack, healthy cereal, wheat cereals), if another class would offer to arrange the collection of the box tops and sort them. We volunteered! It sounded like a great chance for my students to work with a group from a general education class. I worked up a simple collection sheet to monitor the numbers and types of box tops so that they could be collected each week and a monitoring sheet for each of my students who were going to collect and sort the box tops from each classroom. One general education student paired with one of my students was responsible for each section of the school. I incorporated IEP goals for each of my students into their routes. For example, one student practiced wheeling her chair 20 feet down the hallway to another classroom, another recognized and matched room numbers with numbers on the collection sheet, and each student had to make requests by either using words or a switch attached to his or her augmentative and alternative communication device. When we had finished collecting the box tops each day, my students helped sort them and tallied the numbers on their sheets. This information was then graphed on the computer and displayed on a bulletin board. In this activity, all students were working on math but at a variety of levels. To demonstrate this work for inclusion in the alternate assessment, we included individual student-monitoring sheets, graphs of the box tops collected each day, and peer notes.

Our class pets also provided many opportunities for students to work together and provided an excellent activity to document skills for the alternate assessment. Peers helped clean out the cage and assisted my students with pet care. Peers assisted my students in getting leftover food from the kitchen and bringing in items from home. My students would also work with their friends to take care of the pets that belonged to other classes. Both groups of students took aluminum cans to the recycling center and used the money generated to purchase guinea pig food and bedding from the store. I set up monitoring sheets to be completed for each of these activities as evidence of targeted skills. I was also careful to show performance across multiple settings and general education participation, among other requirements for a *distinguished* entry. I also had the peers include a note to describe what they had been doing in this joint activity with my students.

My students were generally scheduled for art, music, and physical education (PE) with their typical peers. With plenty of volunteers coming into my classroom, I had some built-in supports when it came to their general education classes. In each class, I had peers already familiar with my students' concerns and ready to support them when needed. The monitoring and evaluation sheets I set up for these activities reflected the general education participation, and went directly into our alternate assessment entries as documentation of peers working together in a general education environment!

As time progressed, some students began coming to my classroom when they had free time. Soon, a core group of peers congregated in my classroom to spend more time with my students. As the school year wore on, it became evident that genuine friendships were developing. These friendships had developed over time but had begun with general education students volunteering their time as peer tutors.

At this point on the continuum toward inclusive programming, I had participation in the general education curriculum for art, music, and PE, with students working together on core content. I also had students working together on a variety of activities such as attendance, library, recycling, and so forth. It was certainly not full inclusion, but my students were really becoming part of the school. My students were now getting invitations to activities in the general class environment from their peers.

We have since moved further along the continuum, and my students, paired with a general education homeroom, are part of many general education classes and activities within the school day. Collaboration is an important part of the process. I meet with general education teachers on a regular basis to discuss activities and plan how my students can participate in a meaningful way. From a logistical standpoint, it has meant to the general education class an extra pair of hands to assist with students who may be struggling, and to my aide and myself it has added variety to our day! My students appear to enjoy their participation in general education classes, though success has at times varied. Small-group activities with a variety of individualized outcomes have provided the most opportunity for participation. Recently, one of my students participated in an instructional unit that had a dramatic play as the culminating activity. Although this student is nonverbal and has very limited movement, with assistance she was able to press a switch activating a single communication aid so she could contribute at the appropriate time. The peers had recorded the words on the device before the activity started and obviously thought carefully as how best to include her. My student was exposed to the content of the lesson and the group was challenged with how to include an individual with significant needs. As with each content area, the peers helped her complete her activity sheet at the end of the period to document participation in the joint activity, which was included in her portfolio.

To further increase opportunities for my students to be included in extracurricular activities, I started a woodworking club once a week during recess. Because of a variety of reasons, my students were unable to stay at the end of the day to participate in clubs. Our woodworking club provided opportunities for joint activities unrelated to school, with further opportunities for fostering growing relationships with peers. I had a sign-up sheet for general education students, and my students also chose whether to participate. A friend of mine cut out items in wood, and members of the club assembled, sanded, and decorated them. Our high school also offered to help with the wood cutouts. Each student participated to the greatest degree possible—some with hand-over-hand assistance, some by making choices, and others by working independently. The general education students were more than happy to assist those who needed it. We took pictures of our group's work and included documentation of student self-monitoring sheets and notes from peers for inclusion in students' portfolios.

We still struggle with ways to include my, or I should say *our*, students, but I have gained the support of great teachers who are obviously no longer afraid of individual differences and who now accept the challenge of including all students. We have, too, the support of a large number of general education peers who have made all this possible. Three of my students are now fully included. These students, at times with the assistance of technology, are completing their work alongside their peers. We are studying our state's history, math, science, and all the other subjects that make up the general curriculum. The parents of my students are recognizing important gains in their children's attitude toward school, in increased communication skills, and in their children's ability to meet the expectations of the regular class routine. My state's practice of including the alternate assessment in the school accountability index has pushed me as a teacher to make necessary changes in my program, and provided the validation I sometimes needed. The requirements of the alternate assessment have provided the framework with which to do it. For us, the alternate assessment and access to the general curriculum have gone hand in hand!

—Anne Denham, Teacher

MORE TIPS FROM THE FIELD

To what Anne has written, teachers Mike Burdge and Vanessa Groneck add the following suggestions, which are particularly helpful to special education teachers. Their point is that if you want your students to be included and to attain access to the general curriculum, membership with their typical peers, and friendships—you first have to be included yourself!

- **Dress the part**. Sometimes it is easy to pick out the special education teacher when you enter a building. He or she is the only one in jeans and sneakers. Appearance is not everything, but it is your first impression. If special education professionals are not seen as "teachers," their kids are not likely to be seen as "students."

- **Get on school committees** (e.g. textbook, curriculum, site-based council). While you already have plenty to do, your interest in the school as a whole and in students other than those on your caseload will facilitate equal, reciprocal interest in your program and students. Besides that, the knowledge of general education gained by such work can only enhance your ability to adapt the general curriculum and will give you common ground for professional discussions with your general education counterparts.
- **Become a club or team sponsor**. This can foster relationships between yourself and general education students, who are often the leaders in the school. Also, you can be living proof that inclusion can work and, if it can work in a club, why not in a class? Besides, this strategy also allows you to develop your own interests.
- **Be a homeroom teacher**. Homeroom teachers have unique opportunities to teach social skills to all students. For example, some high schools use block scheduling with a flex time immediately following the first class. This block of time was used at one school for an advisor/advisee program, in which students with and without disabilities engaged in learning games, developed and regularly modified their individual graduation plans, ate bag breakfasts, and discussed current events viewed on the state's educational channel. The bag breakfasts (prepared by the cafeteria) not only created opportunities to improve mealtime skills for students with multiple disabilities but also resulted in a larger percentage of students eating breakfast. Some schools also use this flex time for various school clubs to meet, giving students with disabilities even more opportunities to belong and special education teachers more opportunities to evidence/observe the experiences created during that time.
- **Form social/professional alliances**. Search the general education staff for people who share your same interests/values. To do this, be good to yourself—take breaks and eat lunch with the teachers. Alliances and decisions are often made in these staff lounges where teachers spend time with one another. Then, include those people in your circle of friends. Friends work with each other and the mutual benefits to both you and the general education teacher will translate into benefits for all students.
- **Approach inclusion from a skills point of view**. Talk to the general education teacher about the skills (beyond content knowledge) they expect their students to learn or demonstrate. Most of the time, those are the same things that special education educators work on with their students (e.g., organizing, working in a group, using technology, finishing assignments). Then, try to find times when the two sets of students might be able to work on those things together.
- **Offer to teach a related lesson**. What teacher would not like to have an extra period occasionally to just get caught up? Ask the teacher to remain in the room, however. That way you will be modeling just how inclusion can work and demonstrating what skills you can bring to the general education room and students.

- **Use your community-based instruction (CBI) as enrichment for all students.** If you are only permitted to take students with IEPs out of the building for learning, find out what is going on in the general classroom that you might be able to enhance. If the general education students are studying the Renaissance, find a Renaissance recipe, take your students to the grocery store, buy the ingredients, cook enough for everyone, and go down the hall to share. If people bring food, they are usually invited to sit at the table.
- **Coordinate your curriculum.** Brenda Moore from Campbell County Middle School in Alexandria, Kentucky, asks the general education teachers for copies of their lesson/unit plans, which she then adapts or modifies for her students. By having access to some of those adaptations, the general education teacher is able to use the same types of materials for general education students who are struggling.

Although none of these approaches is an end-goal (considering effective inclusive practices), they do demonstrate ways to get your foot in the door and begin to access the general education curriculum and environment. While both the spirit and the letter of IDEA '97 clearly require that instruction within the context of the general education curriculum be an essential focus in the education of all students, the fact is that teachers often need tools to gain that access, strategies to work from the bottom up, to make the promise of IDEA '97 a reality for their own students. In writing this chapter, and especially this section, we have tried to keep that basic reality in mind.

"Friendships Are Nice—But Let's Get Real, They're Not Possible for All Kids...."

Christie had been in a general fourth-grade class for only a few weeks when I got a call from the mother of one of her classmates. She said her daughter, Stacey, had been talking a lot about a new girl in her class and wanted to invite her to stay overnight sometime. She also stated that she got the feeling there was something "different" about this new friend, but wasn't clear what it was. She then asked me if I thought there would be any trouble with inviting her. I swallowed hard and said, "No" (Christie had as many significant disabilities as anyone I had ever taught) and I got her telephone number to exchange with Christie's mom. As the date drew closer, I wanted to find out what was going on but I had promised myself that the families could work it out without a professional, and I stayed out of it. I did discreetly press Stacey for information but it sounded way too "normal." The families had talked on the telephone several times but were meeting for the first time at the school spaghetti dinner. Then Christie was going to Stacey's with big plans for Barbies, pizza, videos, and a midnight bedtime. I tried to wait until the next week at school to find out how things went, but I couldn't. On Sunday, I finally gave up and called Christie's mom. Things had gone better than anyone (especially me!) could ever have expected. Stacey's mom learned to feed Christie at the dinner and when Christie's mom asked about diapering, Stacey's mom interrupted with, "Please! I've had three kids of my own, you know!" Stacey's dad even made Velcro straps so Christie could hold her own Barbies for the first time. Stacey and Christie have kept up their friendship through middle school and have included other friends in their mutual overnights and trips to the mall. Christie's mom said, "I guess I should have been mad when they came home with pierced ears, but she looks so cute!"

—Mike Burdge, Kentucky State Coordinator of Alternate Assessment

---

As the parent of a child with disabilities, you have a lot of dreams taken away from you. The teachers and staff at Fort Wright School (a special school for students with significant disabilities that Christie had previously attended) were wonderful and always willing to help. But having Christie at a general education school has given her a life with friends.... And it has changed my life, too. Now I can talk with other moms in the neighborhood about school, PTA, homework, birthday parties, sleepovers, and school chili suppers. It has given me my life back as a parent."

—Missy Phillips, Parent

REFERENCES

Delaware Department of Education. (1999). *Delaware alternate portfolio assessment: Teacher's training manual (draft)*. Dover: Author.

Falvey, M. (1995). *Inclusive and heterogeneous schooling: Assessment, curriculum and instruction.* Baltimore: Paul H. Brookes Publishing Co.

Falvey, M., Forest, M., Pearpoint, J., & Rosenberg, R. (1992). *All my life's a circle. Using the tools of circles, MAPS, and PATH.* Toronto, Canada: Inclusion Press.

Giangreco, M.F., Cloninger, C.J., & Iverson, V.S. (1998). *Choosing outcomes and accommodations for children (COACH): A guide to educational planning for students with disabilities* (2nd ed.). Baltimore: Paul H. Brookes Publishing Co.

Kentucky Statewide Alternate Portfolio Project. (1999). *Kentucky Alternate Portfolio teacher's guide.* Lexington: University of Kentucky, Interdisciplinary Human Development Institute.

Martin, J., Jorgensen, C.M., & Klein, J. (1998). The promise of friendships for students with disabilities. In C.M. Jorgensen, (Ed.) *Restructuring high schools for all students: Taking inclusion to the next level* (pp. 145–182). Baltimore: Paul H. Brookes Publishing Co.

Perske, R. (1989). *Circle of friends.* Nashville, TN: Abingdon Press.

Schnorr, R. (1990). "Peter? He comes and goes ...": First graders, perspectives on a part-time mainstreamed student. *Journal of The Association for Persons with Severe Handicaps, 15*(4), 231–240.

Schnorr, R. (1997). From enrollment to membership: Belonging in middle and high school classes. *Journal of The Association for Persons with Severe Handicaps, 22*(1), 1–15.

Staub, D., Peck, C., Galluci, C., & Schwartz, I. (2000). Peer relationships. In M. Snell & F. Brown (Eds.), *Instruction of students with severe disabilities* (5th ed., pp. 543–589). Columbus, OH: Charles E. Merrill.

Tennessee Department of Education. (2000). *Tennessee alternate portfolio assessment (Teacher's guide).* Nashville: Author.

chapter 9

*How can I get the community
involved in educating my students?*

DEMONSTRATING PERFORMANCE
ACROSS MULTIPLE ENVIRONMENTS

Harold L. Kleinert, Mark D. Hurte, Vanessa Burke Groneck, Janet M. Fay,
Michele Roszmann-Millican, Meada Hall, Jean Clayton, and Janet M. Lester

The need for students with significant disabilities to receive instruction across school and community environments is well documented (Branham, Collins, Schuster, & Kleinert, 1999; Browder & Snell, 2000; Brown, Schwartz, Udvari-Solner, et al., 1991; Gast & Schuster, 1993; Heward, 2000). Numerous authorities have noted the difficulties that these students experience with generalizing of skills from one context to another. Even if a student with significant disabilities has learned a skill in one environment, one cannot assume that he or she will be able to perform that same skill in other important environments (Brown, Nietupski, & Hamre-Nietupski, 1976).

In fact, the need for students with significant disabilities to receive instruction across environments is so integral to educational programs that a number of states have written this need directly into their participation criteria for their respective alternate assessments. For example, the participation criteria for the alternate assessments in Delaware, Tennessee, and Kentucky all refer to the requirement for "extensive, direct instruction in multiple settings" for students and the application of skills to "school, work, home and community environments." As one of its four parameters for rating skill performance, Indiana requires teachers to consider generalizability, defined as "the capacity to perform skills across environments *and* situations within environments" (Arvidson, Davis, Cunningham, & Bennett, 1999, p. 8); West Virginia also requires evidence of multiple environments in its scoring rubric (West Virginia Department of Education, 1999, p. 9).

THE VALUE OF INCLUSIVE ENVIRONMENTS

Although educators have long recognized the value of community-based instruction, a number of authorities have cautioned about the long-term effects of a curriculum that separates students with moderate and severe disabilities from their same-age peers for significant portions of the school day (Schuh, Tashie, Lamb, Bang, & Jorgensen, 1998; Shapiro-Barnard et al., 1996). Rather, these educators suggest, as an alternative to separate community-based instruction for students with significant disabilities, inclusive opportunities should be made available to students so that they can learn targeted skills throughout the school day with their typical peers. These opportunities can include general classes and other school and extracurricular activities (e.g., working in the school bookstore, as a media aide, on the yearbook staff) as well as inclusive community experiences (e.g., cooperative work experiences, service learning). We agree that, to the maximum extent possible, instruction in multiple environments for students with significant disabilities—including instruction in the community—should occur in the context of cooperative learning activities for other students as well.

The Logical Link Between Learning and Documenting Skills Across Multiple Environments

Given this essential learning need for instruction across multiple environments for students with significant disabilities, it stands to reason that the *documentation* of learning for these students should also occur across multiple school and community environments. Moreover, given the direct relationship of this concept to the participation criteria for many states' alternate assessments, these relevant environments should also be demonstrated in the alternate assessment. With the increasing recognition that *all* students can benefit from instruction in real-life environments and performance-based learning, community-referenced instruction can become a powerful tool for students learning together. Alternate assessment strategies, especially portfolio assessment, can provide an excellent source for documenting and enhancing the results of students learning together across multiple environments. Examples of these enriched learning strategies are presented throughout the chapter.

PRACTICING INDIVIDUALIZED STUDENT OBJECTIVES THROUGH COMMUNITY ACTIVITIES

One way to teach skills in a variety of environments, especially real-life environments, is to gain access to activities planned by the general education teacher, including regularly scheduled field trips. Most field trips are linked to the general education curriculum and require students to complete activities addressing state standards. Because all students will be addressing curriculum concerns during these times, it is very appropriate for the student with a disability to address individualized concerns as a part of the same activity. As the following examples illustrate, the use of field trips to practice targeted skills across multiple environments can be highly effective.

Incorporating an Elementary School Field Trip into the Alternate Assessment

One educator's goal for a fourth-grade field trip to a nature academy was for students to compare the amount and type of insects at the academy with what could be found in the more suburban areas in which the students lived. Prior to the field trip, the students read an article on the effect of urban development on insects' habitats and designed a chart to record that information. While at the academy, the students noted on their chart the type and number of insects observed. Follow-up activities included recording the type and number of insects found around their suburban-area school and using the information to answer an open-response question.

Carlos, a student with a disability, had individualized education program objectives of counting to 10, writing a complete sentence, and identifying high-frequency sight words. While the class was reading the handout on habitats, Carlos was marking familiar words in the article and using the time to work on his sight-word recognition vocabulary. During the field trip, he made a tally mark under the picture of each type of insect as he observed it; as he collected his data, he stopped several times to count "how many" types he had recorded thus far. He followed this same procedure during observation of insects on school grounds, and a peer helped him transfer the data to a final graph. Carlos's open-ended response for this unit was to write three sentences telling how many insects he found at each place and where he observed the most insects. Included in his assessment portfolio were his record of observed insects (both at the nature academy and at school), his graph of his findings, and his open-ended response.

In order to plan for individualized skill practice on field trips, collaboration with the classroom teacher about the goals set for *all* students is necessary. First, the general and special education teachers should review together the student's IEP and select skills that can be addressed within the field trip, especially those objectives that correlate best with already planned activities. For example, a student can practice money skills during a visit to a store, a gift shop, or a concession area. A location with signs posted provides opportunities for sight-word recognition. An activity in which students write their answers offers the student with a disability the opportunity to work on writing skills, too. Communication, social, physical functioning, and behavioral goals typically need to be addressed in every environment, thereby making field trip sites viable environments for instruction and practice in these goals as well.

Some skills clearly correlate with the field trip or activity; others may require more creative thinking. In addition, special *in-school* activities can be used to address IEP objectives including book fairs, assemblies, special interest groups, Junior Achievement, conservation activities (see the middle school example in the next section), and in-school field trips. These occur throughout the building and often have real-life connections. All offer opportunities for demonstrating skills across multiple environments.

A Middle School Field Trip Example

An eighth-grade team went to the local art museum as part of a unit focusing on literature of the European Renaissance period. During their scheduled field trip, students working in small groups were to select five art pieces that they believed evoked a variety of feelings, record information on each piece, and take snap-shots.

Margaret, the student with a disability, had IEP objectives for holding her head up and operating a pressure switch. During the field trip, Margaret was prompted by peers in her group to look at selected art pieces (which reinforced the skill of holding up her head). She operated a tape recorder by holding down a pressure switch while a peer recorded the name of the piece, the artist, and a brief description of the artwork. Back at school, the students used their snapshots to create a *feelings* poster with one-word identifiers and brief descriptions. Margaret and a peer scanned the pictures into PowerPoint (a task for which Margaret used her switch) and added the recorded information. Margaret presented her multimedia poster by using a pressure switch to operate the computer. Included in Margaret's assessment portfolio were the printouts of her PowerPoint slides and the instructional data on her independent switch use in both the community and classroom environments.

As these examples illustrate, to teach everywhere and anywhere only requires that one be on the lookout for every opportunity to address specific skills. Collaborating with school staff and others in planning field trips and accompanying educational activities is an important way to embed individualized student objectives within the context of enriched learning opportunities for all students. The following example takes this principle of generalized learning one step further through the creation of an interdisciplinary study unit.

Inclusive Learning Unit Illustrates Performance Across Multiple Environments

As illustrated in this chapter, for students with significant disabilities the ability to demonstrate acquisition of individualized learning objectives is an essential indicator of a successful educational program. The following example illustrates how Matt, a middle school student with an identified disability, learned to integrate his targeted objectives (including individualized communication, money management, and math skills) across middle school science class, math class, life-management class, and community-based instruction and how all of this was demonstrated in his alternate assessment. Matt even used his targeted skills in a planned presentation to the school principal.

A Middle School Recycling Project   The middle school advisory group to which Matt belonged was working on the concept of economic factors that influence people on a daily basis. The advisees had been involved in a round-table discussion on how to do away with waste at the middle school. They were asked what they could do to improve one aspect of economic waste.

Matt was working on mastering an objective on responding appropriately during a group activity. Specific skills focused on attention to topic, reasonable rate of speech, and enunciation and clarity of words. As a part of this instruction, the general education teacher, the speech-language pathologist, and the special education collaboration teacher had been planning and implementing activities across multiple environments. As a part of this plan, the Life Management teacher and the special education teacher were collaboratively leading a group discussion on recycling as a follow-up to the advisory group discussion. During their round-table discussion, the students were rapidly tossing ideas back and forth about how the middle school did not recycle the aluminum cans from student break and what to do about it.

Proposing the Plan   After 45 minutes of discussion, the students were asked to come up with an innovative plan for the middle school. Matt and a peer partner, Roberto, were appointed to go to the principal and present the group's plan for consideration. Matt and Roberto practiced what they were going to say to the principal through a role-play activity during Language Arts class. After several run-throughs, they were ready to present their plan. The two went to the principal's office and presented the group's proposal—to recycle the aluminum cans at the local recycling center and to save the money for a field trip at the end of the school year.

After the presentation, Matt did a self-evaluation of his identified goals and objectives; he rated each one (e.g., attention to topic, reasonable rate of speech, enunciation and clarity of words) according to how he thought that he did. (Roberto also completed an evaluation of Matt's performance.) Matt and Roberto then discussed his performance with the language arts and the special education teachers, so that Matt could identify the areas in which he wished to improve in his next group presentation. See Figure 9.1 for an example of the peer evaluation Roberto completed for Matt.

As another element of this project (once the group had received the principal's approval), the students worked in math class on estimating how many cans the middle school had thrown away over the past 3 years. The students, in conjunction with the science class, took a sample of the day's consumption of empty soda cans. Matt and four other students collected samples of aluminum cans from the two specially marked trash cans that were placed in the students' common area. (The students had previously gone together to buy the trash cans from the local Wal-Mart; as a part of that community-based activity, Matt had worked on the next-dollar purchasing strategy—in which the student counts out the requested number of dollars and then includes one more dollar for cents—and his identified speech goals and objectives.) The students collected data on disposed aluminum cans for 5 school days and graphed their findings in math class. Matt assisted by typing the information into his computer as the other students read their results to him. They printed out a graph and presented it in Life Management class.

Implementing the Project   After recording their baseline data on wasted resources, the students developed their ongoing recycling project and saved the money from turning the cans in to the recycling center. Once every 2 weeks, Matt and a peer partner from math traveled to the local bank and deposited money into a class savings account. The students kept a budget log and tracked the amount of money deposited each time. This community-based excursion to the bank provided Matt with additional opportunities—and another important community environment—in which to practice both his targeted communication and money management skills.

Matt and his team used an activity-planning matrix to decide how to spend the money that they had saved over the course of the school year. According to their decision matrix, the group had to decide what they wanted to do, what their budget was, and how they would implement their plan. The group decided that, as a part of their end-of-the-year outing, they wanted to ride the go-carts at the local entertainment center. Matt located the telephone number in the telephone

Peer: <u>Roberto Rodriguez</u>   Student: <u>Matt Jones</u>

Date: <u>January 16</u>

Did your partner participate in the presentation? Circle your answer.

(Yes)   No

Use the space following each choice below to describe how your partner interacted in the presentation. You can use the descriptors to evaluate your partner's performance:

My partner took turns when talking.

__✔__ Yes   _____ No

My partner stayed on the same topic of our presentation.

__✔__ Yes   _____ No
All but once!

My partner spoke clearly.

__✔__ Yes   _____ No
Much better

My partner spoke at a slow rate of speech.

_____ Yes   __✔__ No
I had to remind him two times.

My partner did not need help; he or she knew what to say.

_____ Yes   __✔__ No
I needed to help just a little bit by reminding my partner what we were supposed to be talking about.

Figure 9.1.   Peer evaluation for making a presentation for Roberto.

book and wrote it down in his planning sheet. He and his peer partner Roberto practiced making the telephone call during Life Management class. To make the actual call, they went to the school secretary and asked to use the telephone. Roberto and Matt took turns asking for different pieces of information from the entertainment center. They took the information they had obtained back to their class, and Matt presented it to the group with Roberto. Matt then returned to his homeroom advisory group, got out his planning calendar, and marked the date of the go-cart trip. Matt was responsible for bringing and handling the money to pay for the trip and for purchasing the tickets for the class.

Throughout this complex unit, Matt had many opportunities to practice his individualized communication and money management objectives. To document his progress, Matt, with the assistance of his peers and teachers, collected a variety of evidence for his assessment portfolio. That evidence included his own, his teacher's, and his partner's ratings of his presentations (e.g., speaking clearly, speaking at a slow rate, staying on topic); his instructional data on use of the next-dollar strategy in community environments and his accuracy in counting and depositing money at the bank; the recycling bar graphs that he constructed with his peers in math class; and his activity planning sheet for obtaining information and arranging the details for the year-end trip to the entertainment center.

Middle School Vocational Training   Chapter 4 presents an example of a middle school Career Explorations class experience for a student with multiple disabilities and shows how that student included his experience in his alternate assessment portfolio. This chapter presents a similar example for Jay, a student with more moderate disabilities, and explains how Jay's experience, and the subsequent documentation of his learning in the alternate assessment, included evidence across a range of both school and nonschool environments.

Jay's Program   Tuesdays are very busy days for Jay. After breakfast at school, Jay goes to the advisory group (an extended homeroom or "home base" for middle school students) and gets out his schedule planner to organize his daily activities. He reads his schedule to his homeroom peers as he marks down his activities on his schedule sheet. His special education teacher comes in to check with him to see if he has his daily schedule set. They use a planner review sheet to ensure that Jay has put his schedule of classes, "School to Careers" vocational shadowing experience, and lunch in the proper chronological order.

On Tuesdays Jay goes to work at People's Bank of Hustonville for a 2-hour job-shadowing experience. During a previous IEP meeting, Jay and his parents had identified the need for him to get some vocational experience in an area of his interest. Jays vocational interests were identified through a vocational computer screening during an enrichment class, Career Explorations, that focused on the world of work.

Prior to his beginning work at the bank, Jay's team (including Jay and a representative from the bank) had determined modifications and adaptations to help ensure Jay's success at his job. The occupational therapist had designed a sorting tray to help Jay organize bank slips into appropriate categories, while the speech-language pathologist had identified speech phrases necessary for Jay to be able to greet customers and direct them to the head cashier. The special education teacher had identified appropriate social behaviors for Jay to maintain during the 2-hour work period, as well.

A Typical Day   Here is an example of a typical day for Jay: At 9:45 A.M., Jay gets ready for work. Jay's work uniform consists of khakis, a blue button-down shirt, a belt, navy blue socks, penny loafers, and a red pullover sweater with the bank logo. (As part of his community-based instruction, Jay shopped for these clothes. He used a modified guide sheet, designed by his special education teacher, to help him locate his sizes and the appropriate departments.)

After he completes his work at the bank, Jay attends Career Explorations class. Each student in the class takes a turn in a round-table discussion to tell about his or her job experience that day. Jay evaluates his own work as well. He works with a peer partner who reads him the questions on his evaluation sheet and helps him mark his responses. Figure 9.2 presents Jay's self-evaluation sheet.

The Culminating Activity: A Career Fair   Jay's school has a career fair as an end-of-year activity. During this career fair, the students work with representatives from the businesses that they have shadowed. All of the homeroom advisory classes are invited to tour the career fair. Jay had his performance photographed throughout the year at the bank for presentation at the career fair. He includes those photographs, as well other photos from Career Explorations class and the career fair itself, to document his progress toward his goals and objectives on his IEP. These photographs are used in his alternate assessment portfolio, along with data sheets that Jay uses to self-evaluate his work, and his employer evaluations. Jay also includes data sheets indicating his ability to shop for his work uniform (e.g., picking the correct sizes, using the next-dollar strategy) as further evidence of his increasing independence.

High School Peer Tutoring Programs: Evidence of Learning Together

We now present examples of demonstrating learning in multiple environments for high school and postsecondary-age students. Again, the focus for learning across school and community environments for older students should be on activities with typical age-peers.

As Longwill and Kleinert (1998) discussed, high school peer tutor programs—especially those that have been developed to foster students with and without disabilities learning together—can provide valuable supports for evidencing performance across environments and for documenting that evidence in the alternate assessment:

> Peer tutors frequently develop friendships with students with disabilities that go well beyond the classroom. Peers collaborate with students with disabilities within and outside of the school, in such activities as going to youth group, out for pizza on Saturday night, or to the movies; researching topics at the school and public libraries; and going Christmas shopping together. Peers collaborate on community instruction while shopping, banking, eating at a fast food restaurant, and while participating in community recreation and leisure activities. Each of these instances can provide an appropriate context for "showcasing" both learned skills and valued social relations at an exemplary performance level. ... Finally, peer tutors may assist students with moderate and severe disabilities in completing their entries and assembling the entries into a finished portfolio.
>
> As peer tutors provide this support, they also are developing their own portfolio entries. Essays on the meaning and purpose of friendship, the essential need for all students to be an integral part of their community, or what they have learned from their peer tutoring experience have provided the context for outstanding writing entries. Students have even used their peer tutoring assignments as a part of their college admission application, as evidence of their best writing! (1998, pp. 63–64)

Name: _Jay Miller_

Date: _February 8_

Vocational work experience: _People's Bank_

Were you on time today? Circle your answer.

Yes   (No)

If you were not on time, what made you late for work? (For example, "I couldn't find my clothes.")

I had trouble putting my shoes on.

Did you clock in at work? Circle your answer.

(Yes)   No

Make a list of what you did at work today.

Greet customers
Sort coins (quarters and dimes)
Sort bank slips

Give yourself a rating on how you think that you did your job today. (Circle your answer.)

(I did great!)

I did OK!

I needed some extra help.

If you circled "I needed some extra help," what could you work on next time you go to work to make it better?

Figure 9.2.   Jay's self-evaluation sheet.

Longwill and Kleinert also reported other collaborative activities at the high school level among students with significant disabilities and peer tutors, such as working cooperatively on the development of their respective job résumés (at the twelfth-grade level, job résumés are required components of the alternate assessment for several states) and taking general education classes together (a strategy also reported by Hughes, Guth, Hall, Presley, Dye, & Byers, 1999). In at least one high school, all students are required to take a writing workshop in their last year, in preparation for the submission of their final accountability portfolios. In the context of these classes, general education peers (participating in the state's regular educational assessment) and students with significant disabilities (participating in the alternate assessment) work together to develop their respective letters to the reviewer, tables of contents, individual entries, and the construction of their portfolios as a whole (Longwill & Kleinert, 1998).

Finally, Kleinert, Kearns, and Kennedy (in press) discussed how the alternate assessment can itself be a valuable tool for transition by highlighting students' performance across multiple community and vocational environments and by documenting achievement of critical employability skills. For example, one high school student, Tina, included in her alternate assessment portfolio an original employer survey that asked the question "What are the most important skills needed to keep a job?" With the assistance of her peers, Tina developed the survey, which she typed during computer class. Tina and two peers then delivered the surveys to local employers, with the request that the surveys be completed and returned. As the surveys were returned, Tina compiled the results into a database during her accounting class. ("Quality of work" was rated highest by employers, followed by "working well with co-workers.") Tina also included entries related to her own employment: her résumé indicating work experiences at a local department store and a dry cleaner, and recommendation letters from her employers suggesting that she got along well with co-workers and that she worked hard. Alternate assessment evidence included systematic instructional program data, employer ratings of her work, and her own self-reflections.

PERSON-CENTERED PLANNING:
INCORPORATING ACTIVITIES MOST IMPORTANT TO THE STUDENT

Demonstrating performance across multiple environments is important; however, educators should have a clear strategy for choosing, with the student and his family, the multiple environments most significant to the student's education. One such strategy is detailed in *Choosing Outcomes and Accommodations for Children (COACH): A Guide to Educational Planning for Students with Disabilities, Second Edition* (Giangreco, Cloninger, & Iverson, 1998). Another strategy, especially relevant to students in the final years of schooling, is personal futures planning (Mount & Zwernik, 1989). Figure 9.3 presents a personal futures plan for one student— Nan—which was incorporated into her assessment portfolio (with personally identifiable information removed for scoring). This strategy, so important to ensuring the active voice of the student and his or her family in the plans for the future, clearly provides a map for the most relevant environments and activities for skill instruction.

Nan's personal futures plan can itself be part of her alternate assessment, but what is most important is the supporting evidence provided in her portfolio that

Background

Name: Nan
Birthdate: March 5, 1982
Heart operation: 5 months old
Diagnosed with cerebral palsy: 2 years old
Tubes placed in ears: 3 years old
Attended child development center: 3 years old
Public school: Kindergarten
Speech (Ms. Earl)
Special birthday cakes (Peggy)
Special Olympics (Walk and softball throw)
First confession and First Communion
Special Olympics friends
Elementary school (Ms. Carol)
Flower girl and bridesmaid
Walt Disney World
Myrtle Beach vacation
Moved to Spartan County
Started at Spartan County schools

Circle of Support

Family: Joe K., Julia, Mark, Roger, Hannah, Emma, Andy, Andrew, Ina, Matt, Katie, Jacob, Donna, Kevin, Jim, Mary, Donald, Marilyn, Linda, Gary, Grandma S., Grandpa S., Grandma B., Mom, Dad, Anna, Allison

Friends: Cheerleading friends, school friends, church friends, support group, Christy, Missy, Audrey, Jean, Meada, Bryan, April, Linda, Bobby, Billy

Service providers: School teacher and aides, Sunday School teachers, Father Tim, Dr. B., Dr. C., Special Olympics (Debbie and Roberta), Parks and Recreation

Community: Library, chorus, Fazzoli's, St. Luke, 4-H, McDonald's, Wal-Mart, Hoof-n-Nanny, neighbors (Pat, Patrick, and Diana)

Places

Nan's room, and her home with her horses Domino and Dolly

Vacations: Disney World, Myrtle Beach, Daytona Beach, Lake Barkley, Nashville, Houston, Birmingham, Opryland, Busch Gardens

High school: Reading, chorus, Wal-Mart, McDonald's, library, chorus trip (Williamsburg and Busch Gardens)

Community: Haunted Barn, Ham Days, dentist, doctor, St. Luke Festival, cheerleading, 4-H, horseback riding, concerts (Toby Keith, Alan Jackson, Trisha Yearwood).

Dreams

Own apartment
Roommates
Permanent job
Summer job
Make friends
Social group to go out with

(continued)

Figure 9.3. Personal futures plan for Nan.

Figure 9.3   *(continued)*

Personal Preferences

Likes:

Country music
Horseback riding (Dolly)
Animaniacs
Fox Kids Club House
To eat out at Fazzoli's and Hardees
Wal-Mart
Disney store in mall
Buying T-shirts of characters
Videotapes
Pausing the VCR
Halloween and Christmas
Going to Grandma's and Grandpa's
Going to doctor and dentist
Singing in church

Dislikes:

Cleaning my room
Putting dishes away
Having my tapes taken away
Anna's teasing
Getting up early
Fluoride toothpaste (hate it)
Sunday school

Choices

Made by Nan:

What to wear
Where to eat out
Music
Television
How to spend leisure time
Videotapes and CDs

Made by others:

When to go to church
School decisions
When to take baths
When to go to the doctor
When to eat
When to take medications

Made with help:

Horseback riding
When to go to bed
Spending money
Shopping

Made under protest!!

Going to Sunday school
Cleaning bedroom
Being made to stop "bugging"
Putting up tapes

Respect

Skills, gifts, and contributions:

Attractive, gentle, loving, good smile, pretty teeth, funny, easy to get along with, brave and bold, good memory, determined, observant, singing, music, talking about what she likes, physically able, good health, honest, good listener

Barriers to communication:

Lack of programs, transportation, short attention span, shy, allergies, lack of confidence in public, speech, easily frustrated, childlike

Dream day

Sleep late
Eat breakfast and get dressed
Go to part-time job at McDonald's (serve food and clean tables)
Work with animals (feed, water, and walk)
Go out to eat
Dance: Ballet
Exercise
Choir practice
Go to bed

---

shows how Nan and her circle are going about making her dream into a reality. For example, she can include a journal, showing how she is learning to make more of her own decisions in such areas as spending money or spending time with friends on weekends. Entries also can focus on her evidencing targeted skills in such activities as choir practice and ballet classes (both of which Nan had included in her "dream day"). She also can use these activities to demonstrate the existence of her social group.

Her vocational entry can include the steps she has taken, with assistance from her job trainer, to secure a job at McDonald's. Job performance data, including her own self-monitoring data, and employer evaluations also can be included in her vocational entry.

Because Nan is very interested in having her own apartment someday, another entry—perhaps completed in the context of a life science class—can focus on developing a monthly budget, checking apartment listings in the newspaper, and making a list of the things that she would need in her own apartment.

In this way, Nan's personal futures plan can itself become the central focus of what she chooses to place into her culminating portfolio. The personal futures plan describes the valued life outcomes that Nan has chosen, with the support of her family and support circle, and the portfolio provides the evidence of what Nan has accomplished—again with the support of her family and friends—to put her plan into place. What also should be clear is that Nan's personal futures plan provides a range of important environments for Nan to demonstrate her learned skills, including her job at McDonald's, extracurricular activities such as dance and choir practice, and general education classes such as Senior Life Science. Demonstrating performance across multiple environments is essential for students with significant disabilities, but educators have the responsibility to ensure that those environments are the ones most important to the student and her family.

OPPORTUNITIES FOR SELF-ADVOCACY AND LIFELONG LEARNING IN POSTSECONDARY EDUCATIONAL PROGRAMS

Students with significant disabilities, according to a mandate of the Individuals with Disabilities Education Act (IDEA) Amendments of 1997 (PL 105-17), must be educated, to the maximum extent appropriate, in the least restrictive environment. To date, that principle has been applied to public school environments (elementary, middle, and high school programs). Yet a number of authorities (Hall, Kleinert, & Kearns, 2000; Tashie, Malloy, & Lichtenstein, 1998), noting the right of students to a free appropriate public education up to age 21, have discussed the application of this principle to postsecondary education environments, including 2- and 4-year colleges. Students with significant disabilities should have the opportunity to receive their education, according to these authorities, in the environments in which their peers also are learning. Postsecondary education programs can provide valuable opportunities for continuing education, for opening avenues to lifelong learning, and for teaching self-advocacy skills in new and exciting environments. Consider the following examples from teachers with whom we work.

Learning About Students with Varying Ability Levels

EDU 360-01, Educating Exceptional Children in the Regular Classroom, is one section of a required course for all education majors at Northern Kentucky University. It is a 3-hour course that includes a field-based practicum. The course is designed to provide an introduction and overview of special education, legislation, programming, and services, with specific information about exceptional learners. Additional emphasis is placed on the adaptations and modifications that support exceptional learners in the regular classroom.

For purposes of continuity, the entire course can be viewed as a unit of study on exceptionalities. The students (preservice teachers) enrolled in this class have specific learning objectives for each section of the course. These are based on *Kentucky's Beginning Teacher Standards* (Kentucky Department of Education, 1999) and the *Council for Exceptional Children's (CEC) International Standards for Entry into Professional Practice* (CEC, 2000). The first section requires that students recognize and discuss special education in the context of its history, IDEA '97 regulations, placement and service delivery, collaboration, classroom management, learning styles, social acceptance, the learning and physical environments, and technology. The second and third sections focus on the discussion and application of those principles with regard to specific exceptional learning concerns or disability categories. Each section involves topic-related vocabulary and terminology, small-group in-class activities, videotape clips, hands-on experiences and/or practical application sessions, an individual project assignment, and an examination.

LeAnn, who has a significant disability, is working on improving language arts functioning in the sub-skill areas of written language and comprehension. She also is working on improving her vocational skills in the areas of following a schedule and staying on task. Although all of these target skills will not be shown in a single portfolio entry, LeAnn will have the opportunity to work on all of these skills throughout the semester. For this particular example, LeAnn's targeted skills for an alternate assessment entry will be writing/comprehension and staying on task.

The students in EDU 360-01 take notes in class to study for exams. LeAnn uses an adapted class notes form (see Figure 4.5 in Chapter 4) and modified exam questions are then taken from her completed forms. During group activity opportunities, LeAnn goes over her class notes with a classmate, who adds some important items (two or three items maximum) that LeAnn may not have had time to copy. After returning to her high school class, LeAnn writes three sentences about her college experience for the day in her journal, which satisfies her targeted skill of writing. Figure 9.4 includes an excerpt.

Journal entries are used as evidence in LeAnn's alternate assessment to show progress in her writing skills. Her class notes are used as evidence that LeAnn is participating with her same-age peers in a general education environment (as well as evidence of writing and comprehension). LeAnn's modified exams (with instructor comments) and scores are included as evidence of improvement in comprehension skills. Figure 9.5 presents the course instructor's section test, and Figure 9.6 presents LeAnn's modified test.

Preparing for LeAnn's Participation   At the first class meeting, students are given a syllabus. The university instructor and LeAnn's special education teacher

Figure 9.4.   LeAnn's journal entry related to graduation. (It reads: What I think will happen to me after I graduate is that I might get to go to NKU [a university]. And then after I finish going to college, then I can go to NPI [a vocational site] and maybe I can do them both like some people do. Because I kind of know of what I can do. Because I know this much, that I just love school.)

EDU 360–01 Exam #1

Name _____

Date _____

Short answer (3 points each)

1. Define special education and provide an example.

2. Identify and describe one court case that influenced special education.

3. Identify IDEA '97, and list two major provisions of this legislation.

4. List three reasons that support the importance of collaboration for exceptional learners in your classroom.

5. Describe the LRE for a student with mild disabilities.

6. List the four steps in the process and delivery of special education services.

7. List three psychosocial issues that can affect any learner in your classroom.

8. List and describe the three stages of learning.

Figure 9.5. Sample of an EDU 360-01 class exam.

9. List the two problem areas where learners usually require adapted instruction.

10. Describe how you would adapt instruction to accommodate a child's different learning style.

11. Describe how you would adapt your instruction to meet the needs of a student with disabilities who can't complete assignments on time.

12. Identify three aspects/characteristics of your classroom learning environment that will support learning for all children.

13. Identify and describe the two types of behaviors that interfere with classroom operations and/or hinder academic achievement.

14. List the two primary principles of behavior.

15. Identify two important considerations for the use of technology in your classroom.

Brief Essay (5 points each): Answer one of the following; use the back of this page.

a. Describe how you could develop and support social acceptance in your classroom.

b. Describe the important aspects for the physical and the instructional environments of your classroom.

c. Discuss the conditions that can suppress or inhibit learning for any student in your classroom.

EDU 360-01 Exam #1: Modified

Name _____

Date _____

Find underlined items in your class notes:

1. What is <u>special education</u>?

2. What does <u>IDEA</u> stand for? (Circle one.)

   <u>L</u>east <u>R</u>estrictive <u>E</u>nvironment

   <u>In</u>dividuals with <u>Di</u>sabilities <u>E</u>ducation <u>A</u>ct

3. What do teachers do that helps you to learn/remember information?

4. What does <u>LRE</u> stand for? (Circle one)

   <u>L</u>east <u>R</u>estrictive <u>E</u>nvironment

   <u>In</u>dividuals with <u>Di</u>sabilities <u>E</u>ducation <u>A</u>ct

5. From your notes of 1-26-00, list three <u>psychosocial</u> issues that affect any learner in the classroom.

6. If a person is a <u>visual</u> learner, how do they like to get new information?

   See information    Hear information

   2001 © Microsoft

7. What can a teacher do to help a student who cannot get his or her assignments turned in on time? (Circle one.)

   Send student to detention   Give student more time

8. What characteristics/aspects of a classroom support learning for all students? (Circle two.)

   A variety of books   Teachers always lecture in class

   Teachers yell at those who misbehave   Teachers give encouragement

9. What could you use <u>technology</u> (computers, TV) for in a classroom?
   <u>Essay</u>

10. What kinds of conditions in a classroom can keep/stop students from learning? Write three sentences about these conditions. (In other words, tell me some not-so-good things that teachers should *not* do).

Figure 9.6.   A modified EDU 360-01 exam for LeAnn.

have collaborated prior to the second week of classes and have decided on a schedule of attendance for LeAnn. Those are highlighted on LeAnn's syllabus and LeAnn puts them on her calendar. She crosses off each day on her calendar that she attends class. Calendar checklists are used as portfolio evidence of LeAnn's ability to manage her own schedule.

To work on staying on task, LeAnn is expected to include five items covered in class by writing those items in the blanks on her class notes form. After class, LeAnn graphs the number of items she has recorded as a visual chart of her progress toward that targeted skill. Copies of the graphs are included in her alternate assessment portfolio as evidence of improvement on her targeted skill of staying on task; instructor comments on improvement in this area will also be included as evidence.

It is important to note that LeAnn's performance in this age-appropriate, inclusive environment illustrates her reliance on natural supports. This class also serves other purposes for LeAnn. As she learns with her typical peers, she is developing important skills in mapping her own learning style (see her unit test questions on learning style, as illustrated in Figure 9.6), and she is gaining knowledge in essential civil rights for people with disabilities. It is this content knowledge, richly embedded in a university general curriculum course for preservice teachers, that furthers LeAnn's path to self-advocacy and self-determination. This point of learning to speak for oneself is illustrated with another journal entry, shown in Figure 9.7, also included in LeAnn's accountability portfolio. As indicated in Chapter 6, self-advocacy is itself an important outcome of education.

LeAnn has shown that she can communicate appropriate adult feelings and needs related to events in her life. This example also shows her skill in the area of taking control over her own education. LeAnn's response to Mrs. Groneck (who was not LeAnn's IEP teacher of record and who was thus less familiar with LeAnn's support needs) is an excellent example of the types of self-assertive behaviors that will lead LeAnn into a more independent adulthood.

Finally, this class has important career implications for LeAnn. As part of her course, she is completing a practicum as a teacher assistant in a preschool environment. There she has the opportunity to apply the course content by constructing a positive learning environment for her "own" students, whom she serves in the preschool class. At the end of her practicum experience each day, she completes the self-reflection form presented in Figure 9.8. This form, too, is included in LeAnn's alternate assessment. Taken as a whole, the sum of this alternate assessment evidence provides documentation of LeAnn's growing maturity in her academic and vocational skills and the greater role she is taking in her own learning across multiple real-life environments.

A Postsecondary Physical Education Class:
Taking Steps Toward Life-Long Exercise Habits

Stephanie and David, who both have significant disabilities, are students in a postsecondary class called PHE 108, Beginning Conditioning. Each student is 19 years old, and while they are still officially in high school, both attend NKU for part of the day. Both students are working on developing appropriate leisure skills that they can continue to use after they graduate, as well as on improving their physical skills and endurance.

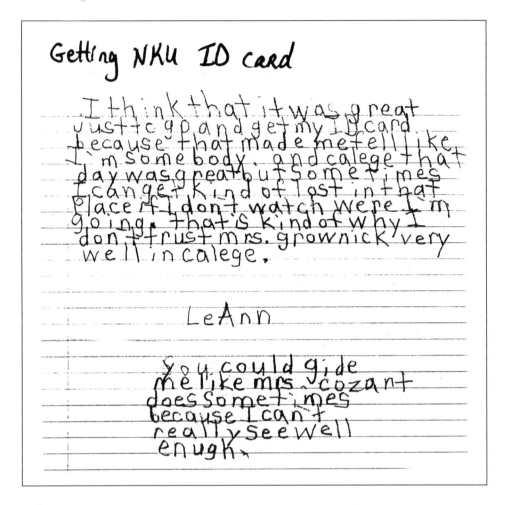

Figure 9.7. LeAnn's Journal entry: Getting the NKU student ID. (It reads: I think that it was great just to go and get my ID card because that made me feel like I'm somebody. And college that day was great, but sometimes I can get kind of lost in that place if I don't watch where I'm going. That is kind of why I don't trust Mrs. Groneck very well in college.
LeAnn
P.S. You could guide me like Mrs. Cozart does sometimes because I can't really see well enough. [This last part was added as a note to Mrs. Groneck, after she asked LeAnn how she could gain LeAnn's trust and give her better support at NKU.])

David and Stephanie are fully participating members of PHE 108 and participate in the same learning activities as the other students. Their high school special education teacher or an instructional assistant accompanies them to each class. After the course instructor gives overviews and demonstrations of the various areas available for use in the health center, students are assigned to develop and follow their own fitness program during each class meeting. Each student's program is designed to help him or her improve in each of five components of fitness. Because all students complete individual workouts at their own pace, modifications are needed for Stephanie and David only when doing certain exercises and when taking quizzes.

All students are required to keep journals recording their progress. Stephanie and David first choose which exercises/routines to include in their programs and

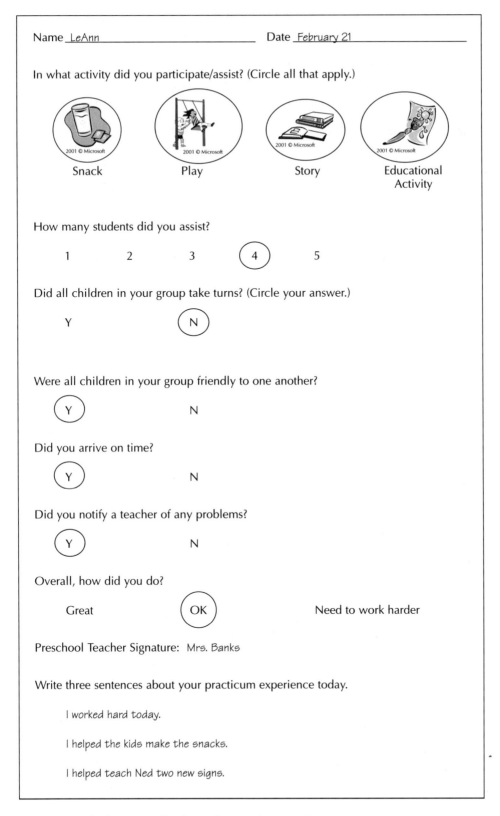

Name **LeAnn**   Date **February 21**

In what activity did you participate/assist? (Circle all that apply.)

Snack   Play   Story   Educational Activity

How many students did you assist?

1   2   3   (4)   5

Did all children in your group take turns? (Circle your answer.)

Y   (N)

Were all children in your group friendly to one another?

(Y)   N

Did you arrive on time?

(Y)   N

Did you notify a teacher of any problems?

(Y)   N

Overall, how did you do?

Great   (OK)   Need to work harder

Preschool Teacher Signature: Mrs. Banks

Write three sentences about your practicum experience today.

I worked hard today.

I helped the kids make the snacks.

I helped teach Ned two new signs.

Figure 9.8. Preschool practicum self-evaluation for LeAnn.

in which order they would like to perform the routines. A printed model listing each component of their workout and three evaluation questions are then prepared for them to copy into their journals. (For Stephanie, this includes picture cues, which are gradually faded out as the class progresses.) Both students complete this preparation of their daily journal entry before going to class. During workout sessions, Stephanie and David check off each component as they complete it and later, back at their high school, finish the entry by answering the evaluation questions. Also included as part of their journal is a Nautilus weight chart on which they keep track of progress on the weight machines they use. Informal notes from other classmates are included when they act as exercise partners with either student or give assistance by demonstrating specific exercises.

These journal entries will be used in Stephanie's and David's alternate assessments as evidence of self-planning, self-evaluation, sustained interactions with age-peers, and participation in activities that promote physical health and well-being. A blank sample of the printed journal entry guide is presented in Figure 9.9. Results of quizzes and health component tests with instructor com-

---

Name_____   Date _____

Circle the things that you did:

    Stretching

    Cardiovascular exercise

    Weight machines

    Walk track

Program completed?

Did I improve?

     Y   N

Next time I will work harder on:

Figure 9.9.   Sample of a daily journal entry guide.

ments also are used as evidence of class participation and progress toward student goals/objectives.

WORKING WITH FAMILIES TO DEMONSTRATE
A STUDENT'S PERFORMANCE AT SCHOOL AND AT HOME

Throughout this chapter, we emphasize how important it is for students with significant disabilities to perform targeted skills across multiple school and community environments. We have discussed how this performance can be demonstrated in the context of important learning for all students—at the elementary, middle, high school, and postsecondary levels—and how such performance can be incorporated into alternate assessment practice. Yet, there is still one environment we have failed to discuss—one that is of crucial importance to students of all ages—the student's own home! We now turn to the importance of carryover between school and home, between teachers and families, and how teachers are documenting that carryover as a part of their students' alternate assessments. Janet Fay, a teacher with students in her state's alternate assessment, discusses what this has meant for one of her students:

The summer before I started working with James, I met him and his mother, Terri, at a summer program where James was enrolled. His mother wanted me to see the activities in which James was involved, and how the occupational therapist was working with him.

As the school year began, Terri and I used a notebook to send messages back and forth, as well as e-mail, which I subsequently copied for my own notes. Terri often called me before or after school and gave me articles to read about James's disability and promising new interventions. She often asked if I would try things after reading the information, and I was usually willing because she knew James best and most of the things we discussed were backed by research. She would always say, "I hope I'm not being pushy." It never seemed that way to me, knowing that parents should be an integral part of any educational team.

During that first year, our speech-language pathologist and Terri attended a Picture Exchange Communication System (PECS) (Bondy & Frost, 1994) training. I originally thought of this approach as having more of a speech therapy function. Terri wanted to start using this approach at home and paid for someone from PECS to spend the day at school and train the teaching assistant and myself. This was a good lesson for me that we *all* needed to be a part of James's whole program.

Last year, we had some difficulty with James acting out. Terri came to the class and brought James's favorite treats for the class—Twinkies. Then, she explained to the children about autism and how James's disability affected him. Even now, those students continue to bring up little things that they learned from her. For example, Terri asked if they noticed that Ms. Fay (that's me!) gave James a lot of hugs. She explained that he needed tactile input, and the students still mention that from time to time.

I have placed notes from some of his peers in James's portfolio to document his facility with relationship building.

This past summer, Terri met with the teaching assistant, Vivian, and me to discuss what James had been doing over the summer. I gave Vivian my PECS manual and a book on autism. This information has helped Vivian to form a close relationship with James, which has helped to cement our relation with James's mother. Vivian now has a better understanding of James and his whole life. She's learned from Mom about what goes on at home and how James handles things at home. Of course, what she has learned is carried over in the classroom. And Terri also has better feelings about school because she knows every aspect of James's education and what we are doing.

We continue to write in the notebook and correspond through e-mail. Some of the notes and mail are placed in his portfolio, as evidence of instruction and carryover in multiple environments. We coordinate his program by mutually reinforcing James's learning across both environments. For example, when we started his reading words, I used pictures Terri had taken of his favorite foods, house, animals, and relatives. I used block letters (such as we do with spelling), but blocked the word as a whole because I learned from in-services that children with autism often see things as a whole—and often do not attend to individual letters. Every time I make a new work card, I ditto it, send a copy home, and keep a copy for James's portfolio. The data I collect from my own instruction and from Terri at home regarding his learning of new words are placed into the portfolio as well.

Whenever we (as a team) think James is ready to go to the next step in PECS, we either discuss it in person or through the notebook or on the telephone. Whatever Terri is doing at home, we reinforce at school, if at all possible. We also use the same symbols. I made up a weekly progress form to send home (see Figure 9.10). That form becomes portfolio evidence, too. I'm starting to use this format so that Terri will know where James is in relation to his IEP goals. Hopefully, this will keep her even better informed!

Now that James is speaking more, it is sometimes difficult to know exactly what he's talking about. He recently went to Disney World, and Terri sent pictures of the trip to school. That way we could talk with James about his trip; this also gave his peers the opportunity to talk to him about it! We had him describe his trip to one of his peers during journal-writing time; a copy of his dictated journal entry also is placed into his portfolio.

Recently, when Terri gave a pizza party at school, James started using attributes or *describing* words. This was an opportunity to show the other students how PECS worked for James. She had plain, pepperoni, and mushroom pizza, as well as soft drinks. All of his classmates had PECS symbols to use to request the type of pizza they wanted. The kids had to form the sentences such as, "I want pepperoni pizza," "I want

Home–School Progress Report

Name: _____   Date: _____

IEP goals	% and/or anecdotal notes

Comments:

Comments and suggestions from home:

Figure 9.10.   Sample home–school progress report.

soda," and so forth, using the same symbols that James uses. (This activity also fit in perfectly with the classroom teacher's lesson on parts of speech.) Some of the kids wrote about the activity in their journals the next day, and I placed their entries into James's portfolio to show natural supports, inclusive environments, and relationships (along with all of the neat pictures we took of the activity).

As I have shown in my description of the close working relationship between home and school for James (and how that relationship has created new learning opportunities that we have demonstrated in his accountability portfolio), it is not always easy to say where instruction ends and assessment begins. And maybe there shouldn't be a clear distinction between the two! I think our work with James shows how school and home collaboration can be used effectively in the instruction/assessment process. I know James wouldn't have done as well as he has if we—home and school—hadn't worked so closely together.

—Janet M. Fay, Special Education Teacher

SUMMARY

Throughout this chapter, we have provided examples of how to demonstrate student performance across multiple, age-appropriate environments. These environments should always include the presence of typical peers and the provision of natural supports. In each example, we have shown how teachers and students can collect performance data for the student's alternate assessment and how such performance results are consistent with the alternate assessment content and scoring requirements of several states that have taken the lead in this area. Finally, performance across multiple environments is not something to demonstrate in isolation of the other critical dimensions of alternate assessments but rather is inseparable from those other dimensions. Thus, alternate assessments to demonstrate performance across multiple environments should always include opportunities for student choice-making, planning, and self-evaluation and for developing one's own schedule. They also should include opportunities for increasing self-determination, forming a rich network of social relationships, and fostering a true sense of membership with typical peers. Although the elements of effective performance can be separated into discrete categories for scoring purposes, real life does not work that way. These elements must all be present if students are to achieve the overarching outcome of increased participation in valued life roles.

REFERENCES

Arvidson, H.A., Davis, M.A., Cunningham, J.N., & Bennett, D.E. (1999). *Indiana Assessment System of Educational Proficiencies (IASEP) training manual.* West Lafayette, IN: Purdue University, Department of Educational Studies.

Branham, R., Collins, B., Schuster, J., & Kleinert, H. (1999). Teaching community skills to students with moderate disabilities: Comparing combined techniques of classroom simulation, videotape modeling, and community-based instruction. *Education and Training in Mental Retardation and Developmental Disabilities, 34*(2), 170–181.

Bondy, A., & Frost, L. (1994). The picture exchange communication system. *FOCUS on Autistic Behavior, 9*(3), 1–19.

Browder, D., & Snell, M. (2000). Teaching functional academics. In M. Snell & F. Brown *Instruction of students with severe disabilities* (5th ed., pp. 493–542). Columbus, OH: Charles E. Merrill.

Brown, L., Nietupski, J., & Hamre-Nietupski, S. (1976). The criterion of ultimate functioning and public school services for severely handicapped children. In M.A. Thomas (Ed.), *Hey, don't forget about me!* Reston, VA: Council for Exceptional Children.

Brown, L., Schwartz, P., Udvari-Solner, A., Kampschroer, E., Johnson, F., Jorgensen, J., & Gruenewald, L. (1991). How much time should students with severe intellectual disabilities spend in regular education classrooms and elsewhere? *Journal of The Association of Persons with Severe Handicaps, 16*(1), 39–47.

Council for Exceptional Children. (2000). *International standards for entry into professional practice* [On-line]. Available: http://www.cec.sped.org/ps/ps-entry.htm

Gast, D., & Schuster, J. (1993). Students with severe developmental disabilities. In A. Blackhurst & W. Berdine (Eds.). *An introduction to special education* (3rd ed., pp. 454–491). New York: HarperCollins.

Giangreco, M.F., Cloninger, C.J., & Iverson, V.S. (1998). *Choosing outcomes and accommodations for children (COACH): A guide to educational planning for students with disabilities* (2nd ed.). Baltimore: Paul H. Brookes Publishing Co.

Hall, M., Kleinert, H., & Kearns, J. (2000). College connection: New directions in post-secondary programs for students with moderate and severe disabilities. *Teaching Exceptional Children 32*(3), 58–65.

Heward, W. (2000). *Exceptional children: An introduction to special education* (6th ed.). Columbus, OH: Charles E. Merrill.

Hughes, C., Guth, C., Hall, S., Presley, J., Dye, M., & Byers, C. (1999). "They are my best friends": Peer buddies promote inclusion in high school. *Teaching Exceptional Children, 31*(5), 32–37.

Individuals with Disabilities Education Act (IDEA) Amendments of 1997, PL 105-17, 20 U.S.C. §§ 1400 *et. seq.*

Kentucky Department of Education. (1999). *New teacher standards for preparation and certification* [One-line]. Available: http://www.kde.state.sy.us/otec/epsb/standards

Kleinert, H., Kearns, J., & Kennedy, S. (in press). Including all students in educational assessment and accountability. In W. Sailor (Ed.), *Inclusive education and school/community partnerships.* New York: Teachers College Press.

Longwill, A., & Kleinert, H. (1998). The unexpected benefits of high school peer tutoring. *Teaching Exceptional Children, 30*(4), 60–65.

Mount, B., & Zwernik, K. (1989). *It's never too early—it's never too late: A booklet about personal futures planning.* Minneapolis: Minnesota Governor's Planning Council on Developmental Disabilities.

Schuh, M., Tashie, C., Lamb, P., Bang, M., & Jorgensen, C.M. (1998). Community-based learning for all students. In C.M. Jorgensen, *Restructuring high schools for all students: Taking inclusion to the next level.* (pp. 233–260). Baltimore: Paul H. Brookes Publishing Co.

Shapiro-Barnard, S., Tashie, C., Martin, J., Schuh, M., Malloy, J., Piet, J., Lictenstein, S., & Nisbet, J. (1996). *Petroglyphs: The writing on the wall.* Durham: University of New Hampshire, Institute on Disability.

Tashie, C., Malloy, J., & Lichtenstein, S. (1998). Transition or graduation? Supporting all students to plan for the future. In C.M. Jorgensen, *Restructuring high school for all students: Taking inclusion to the next level* (pp. 233–260). Baltimore: Paul H. Brookes Publishing Co.

West Virginia Department of Education. (1999, October). *West Virginia alternate assessment: Pilot project administration manual.* Wheeling: West Virginia Department of Education, Office of Student Services and Assessment and Office of Special Education.

chapter 10

*In the big picture, what
does this move toward assessing
all students mean for me and my students?*

RESEARCH ON THE IMPACT
OF ALTERNATE ASSESSMENT

Harold L. Kleinert, Jacqui Farmer Kearns,
Kimberly Ann Costello, Karen Nowak-Drabik, Michelle Marilyn Garrett,
Leah S. Horvath, Stephanie H. Kampfer, and Matthew D. Turner

In this chapter, we briefly review what we have learned about alternate assessments from our research. We discuss a number of questions, which we believe have the most significance for educators, in a question-and-answer format. Although we certainly cannot claim to have definitive answers to any of these important concerns, through various studies we have done preliminary research into each of these questions, and we hope that what we have found will be of value to you as a teacher or practitioner.

FINDINGS FROM RESEARCH

In this chapter, we summarize what we have found in each of these areas:

Q: *Is there consensus within our field as to the performance criteria or yardsticks that should be used in evaluating the learning of students with significant disabilities, as well as the quality of supports provided in the context of their education?*

A: As we have noted elsewhere, essential to the practice of developing any alternate assessments is deciding *how to score* that assessment (i.e., what standards or performance criteria to use) (Kleinert & Kearns, 1999). In this study, we surveyed 44 national authorities in best practices for students with moderate and severe cognitive disabilities. These experts' responses did reveal a high degree of professional congruence on the core of best practices embodied in the performance criteria for Kentucky's alternate assessment. On a five-point Likert scale (5 representing *highest importance* for students with significant disabilities and 1 representing *lowest importance*), mean ratings for Kentucky's performance or scoring criteria by these national experts ranged from a high of 4.91 for "performance in integrated environments" to a low of 3.34 for "student uses computer technology." Of the 16 performance indicators, 11 had mean scores higher than 4.5 (see Table 10.1). So noted in that table, the two performance indicators rated highest were "performance in integrated environments" (mean 4.91) and "functional outcomes that are meaningful in current and future settings" (mean 4.89).

Several respondents commented about the importance of students with significant disabilities' demonstrating that they could meet the same academic expectations as all other students. For example, one respondent noted that "the more these indicators are tied to your standards, the more important I believe they are" (Kleinert & Kearns, 1999, p. 105).

Although even the lowest rated performance indicators were judged to be important (mean ratings above 3 on the five-point scale), expert respondents indicated a considerably more divergent range of opinions on most of the lower rated indicators. For example, for the indicator "student activities represent all domain areas," more than 20% of the respondents indicated that the domain-based approach (e.g., vocational, personal management, recreation/leisure) within Kentucky's alternate assessment was too narrowly defined if that indicator did not also consider a student's access to the general curriculum as one of those key domains. As Kleinert and Kearns noted, "An analysis of the written

Table 10.1. Kentucky Alternate Assessment performance indicator expert ratings

Performance indicator	Minumum rating	Maximum rating	Mean	Standard deviation
Integrated environments	4.00	5.00	4.91	.29
Functionality	2.00	5.00	4.89	.49
Age appropriate	3.00	5.00	4.81	.45
Choice-making	4.00	5.00	4.80	.41
Multiple settings	3.00	5.00	4.80	.51
Communication	3.00	5.00	4.79	.53
Academic Expectations	2.00	5.00	4.78	.57
Natural support	2.00	5.00	4.67	.65
Targeted skills	3.00	5.00	4.63	.63
Friendship	3.00	5.00	4.59	.69
Parent involvement	3.00	5.00	4.59	.69
Assistive technology	3.00	5.00	4.42	.76
All domains	1.00	5.00	3.88	1.27
Plan/monitor/evaluate	1.00	5.00	3.80	.93
Evaluate own performance	1.00	5.00	3.69	.92
Computer technology	1.00	5.00	3.34	1.12

From Kleinert, H., & Kearns, J. (1999). A validation study of the performance indicators and learner outcomes of Kentucky's alternate assessment for students with significant disabilities. *Journal of The Association for Persons with Severe Handicaps, 24*(2), 105; reprinted by permission.

comments suggested that respondents viewed general education, academic classes as important vehicles for achieving functional outcomes for students with significant disabilities" (1999, p. 108).

More than 20% of the respondents cautioned about the use of scoring criteria that only reflected a functional domains-based curricular approach, if that approach did not also consider a student's participation in general academic classes and progress in the general curriculum. Respondents also noted that performance indicators cannot be taken in isolation, but had to be used concurrently to be meaningful (e.g., age-appropriate choices should occur in the context of activities with peers without disabilities, targeted skills should be evidenced across multiple school and community settings). Assessing isolated instances of each best practice indicator would defeat the intent of the assessment.

Q: *How advisable is it for teachers to base learner outcomes for students with significant disabilities on the same educational standards that states and school districts are identifying for all students?*

A: One of the most important considerations in conceptualizing alternate assessments "is whether the content standards (or core learning outcomes) identified for all students can and should be applied to students participating in the alternate assessment; or conversely, whether alternate assessments should be based on a separate, more 'functional' set of learner outcomes" (Kleinert & Kearns, 1999, p. 100). We have contended that if we do apply the same learner outcomes to all students, then we still need to ask "if *differential* benchmarks or performance indicators should be used for students in the alternate assessment to measure their progress on those essential outcomes" (Kleinert & Kearns, 1999, pp. 100–101).

Kentucky's alternate assessment, similar to that of a number of states, is based on a *subset* of the learner outcomes identified for all students. In the initial development of the state's alternate assessment, a group of Kentucky educators reviewed each of the state's Academic Expectations and chose those that appeared to have the greatest applicability to the educational needs of students with significant disabilities. In making this determination, the educators first considered the underlying or *critical function* associated with each of the Academic Expectations. For example, *using patterns to understand past and present events and predict future events* for a student with significant disabilities could be documented by that student's independently maintaining his or her own daily schedule of activities (using a pictorial or printed personal schedule or an object symbol-shelf). The Academic Expectation of *student communicates ideas through speaking* could be evidenced by a student communicating his or her basic needs across environments, situations, and people.

As part of the same study discussed in Question 1, we asked the 44 survey respondents to rate the importance of the 25 Academic Expectations (i.e., learner outcomes) that form the basis for Kentucky's alternate assessment for students with significant disabilities. Respondents evaluated the importance of each of these learner outcomes with the same five-part Likert scale used for rating the performance indicators. The highest rated Academic Expectations (in terms of their importance for students with moderate and severe disabilities) were *mental and emotional wellness* (4.80), *speaking* (4.79), *interpersonal relationships* (4.71), *democratic principles* (4.69), *accessing information* (4.67), and *postsecondary opportunities* (4.66). Table 10.2 presents the rating for each of Kentucky's Academic Expectations.

We should note, however, that respondents made numerous comments about the critical functions or "functional interpretations" that Kentucky educators had assigned to each of the Academic Expectations represented within the state's alternate assessment. Respondents questioned the necessity of establishing functional applications for students with moderate and severe disabilities if, in fact, the Academic Expectations have been determined to be important for *all* Kentucky students. Respondents also were concerned that functional applications or critical functions were being too narrowly construed for students with significant disabilities, especially considering the breadth of Kentucky's Academic Expectations in general, and that narrowly interpreted applications of broadly expressed standards could well result in expectations for these students that were "too low" or not sufficiently tied to the general curriculum.

The results of this national survey clearly indicated that 1) experts in educational programs for students with significant disabilities believed strongly that alternate educational assessments should be based on the same learner outcomes (or a subset of those learner outcomes) identified for all students, and 2) although students with significant disabilities may evidence those same outcomes in adapted ways, educators should be careful that our functional interpretations of those adapted ways do not result in lowered expectations or a narrowing of curricular options for these students.

Table 10.2.   Kentucky Academic Expectations: Experts' ratings

Academic Expectations	Minimum rating	Maximum rating	Mean	Standard deviation
Mental and emotional wellness	3.00	5.00	4.80	.46
Speaking	1.00	5.00	4.79	.72
Interpersonal relationships	3.00	5.00	4.71	.55
Democratic principles	3.00	5.00	4.69	.56
Accessing information	2.00	5.00	4.67	.65
Postsecondary opportunities	3.00	5.00	4.66	.65
Family life/parenting	3.00	5.00	4.59	.67
Physical wellness	3.00	5.00	4.55	.66
Nature of scientific activity	3.00	5.00	4.54	.71
Identifying/using patterns	3.00	5.00	4.50	.71
Reading	2.00	5.00	4.44	.67
Lifetime physical activities	3.00	5.00	4.41	.66
Using electronic technology	2.00	5.00	4.38	.83
Accessing community health	2.00	5.00	4.26	.82
Selecting career path	3.00	5.00	4.26	.79
Employability attributes	2.00	5.00	4.23	.93
Structure/function political	2.00	5.00	4.17	1.05
Writing	2.00	5.00	3.98	1.05
Psychomotor skills	1.00	5.00	3.95	1.01
Understanding constancy	1.00	5.00	3.93	1.15

From Kleinert, H., & Kearns, J. (1999). A validation study of the performance indicators and learner outcomes of Kentucky's alternate assessment for students with significant disabilities. *Journal of The Association for Persons with Severe Handicaps, 24*(2), 107; reprinted by permission.

Q: *At the school level, is there any relationship between student performance in the alternate assessment and the performance of all the other students in that school in the regular assessment? Has research shown that schools whose students do well in the alternate assessment also produce students who receive high scores in the regular assessment?*

A: Turner, Baldwin, Kleinert, and Kearns (2000) compared the individual Alternate Portfolio score for 60 students with the overall school accountability index for each student's school as well as the amount of improvement in each school's accountability index in the last 2-year cycle. A total of 36 schools were involved in the study, including equal numbers of elementary, middle, and high schools, and were chosen from schools that in previous years had average performance scores within the alternate assessment in each of the state's performance levels (i.e., Novice, Apprentice, Proficient, and Distinguished).

First, the Alternate Portfolio score for each student was correlated with the actual Kentucky Instructional Results Information System (KIRIS), or schoolwide accountability score, for the student's school. (The KIRIS score is a composite index of the scores of all of the students in that school.) Second, Alternate Portfolio scores were correlated with the amount of KIRIS score *improvement* (expressed as percentage of goal obtained) for each school over the last 2-year accountability cycle. In Kentucky, schools are rewarded or sanctioned based on improvement over previous years' scores. Each school must meet its individual improvement goal for that particular cycle to receive rewards. A school that started at a baseline level of 50 might be assigned a goal of 55 for the next 2-year cycle. If that school achieved a score of 55 within that cycle, the school would have met 100% of its goal; if it improved to a score of 60 in that cycle, it would have doubled the amount of improvement required, or achieved 200% of its goal. Turner et al. were interested both in the strength of the relationship between a school's alternate assessment scores and the school's absolute KIRIS score for all students, as well as between the school's improvement measure (percentage of current goal obtained for all students) and its alternate assessment scores.

The study found that, even though students in the Alternate Portfolio make up less than 1% of all the students in Kentucky's educational assessment and accountability system, Alternate Portfolio scores within each of these 36 schools correlated significantly with the total KIRIS school score for each school as well as with the percentage performance gain for *all* students within the school. Specifically, Turner et al. found a significant correlation ($r = .48$, $p < .001$) between Alternate Portfolio scores and KIRIS scores for each school and an even stronger relation ($r = .57$, $p < .001$) between Alternate Portfolio scores and the percent of KIRIS goal attained, or school improvement, for each school.

Given the small numbers of students in the alternate system, it is unlikely that the Alternate Portfolio scores themselves would have had the impact on overall school improvement scores to produce correlations of this magnitude. A more likely explanation for this relationship is that best practices instructional opportunities for students with moderate and severe disabilities are integrally related to enhanced learning opportunities for all students (Turner et al., 2000). Scores at the Distinguished level, for example, require a high degree of collaboration between general and special education staff. A number of authorities in both moderate and severe disabilities and in the general education school reform literature suggested that best practices for students with significant disabilities (e.g., cooperative learning groups with individualized student outcomes, mixed-ability grouping, positive behavioral supports, instruction in prosocial skills) result in improved instruction for *all* students (Coots, Bishop, Grenot-Scheyer, & Falvey, 1995; Jorgensen, 1998; Lipsky & Gartner, 1997). Although the results of this study do not conclusively prove this hypothesis, they certainly support it.

Q: *What will schools actually do with the alternate assessment results of students with significant disabilities, especially given the fact that so few students will actually participate in the alternate assessment (in comparison to the number of students participating in the regular assessments) in any given school? Will schools really care about the performance of their students in the alternate assessment, and will the inclusion of these students result in changes in instructional practices?*

A: In order to answer the question "What changes are occurring in instructional practices or administrative support as a result of participation in the alternate assessment?", Costello, Turner, Kearns, and Kleinert (2001) contacted special education teachers and principals in 36 schools. Schools were randomly selected according to the following three components: 1) each school had an individual student in the Alternate Portfolio (an equal number of High–Proficient or Distinguished, and Low–Novice or Apprentice, Alternate Portfolios were chosen), 2) the grade level of students participating in the alternate assessment (an equal number of students at the fourth-, eighth-, and twelfth-grade levels), and 3) the *school's* percentage of goal met in Kentucky's accountability system (an equal number of schools that had met or exceeded their performance goal and an equal number that had not attained their accountability goal). The principal's interview consisted of questions that examined the impact of alternate assessment requirements on school accountability and educational practices, as well as his or her general perception of the alternate assessment. The teacher's interview examined similar questions but contained additional questions on the impact of the alternate assessment on the student's IEP goals and on instructional interventions. A total of 29 teachers and 22 principals participated in the study.

School interviews were categorized by the Alternate Portfolio score and the school's achieved percentage of its accountability goal for *all* of its students in Kentucky's statewide assessment according to the following four groups: 1) Low AP/Low % goal schools = Low Alternate Portfolio score and low percentage of overall school goal, 2) High AP/Low % goal schools = High Alternate Portfolio score and low percentage of overall school goal, 3) Low AP/High % goal schools = low Alternate Portfolio score and high percentage of overall school goal, and 4) High AP/High % goal schools = High Alternate Portfolio and high percentage of overall school goal. Table 10.3 presents these four groupings. The authors analyzed the interviews for thematic content in the following five areas:

- Impact and inclusion of the Alternate Portfolio in the school's Accountability Index
- Principals' and teachers' perception of changes that have occurred as a result of students' inclusion in the alternate assessment

Table 10.3.   A study of how schools respond to the inclusion of students in the alternate assessment

	Low percentage of accountability goal achieved for all students in school	High percentage of accountability goal achieved for all students in school
Schools with low student Alternate Portfolio score	Low Alternate Portfolio Score and Low Overall Percentage of School Goal (Low/Low Schools) (*n* = 11)	Low Alternate Portfolio Score and High Overall Percentage of School Goal (Low/High Schools) (*n* = 3)
Students with high student Alternate Portfolio score	High Alternate Portfolio Score and Low Overall Percentage of School Goal (High/Low Schools) (*n* = 5)	High Alternate Portfolio Score and High Overall Percentage of School Goal (High/High Schools) (*n* = 10)

From Costello, K., Turner, M., Kearns, J., & Kleinert, H. (2000). *Teacher and principal perceptions of the impact of alternate assessments on school accountability and instructional practices.* Manuscript in preparation.

- The alternate assessment's strength and weaknesses
- The alternate assessment's impact on IEP and program development
- Teachers' perceptions of the extent to which they felt supported by the school administration and by other school staff

As might be expected, Costello et al. found the greatest difference in these variables between Low/Low and High/High schools. The majority of teachers and principals in Low/Low schools indicated that Alternate Portfolios had no impact or minor negative influence, and they did not want the Alternate Portfolio included in the school accountability index. In contrast, teachers in High/High schools indicated that Alternate Portfolios *did* have a positive impact, and that the Alternate Portfolio should be included in the school accountability index. Costello et al. noted, however, that even for High/High schools, principals had mixed opinions on the inclusion of the alternate assessment in the school's overall index.

Across all *four* groups of schools, Costello et al. found a general lack of knowledge about the alternate assessment among principals. These researchers also found common concerns across all four groups of teachers, including the amount of time involved in completing alternate assessments, the extent to which the student's portfolio represented teacher and not student work, and the extent to which the state's academic expectations could be documented—even in the context of an alternate assessment—for students with the most significant disabilities.

Perhaps the most striking differences Costello et al. found between Low/Low and High/High schools were the perceptions of teachers along three critical variables: 1) changes in school practice as a result of the alternate assessment, 2) impact of the alternate assessment upon IEPs and instructional interventions, and 3) teacher perceptions of the extent they themselves were supported in their school communities. Table 10.4 summarizes those differences.

IMPLICATIONS FOR TEACHERS

What are the implications of Costello et al.'s study for teachers? First, it is critical that teachers convey to administrators the importance of the Individuals with Disabilities Act (IDEA) Amendments of 1997 (PL 105-17) mandate for the inclusion of all students in state- and district-level educational assessments, including the

Table 10.4. Differences in teachers' perceptions in Low-Low and High-High achieving schools

	Special education teacher perceptions in Low-Low schools (n = 11)	Special education teacher perceptions in High-High schools (n = 13)
Teacher perception of change as a result of the alternate assessment	Majority of teachers said that the performance data from their alternate assessments were not used as part of their school's instructional improvement plan, or that they were unsure of the use of the alternate assessment data.	50% of these teachers (5 of 10) said that the alternate assessment data were used as part of school improvement planning; 50% said that the data were not used, or that they were unsure of the use of these data.
	Majority of teachers in this category said that the alternate assessment had no impact on inclusion.	All of these teachers said the alternate assessment had increased inclusion and/or collaboration with general education teachers.
Impact of the alternate assessment on the individualized education program (IEP) and instructional interventions	Majority of these teachers said that the alternate assessment had no impact on either the student's IEP or instructional interventions.	All of these teachers said that there was some connection between the alternate assessment and the student's IEP; 5 of the 8 teachers who replied to this question said that the alternate assessment also had an impact on instructional interventions.
Teachers' perceptions of their support within the school	Support systems were limited to special education teachers and assistants; one teacher noted, "It's just me."	Majority of these teachers said that other teachers were a source of support, including regular and special education teachers, though a few of these teachers also indicated that they had little support.

From Costello, K., Turner, M., Kearns, J., & Kleinert, H. (2000). *Teacher and principal perceptions of the impact of alternate assessments on school accountability and instructional practices.* Manuscript in preparation.

use of alternate assessments for those students who cannot participate in the regular assessment. Second, we believe this study illustrates the critical nexus between successful outcomes for students with significant disabilities and schoolwide educational reform. Teachers from Low/Low schools reported little or no impact from the inclusion of their students in the school's accountability index and little or no impact on the development of the student's IEP and educational interventions, as a result of the student's participation in the alternate assessment. However, teachers from High/High schools *did* perceive a positive impact, including a positive relationship between the alternate assessment and the development of the student's IEP and instructional interventions. Because Kentucky's alternate assessment is based on a subset of the state's learner outcomes for *all* students, we believe this suggests that teachers in High/High schools perceived a relationship between the student's individualized educational objectives and those Academic Expectations for all students integrated in the general curriculum. Conversely, teachers in Low/Low schools did not see this relationship; for them, special education was just that, "special" education. Finally, teachers in Low/Low schools reported being out there on their own, with support only from other special educators or paraprofessionals. Special Education teachers in High/High schools clearly believed themselves to be more supported by general education teachers, and more connected to their school community. They reported that the alternate assessment supported inclusion and collaboration; for these teachers, the alternate assessment supported the development of a schoolwide community of learners.

Q: *What about the amount of work involved in developing alternate assessments? Teachers already are responsible for mountains of paperwork. Are alternate assessments just another situation in which the more time teachers put into it, the higher their students' scores? And if teacher time is not the most important variable in the alternate assessment, what variables do predict how well students will score?*

A: During the spring of 1999, immediately after statewide scoring of all of Kentucky's Alternate Portfolios, Kampfer, Horvath, Kleinert, and Kearns (in press) surveyed all special education teachers in the state who had a student participating in the alternate assessment program in that school year. Specifically, these researchers wanted to know if there is a relationship between portfolio score and the amount of time spent working on the portfolio; which portfolio items require the most teacher effort; to what extent teacher variables (e.g., experience, amount of training) and instructional variables (e.g., amount of student involvement in the construction of the portfolio) predict portfolio score; and what aspects of the alternate assessment tend to be of most concern for teachers. Of 400 surveys sent, 206 surveys (51.5%) were returned.

Kampfer et al. (in press) found that teachers reported spending considerable effort outside of instructional time, even for one portfolio. The development of the individual portfolio entries was rated as requiring the most effort (i.e., *"extensive effort,"* an average response of 4.2 on a scale of 1–5), while "facilitating social relations," "documenting progress," and "developing natural supports" all were rated above 3.6 (*moderate* to *extensive* effort). Finally, "accessing multiple settings" also was rated as requiring *moderate* to *extensive* effort (an average response of slightly above 3.4).

For this sample of teachers, the mean number of years teaching was 11–15, the average amount of experience with the Alternate Portfolio was 4 years, and the mean number of hours spent developing each portfolio outside of instructional time was 25–35. When we conducted a hierarchical regression analysis,[1] with "score" as the outcome variable and the sets of 1) "instructional variables" (i.e., level of student involvement in the development of the portfolio, portfolio elements embedded into instruction, and benefit to student), 2) "teacher variables" (e.g., number of years teaching, years of experience with the Alternate Portfolio, and number of scoring and training sessions attended), and 3) "time" (e.g., number of teacher hours spent outside of instructional time on the Alternate Portfolio), we found that these variables accounted for 27.5% of the variance in score. Most significant, "instructional variables" *alone* accounted for 24.1% of the variance. "Teacher variables" and "hours spent outside of instructional time" did not add any additional predictive power.

In other words, although teachers reported that their students' Alternate Portfolios required a great deal of their own time, the amount of time teachers

---

[1]Hierarchical regression analysis is a way to examine the effects of a group of independent variables on an outcome variable, such as an alternate assessment score. The results of this analysis explain how much each variable contributes to a "prediction" of what that outcome, or score, will be.

actually spent on those portfolios did not appreciably affect the portfolio's score ($r = .15$, $p < .05$). Only 2.3% of a student's score was accounted for by teacher time spent. Teacher experience in the classroom and experience with the alternate assessment likewise did not predict portfolio scores. The critical variables in predicting the variance in scores were the *instructional elements* associated with the alternate assessment: To what extent did teachers *actively embed* the development of the alternate assessment into their daily instruction, to what extent was the *student* him- or herself actually involved in the construction of the portfolio, and what was the perceived *benefit* of the alternate assessment to the student.

Of note, when we analyzed teachers' written comments on the survey, we found that amount of time required for the portfolio seemed to be of most concern for teachers, with 33% of all of the written comments focusing on time. This finding echoed the results of a previous teacher survey on alternate assessment (see Kleinert, Kennedy, & Kearns, 1999). It may thus surprise some teachers to learn that research shows it is instructional variables and *not* teacher time that predict the success of alternate assessment scores. It may be that teachers need more concrete strategies for embedding portfolio development into ongoing, daily instruction and strategies to increase students' involvement in their own portfolios. Not only will these strategies reduce the time burden for teachers but also they should result in higher scores for their students. We focused especially on these strategies for instruction and student involvement in Chapters 5 and 6.

Q: *Have instructional practices actually changed as a result of the inclusion of students with significant disabilities in large-scale educational assessments? After all, a major premise of assessment and accountability systems is that classroom practices will change to reflect the skills being measured (Guskey, 1994).*

A: A great deal more can be learned about how teachers are changing instructional practices as a result of the participation of their students in the alternate assessment. One study (Kleinert et al. 1999) indicated how instructional practices might be changing. In that study, the researchers surveyed 331 teachers who had students participating in Kentucky's alternate assessment. Kleinert et al. found that the majority of teachers reported implementing instructional practices required as evidence in the alternate assessment. For example, 53.9% of the teachers agreed or strongly agreed that they had their students check their schedules before changing activities throughout the day (only 19.0% disagreed or strongly disagreed with this statement). Furthermore, 56.6% of teachers agreed or strongly agreed that their students used adapted checklists to record or evaluate their own progress on at least two instructional activities (with only 20.0% disagreeing or strongly disagreeing with this statement). Given what we know about the importance of teaching students to manage their daily schedules and to evaluate their own progress as component skills of the broad outcome of self-determination (see Browder & Bambara, 2000, and Chapter 6), these are encouraging signs that teachers do incorporate the elements of their statewide alternate assessment into their daily practice.

Kleinert et al. (1999) also asked the teachers in this study whether their students who were participating in the alternate assessment had 1) intelligible speech, 2) an augmentative or alternative communication (AAC) system, or 3) no formal means of communication. These researchers were especially interested in the communicative status of the students without intelligible speech. In a study immediately preceding the implementation of the alternate assessment in Kentucky, Wheatley (1993) found that only 42% of students eligible for the alternate assessment who were not capable of intelligible speech had augmentative systems. In our study, conducted 5 years later, teachers reported that, of their nonverbal students, 62.8% did have AAC systems. Teacher responses in both surveys were anonymous. Although the teacher respondents in the two studies were not identical so these results must therefore be interpreted with caution, the reported increase in student AAC systems in the second study is nevertheless encouraging. These results are especially noteworthy in light of the fact that Kentucky's alternate assessment now requires that teachers show direct evidence of students' communication systems within the students' portfolios.

Q: *Including students with significant disabilities in measures of school and district educational performance is a nice idea, but what's in it for the students? Is it accurate to say that doing well in the alternate assessment will help them? Is there any evidence that alternate assessment scores for students in their last year of school are related to postschool outcomes, including such important issues as employment, friendships and relationships, choice making, self-determination, and community participation?*

A: As this book goes to press, this is a study in process. Over a 2-year period, Kleinert, Garrett, et al. (2001) have interviewed 41 former students who had participated in the alternate assessment in their final year of school. These graduates were chosen randomly from each of the four alternate assessment scoring levels (Novice, Apprentice, Proficient, and Distinguished). The participants included 4 former students who had scored at a Novice (lowest) level in their final Alternate Portfolio, 14 at an Apprentice level, 15 at a Proficient level, and 8 at the Distinguished (highest) level. These former students were interviewed in their homes, with a family member present, approximately 9 months to 1 year after they had graduated. The home visit interview protocol was based on O'Brien and Lyle's (1987) Five Life Accomplishments and included questions about community integration, choice and decision making, friendships and relationships, and employment. As the interview took place, individual maps based on personal futures planning (Mount & Zwernik, 1989) were drawn of each of the Life Accomplishment categories, as a visual representation of these accomplishments and as a means of confirming the interview responses with the former student and his or her family member.

Kleinert et al. (2000) then scored the results of each interview with a "Life Dimensions Scoring Rubric" that was developed based on the work of Schalock (1996), Hughes and Hwang (1996), and Conroy (1998). The Life Dimensions Scoring Rubric (Table 10.5) was designed to examine broad dimensions of postschool outcomes and was constructed after researchers had completed the initial set of eight interviews. Each of the two interviewers then scored the life-outcomes for each of the former students based on the criteria of the Life Dimensions Scoring Rubric. Inter-rater reliability on the Life Dimension Scoring Rubric was 84% (with a range of 78%–90% inter-rater reliability within each of the Life Dimensions); areas of disagreement were reconciled by discussion between the interviewers.

Table 10.5. The Life Dimensions Scoring Rubric

Life dimensions or standards	Novice	Apprentice	Proficient	Distinguished
Choice and decision making	Few or very limited choices, confined to incidentals (e.g., what to drink with meals, what to have as a snack, what to watch on TV)	Clearly makes daily/weekly choices in at least three areas of functioning (e.g., in which community activities to participate, what clothes to wear, how to spend money)	Clearly makes daily/weekly choices in at least three areas of functioning AND participates in making major life decisions (e.g., where to work, who to be friends with, on what to make major expenditures of own money)	As noted in proficient level, AND chooses own life goals (clearly has the lead in these decisions); makes own plans to achieve those goals and advocates for self with family and others
Friendships and relationships	Friends limited to family and extended family and/or people with disabilities	Has other friends, including same-age peers without disabilities, but sees friends less than once per week	Has a clearly defined set of friends (the majority of whom do not have disabilities); sees friends one or more times weekly	Friendships occur across multiple life areas (e.g., work, recreation interests, church, etc.); sees friends at least two times per week
Community integration	Actively[a] participates in less than one community activity per week	Participates actively in at least one weekly activities	Participates actively in at least three activities per week on average, some of which are not with the immediate family or with paid providers	Five or more community activities per week; activities, settings, and the person or people with whom the activities are done reflect a rich variety in the person's life
Employment	No integrated work or volunteer activity within the community; OR less than 25 hours of paid work within a sheltered setting	Regular but less than 15 hours a week of integrated, paid employment or volunteer work; OR at least 25 hours of paid work in a sheltered setting	15–25 hours per week of integrated, paid employment	At least 25 hours per week of integrated, paid employment with typical wages

Note: Probe, if necessary, to determine the extent to which the student makes active responses, communicates with others, makes choices, etc., within the context of the activity.
[a]Active participation examples: ordering own food at restaurant, selecting own purchases while shopping.

The Life Dimension Scoring Rubric uses a scale from 4 (lowest) to 16 (highest), based on individual scores from 1 (lowest) to 4 (highest) for each of the four Life Dimensions. In the preliminary data analysis for this study, overall scores that were 10 and above (i.e., an average Life Dimension score of 2.50 or greater across the four individual dimensions) were considered "more successful" life outcomes; scores of less than 10 (an average Life Dimension score of 2.25 or less) were considered "less successful" life outcomes. Thirty-three students, or 80% of the sample, had postschool Life Dimension scores of less than 10. Only nine students had postschool scores of 10 or greater.

As this book goes to press, Kleinert et al. were still in the process of analyzing these data. Yet there were two initial findings that these authors believe have important implications for practitioners. First, for the former students in this study, life outcomes (as measured by the Life Dimensions Scoring Rubric) in general were low, consistent with other postschool adjustment studies of students with significant disabilities (Blackorby & Wagner, 1996). This was generally the case, regardless of the student's final Alternate Portfolio score. A higher portfolio score before graduation was hardly a guarantee of more positive life outcomes after school, however. Students who had a Proficient or Distinguished portfolio were not more likely to demonstrate higher outcomes after graduation than students with Novice or Apprentice portfolios. Only 1 of 4 Novice portfolio students (25%) and 2 of 14 Apprentice portfolio students (14%) scored a 10 or above on the post-school Life Dimensions measure; 3 of 15 Proficient portfolio students (20%, including the 3 highest Life Dimension scores in the entire sample) and 2 of 8 Distinguished portfolio students (25%) scored at that level.

A second finding worth noting is the relationship of employment (one of the four postschool Life Dimensions) to the other three Life Dimensions measured in this study. For this sample of 41 former students, 8 of the 10 who reportedly were not working at all had scores at the very bottom (a score of 4, 5, or a 6) on the overall Life Dimensions measure. In contrast, of the 11 graduates with integrated, community employment, overall Life Dimension scores were distributed across nearly every level. Nevertheless, more than half (7 of 11) of those who *had* achieved community employment scored in the lower portion (below 10) on the overall Life Dimensions measure.

Not having any employment or work status was thus associated with poor outcomes in the other Life Dimensions (choice and decision making, community integration, and friendships and relationships), but community employment in itself was not sufficient to guarantee higher outcomes in these other Life Dimensions. Clearly, high school teachers need to focus upon not only integrated community employment for their students with significant disabilities but also on other factors essential to achieving a measure of autonomy and life satisfaction, including choice and decision making, community integration, and friendships and relationships.

SUMMARY

Performance-based assessment strategies for students with significant disabilities are hardly new (consider our field's emphasis on the application of learned skills to real-life environments; our use of databased, continuous measurement of observable behavior; and our emphasis on enhanced life outcomes for our students). What *is* new, however, is the inclusion of students with significant disabilities in large-scale educational assessments, especially through the use of alternate assessments. We do not pretend to have the definitive answers as to how closely alternate assessments for these students can be tied to the learner outcomes identified for all students or what the performance and scoring criteria for these assessments should be. We do not know to what extent schools will use the information obtained from alternate assessments to improve instruction for students with significant disabilities or whether alternate assessments will be viewed as integral—or wholly separate from—school reform efforts for all students. And we cannot answer with certainty whether scores obtained on alternate assessments, especially those obtained in the student's final year of school, are predictive of meaningful postschool outcomes. Research in each of these areas is in its infancy but fortunately these important questions are now being addressed for the good of all students now and in the future.

REFERENCES

Blackorby, L., & Wagner, M. (1996). Longitudinal postschool outcomes of youth with disabilities: Findings from the National Longitudinal Transition study. *Exceptional Children, 62*(5), 399–414.

Browder, D., & Bambara, L. (2000). Home and community. In M. Snell & F. Brown (Eds.), *Instruction of students with severe disabilities* (5th ed., pp. 543–589), Columbus, OH: Charles E. Merrill.

Conroy, J. (1998). *Personal life quality protocol* (Family version 4.4). Delaware County, PA: Office of Mental Health and Mental Retardation: Self-Determination Project.

Coots, J., Bishop, K., Grenot-Scheyer, M., & Falvey, M. (1995). Practices in general education: Past and present. In M. Falvey (Ed.), *Inclusive and heterogeneous schooling: Assessment, curriculum, and instruction* (pp. 7–22). Baltimore: Paul H. Brookes Publishing Co.

Costello, K., Turner, M., Kearns, J., & Kleinert, H. (2000). *Teacher and principal perceptions of the impact of alternate assessments on school accountability and instructional practices.* Manuscript in preparation.

Guskey, T. (1994). What you assess may not be what you get. *Educational Leadership, 51*(6), 51–54.

Hughes, C., & Hwang, B. (1996). Attempts to conceptualize and measure quality of life. In R. Schalock (Ed.), *Quality of life: Vol. I. Conceptualization and measurement* (pp. 51–62). Washington, DC: American Association on Mental Retardation.

Individuals with Disabilities Education Act (IDEA) Amendments of 1997, PL 105-17, 20 U.S.C. §§ 1400 *et. seq.*

Jorgensen, C.M. (1998). *Restructuring high schools for all students: Taking inclusion to the next step.* Baltimore: Paul H. Brookes Publishing Co.

Kamfer, S., Horvath, L., Kleinert, H., & Kearns, J. (in press). Teachers' perceptions of one state's Alternate Portfolio Assessment System: Implications for practice and teacher preparation. *Exceptional Children.*

Kleinert, H., Garrett, B., Towles, E., Garrett, M., Nowak-Drabik, K., Waddle, C., & Kearns, J. (2001). *Alternate assessment scores and post-school outcomes: Is there a relationship?* Manuscript in preparation.

Kleinert, H., & Kearns, J. (1999). A validation study of the performance indicators and learner outcomes of Kentucky's alternate assessment for students with significant disabilities. *Journal of The Association for Persons with Severe Handicaps, 24*(2), 100–110.

Kleinert, H., Kennedy, S., & Kearns, J. (1999). Impact of alternate assessments: A statewide teacher survey. *Journal of Special Education, 33*(2), 93–102.

Lipsky, D.K., & Gartner, A. (1997). *Inclusion and school reform: Transforming America's classrooms.* Baltimore: Paul H. Brookes Publishing Co.

Mount, B., & Zwernik, K. (1989). *It's never too early—it's never too late: A booklet about personal futures planning.* Minneapolis: Minnesota's Governor's Planning Council on Developmental Disabilities.

O'Brien, J., & Lyle, C. (1987). *Framework for accomplishment.* Decatur; GA: Responsive Systems Associates.

Schalock, R. (1996). Reconsidering the conceptualization and measurement of quality of life. In R. Schalock (Ed.), *Quality of life: Vol. I. Conceptualization and measurement.* (pp. 123–139). Washington, DC: American Association on Mental Retardation.

Turner, M., Baldwin, L., Kleinert, H., & Kearns, J. (2000). An examination of the concurrent validity of Kentucky's alternate assessment system. *Journal of Special Education, 34*(2), 69–76.

Wheatley, S. (1993). *Communication systems for students with intellectual disabilities: A statewide survey.* Unpublished manuscript, University of Kentucky at Lexington.

PHOTOCOPIABLE FORMS

Adapting a General Education Lesson or Unit

Student: _____   Date: _____

Level: _____

Class: _____

Standard: _____

Learner Objectives (for all students): _____

Classroom activity	IEP goal:	Who	IEP goal:	Who	IEP goal:	Who	Additional Learning Outcomes:	Who

Alternate Assessment: Measuring Outcomes and Supports for Students with Disabilities by Harold L. Kleinert and Jacqui Farmer Kearns
© 2001 Paul H. Brookes Publishing Co.

Job Shadowing Report

Name: _____ Date: _____

Answer the following using information from a job shadowing experience.

1) Name of occupation: _____

2) Name of business (or attach business card):

_____

3) Can you ride a bus to this job? (Circle one.)

              Y   N

4) Do you work nights? (Circle one.)

              Y   N

5) What days do you work? (Circle those that apply.)

        S   M   T   W   Th   F   S

6) Is training for your job   On the job   Videotape training
   (circle one or both):

7) Is your job (circle one):   Full time   Part time

8) Use a magazine to cut out pictures associated with two job duties for this occupation.

9) Starting pay for this job is approximately: $_____

10) Do you wear a uniform for this job?
    (Circle one.)   Y   N

11) How old must you be to hold this job? (Circle one.)   16   18   21+

12) Does this job require a high school diploma?
    (Circle one.)   Y   N

Signature/title _____ Date _____

Alternate Assessment: Measuring Outcomes and Supports for Students with Disabilities
by Harold L. Kleinert and Jacqui Farmer Kearns © 2001 Paul H. Brookes Publishing Co.

Classroom Questionnaire

Name: _____ Date: _____

Class: _____

1) How was today's class material presented? (Circle all that apply.)

Videotape   Overhead   Audiotape

Computer   Lecture   Group activity

2) Which presentation mode do you prefer?

_____

3) Today in class, I heard/learned about:*

_____

_____

*Attach a copy of anything you produced in class today.

Alternate Assessment: Measuring Outcomes and Supports for Students with Disabilities by Harold L. Kleinert and Jacqui Farmer Kearns © 2001 Paul H. Brookes Publishing Co.

Student Book Journal/Report Form: Sample 1

Name: _____ Date: _____

Book title: _____

Book author: _____

Does this book look good or interesting?

_____ Yes   _____ No

Do you see information from class listed in the "Table of Contents"?

_____ Yes   _____ No

Look at "Chapter 1." Is it divided into sub-headed sections?

_____ Yes   _____ No

Are important words colored or in **bold** print?

_____ Yes   _____ No

Are there charts or pictures in the chapters?

_____ Yes   _____ No

Does this book cover information learned in class?

_____ Yes   _____ No

Your overall opinion of this book:

_____ Very useful   _____ Satisfactory   _____ Not very useful

Alternate Assessment: Measuring Outcomes and Supports for Students with Disabilities
by Harold L. Kleinert and Jacqui Farmer Kearns © 2001 Paul H. Brookes Publishing Co.

Student Book Journal/Report Form: Sample 2

Name: _____ Date: _____

Book title: _____

Book author: _____

Main characters: _____

New words I learned (5): _____

_____

How I chose to complete the book (circle one):

With a buddy   Audiotape   On my own   Videotape

The book ended (circle one or both):

Happily   Sadly

The book was (circle one):

Great!   Good   Okay   Poor (not so good)

****   ***   **   *

Next time, I will use this strategy (circle one):

With a buddy   Audiotape   On my own   Videotape

Does this book discuss anything you heard in class? (Circle one.)   Y   N

It discusses: _____

_____

Write a short summary of the story on the back of this sheet (over).

Alternate Assessment: Measuring Outcomes and Supports for Students with Disabilities by Harold L. Kleinert and Jacqui Farmer Kearns © 2001 Paul H. Brookes Publishing Co.

Alternate Assessment Outline

Student name:_____ School year:_____

Target skill #1:_____

  Strategies/activities

    1. _____

    2. _____

    3. _____

    4. _____

Target skill #2:_____

  Strategies/activities

    1. _____

    2. _____

    3. _____

    4. _____

Target skill #3:_____

  Strategies/activities

    1. _____

    2. _____

    3. _____

    4. _____

Target skill #4:_____

  Strategies/activities

    1. _____

    2. _____

    3. _____

    4. _____

Target skill #5:_____

  Strategies/activities

    1. _____

    2. _____

    3. _____

    4. _____

Alternate Assessment: Measuring Outcomes and Supports for Students with Disabilities
by Harold L. Kleinert and Jacqui Farmer Kearns © 2001 Paul H. Brookes Publishing Co.

Planning, Monitoring, and Self-Evaluation Form
Science

Name: _____ Date: _____

Today I will work on:

Looking/listening   Math/counting   Finishing working/asking for help

How will I practice this skill?

Working with peers   on my own   Working with my science teacher

		100	100

Teacher/peer initials: _____

Evaluation: My performance (circle one):

Improved

Remained the same

Needs to be better

100	100
90	90
80	80
70	70
60	60
50	50
40	40
30	30
20	20
10	10
% of questions Last time	% of questions Today

New science words:

1. _____
2. _____
3. _____
4. _____

Compare the percentage of study questions correct today with last time by shading in blocks above.

Next time I plan to work on:

Looking/listening   Math/counting   Finishing working/asking for help

Alternate Assessment: Measuring Outcomes and Supports for Students with Disabilities by Harold L. Kleinert and Jacqui Farmer Kearns © 2001 Paul H. Brookes Publishing Co.

Planning, Monitoring, and Self-Evaluation Form
Reading

Subject/class: _____

Name: _____

Date: _____

I need to work on (circle all that apply):

1. Looking at the question again (reading each question twice)

2. Reading each paragraph again

3. Highlighting the important part of the sentence

Today I will work on reading comprehension in (circle one):

Health   Social Studies   Humanities   Language Arts   Science

I will practice by (circle all that apply):

100	100
90	90
80	80
70	70
60	60
50	50
40	40
30	30
20	20
10	10
% of study questions correct last time	% of study questions correct today

1. Studying with a friend

2. Working on the computer

3. Doing homework

4. Other

Day	Teacher/peer initials
Monday	
Tuesday	
Wednesday	
Thursday	
Friday	

How did I do today? (Circle one.)

I improved

I stayed the same

I did worse

Compare the percentage of study questions correct today with last time by shading in blocks above.

Next time I will work on (circle one):

1. Looking at the question again

2. Reading each paragraph again

3. Highlighting the important part of the sentence

Alternate Assessment: Measuring Outcomes and Supports for Students with Disabilities by Harold L. Kleinert and Jacqui Farmer Kearns © 2001 Paul H. Brookes Publishing Co.

Planning, Monitoring, and Self-Evaluation Form
Social Studies

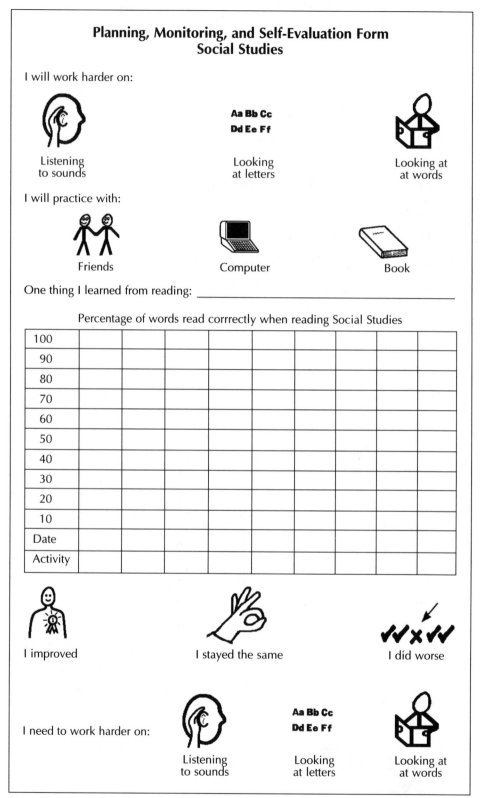

I will work harder on:

Listening to sounds　　　Looking at letters　　　Looking at at words

I will practice with:

Friends　　　Computer　　　Book

One thing I learned from reading: _____

Percentage of words read corrrectly when reading Social Studies

100									
90									
80									
70									
60									
50									
40									
30									
20									
10									
Date									
Activity									

I improved　　　I stayed the same　　　I did worse

I need to work harder on:　　　Listening to sounds　　　Looking at letters　　　Looking at at words

Alternate Assessment: Measuring Outcomes and Supports for Students with Disabilities
by Harold L. Kleinert and Jacqui Farmer Kearns © 2001 Paul H. Brookes Publishing Co.

Planning, Monitoring, and Self-Evalutation Form
Writing in _____

I need to work harder on:

Studying	Listening	Reading	Typing capital letters

Important things to learn:

1. _____
2. _____
3. _____
4. _____
5. _____

Did I use a capital letter when typing about _____? (Place a ✓ if correct, 0 if incorrect)

1. _____   6. _____
2. _____   7. _____
3. _____   8. _____
4. _____   9. _____
5. _____   10. _____

% of correct responses						Date	Setting/activity
100							
90							
80							
70							
60							
50							
40							
30							
20							
10							
Date							

I will practice with:

Friend   Computer   Book

I improved   I stayed the same   I did worse

Next time, I need to work harder on:

Studying	Listening	Reading	Typing capital letters

(Picture Communication Symbols © 1981–2000, Mayer-Johnson, Inc., Solana Beach, CA. Used with permission.)

Alternate Assessment: Measuring Outcomes and Supports for Students with Disabilities by Harold L. Kleinert and Jacqui Farmer Kearns © 2001 Paul H. Brookes Publishing Co.

Planning, Monitoring, and Self-Evaluation Form
Keyboarding Class

Name: _____ Date: _____

I will work on (circle one):

> Placing my fingers correctly in home key position
>
> Following directions
>
> Completing tasks
>
> Speeding up my work pace

I will work on this by (circle one):

> Practicing with a peer before starting
>
> Asking teacher to repeat/explain directions (say, "I don't understand")
>
> Not looking at my neighbors in class while typing

		Teacher/peer comments
10	10	
9	9	
8	8	
7	7	
6	6	
5	5	
4	4	
3	3	
2	2	
1	1	
Number of teacher cues last time	Number of teacher cues today	

How did I do today? (Circle one.)

> I improved   I stayed the same   I did worse

Next time I will work on (circle one):

> Placing my fingers correctly in home key position
>
> Following directions
>
> Completing tasks
>
> Speeding up my work pace

Alternate Assessment: Measuring Outcomes and Supports for Students with Disabilities by Harold L. Kleinert and Jacqui Farmer Kearns © 2001 Paul H. Brookes Publishing Co.

Generalized Student Planning, Monitoring, and Self-Evaluation Form

I need to work harder on:
(Place two or three symbols representing subskills of targeted skill.)

My plan to practice:
(Place two or three symbols representing instructional activities or ways to practice.
Circle plan and then check off as completed.)

% of correct responses						Date	Setting/activity
100							
90							
80							
70							
60							
50							
40							
30							
20							
10							
Date							
Activity							

I improved   I did not improve

Next time, I need to work harder on:
(Place same symbols from the top and circle here and then again on the next sheet.)

Alternate Assessment: Measuring Outcomes and Supports for Students with Disabilities
by Harold L. Kleinert and Jacqui Farmer Kearns © 2001 Paul H. Brookes Publishing Co.

Elementary-Level Job Checklist

Activity	Date	Date	Date	Documentation to demonstrate . . .
I am working on . . .				
Did I use my schedule?				
Did I get what I needed?				
What must I do first?				
What will I do next?				
Have I completed my work?				
Have I put everything away?				
Have I checked my work and completed my self-evaluation?				

(Picture Communication Symbols © 1981–2000, Mayer-Johnson, Inc., Solana Beach, CA. Used with permission.)

Alternate Assessment: Measuring Outcomes and Supports for Students with Disabilities by Harold L. Kleinert and Jacqui Farmer Kearns © 2001 Paul H. Brookes Publishing Co.

Student Data Form
Average Prompt Level Across Activities

Dates: _____ Student: _____ Objective number: _____

Date	Content	Prompt	+/-	Activity	Date	Content	Prompt	+/-	Activity

Content area		**Prompts**	
Math	M	Independent	I
Science	S	Verbal	V
Language arts	LA	Gesture	G
PE	PE	Partial physical	P
		Full physical	F

Alternate Assessment: Measuring Outcomes and Supports for Students with Disabilities
by Harold L. Kleinert and Jacqui Farmer Kearns © 2001 Paul H. Brookes Publishing Co.

Home–School Progress Report

Name: _____ Date: _____

IEP goals	% and/or anecdotal notes

Comments:

Comments and suggestions from home:

Alternate Assessment: Measuring Outcomes and Supports for Students with Disabilities
by Harold L. Kleinert and Jacqui Farmer Kearns © 2001 Paul H. Brookes Publishing Co.

INDEX

Page numbers followed by *f* indicate figures; those followed by *t* indicate tables.

AAC, *see* Augmentative and alternative communication (AAC) systems
Academic expectations, 11, 74, 127*t*, 215–216, 216*t*
Accommodations, *see* Adaptations
Accountability, *see* Documentation of performance; Outcomes
Adaptations
    in college courses, 199, 200*f*–202*f*, 203–204
    guidelines for developing, 83, 85–87
    in individualized education programs (IEPs), 4, 23–24, 24*f*
    use in instructional strategies, 81–83, 85–87
    use in multiple environments, 86
    see also Assistive technology; Augmentative and alternative communication (AAC) systems; Keyboards; Overlays, keyboard; Software; Supports
Assessments, alternate
    augmentative and alternative communication (AAC) systems in, 222–223
    documentation issues, 77–78, 79–80, 83, 84*f*, 128
    effect on instructional practices, 218, 219*t*, 220*t*, 222–223
    eligibility for, 9–10
    historical perspective on, 2–3
    integrating with instruction, 46–47, 78–83, 87, 88*f*, 121, 124–126, 125*t*, 126*t*, 127*t*, 221–222
    journals, 204, 206–207, 206*f*
    multiple environments, use in documenting, 185–186, 210
    overview, 6–14
    relationship to life dimensions, 223, 224*t*, 225
    relationship to performance on regular assessments, 217–218
    scoring issues, 77, 158*t*, 213–215, 221–222, 223, 224*t*, 225
    separate learning outcomes, 215–216, 216*t*

social relationships as outcomes, 173–174
    state and district, 4–5, 29–30
    strategies, 6–8, 12–14
    student schedule management skills, 117–119, 118*f*, 119*f*, 120*f*, 121, 122*f*–123*f*
    teacher time and effort, 77–78, 221–222
    teacher verification of data, 157
    technology use, 138–141, 139*t*, 140*f*, 141*f*, 144–145, 144*f*, 145*f*, 146*f*
    timetable for development, 87, 89*f*
    see also Portfolios
Assessments, standards-based
    and elementary school curriculum, 50, 52*f*, 53–56
    and high school curriculum, 62, 63*f*, 64–65, 66*f*, 67*f*, 68–69, 70*f*, 71–73
    and middle school curriculum, 56, 57*f*, 58–59
Assistive technology
    keyboards, 138*f*, 136–138
    overlays, 138, 138*f*, 139–141, 140*f*, 141*f*, 144*f*, 145*f*, 146*f*
    software, 138–139, 141
    see also Augmentative and alternative communication (AAC) systems
Audiotapes, *see* Electronic portfolios
Augmentative and alternative communication (AAC) systems
    in alternate assessments, 222–223
    examples of use, 62, 63*f*, 64, 113
    use of cheek switch, 62, 63*f*, 64
Authentic activities
    assessments using, 22–23, 186
    definition of, 22–23
    standards for, 33–37, 34*t*
    use in individualized education programs (IEPs), 23
    see also Critical skills
Autism, 207–210

Calendars, *see* Daily schedules

Careers,
　　learning about, 58–59, 60f, 61f,
　　　203
　　on-line resources, 73
　　see also Vocational training
Certificate-of-completion programs,
　　9–10
Choices, making,
　　documentation of, 114
　　impact of, 112–113
　　instructional strategies, 110,
　　　112–114
　　life dimensions scoring rubric,
　　　224t
　　relationship to alternate assess-
　　　ment scores, 223
　　self-determination and, 107, 110
　　see also Daily schedules; Self-
　　　determination
Choosing Outcomes and Accommodations
　　for Children (COACH), Second
　　Edition, 25, 38f–41f, 110, 169,
　　194
Clip art, on-line resources, 73, 116
COACH, Second Edition, see Choosing
　　Outcomes and Accommodations for
　　Children, Second Edition
College courses, see Postsecondary
　　education
Communication
　　as individualized education pro-
　　　gram (IEP) priority, 24f, 25–26,
　　　26t, 27t
　　skills acquisition as standard, 19f
　　skills activities, 22, 38f–41f
Community-based instruction
　　facilitating inclusion, 182
　　field trips, 186–188
　　multiple environments, 186–189,
　　　191–192, 193f, 194
　　relationship to alternate assess-
　　　ments scores, 223, 224t
　　value of, 185–186
Constant time delay, 80
Criteria, performance, see Outcomes
Critical skills
　　academic expectations, 11, 74,
　　　127t, 215–216, 216t
　　in individualized education pro-
　　　grams (IEPs), 19–21, 23, 25, 27t
　　linking with standards, 7–8, 11,
　　　22f, 27t, 30–33, 36–37, 36f
Culminating performances, 43, 44f
Curriculum, general education
　　community-based instruction,
　　　186–189, 191–192, 193f, 194
　　elementary school examples, 38f,
　　　50, 52f, 53–56, 74

forms for adapting lessons, 51f,
　　52f, 57f, 63f
high school examples, 40f, 62,
　　63f, 64–65, 66f, 67f, 68–69, 70f,
　　71–73
identifying unit organizers, 42–43,
　　44f–45f
inclusion, 5–6, 176–182
integrating alternate assessment
　　with, 46–47, 78–83, 87, 88f,
　　121, 124–126, 125t, 126t, 127t
linking standards with, 30–36
middle school examples, 39f, 56,
　　57f, 58–59
participation of students with dis-
　　abilities, 33–37, 35f, 36f,
　　38f–41f, 42–43, 46
planning guide, 44f–45f
raising expectations, 74
relationship to individualized edu-
　　cation programs (IEPs), 3–4, 18,
　　24f
reverse planning, 37, 42–43

Daily schedules
　　designing individualized sched-
　　　ules, 115–117, 118f, 119f, 120f
　　examples, 118f, 119f, 120f, 121
　　student management of, 115–119,
　　　118f, 119f, 120f, 121, 122f–123f
Decision making, see Choices, making
Delaware
　　alternate assessment require-
　　　ments, 174
　　social relationships as educational
　　　outcomes, 174
　　student performance in multiple
　　　environments, 185
Digital portfolios, see Electronic port-
　　folios; Portfolios
Documentation of performance
　　across multiple environments, 186
　　choice-making, 114
　　data organization, 79–80, 83, 84t
　　data security, 164
　　example, 128t, 129f, 131f, 132f
　　Indiana Assessment System of
　　　Educational Proficiencies
　　　(IASEP), 154–158, 159f,
　　　160–164, 161f, 162f, 163f
　　time spent on, 77–78, 221–222
　　see also Forms; Portfolios

Education reform, 2–3, 148
Electronic Portfolio, The, 151
Electronic portfolios, see also Portfolios

critical issues, 152–154
data security, 164
effect on instruction, 153–154
feasibility of, 149–150
on-line resources, 150
software, 150–151, 151*f*
technology for creating, 150–152,
  151*f*
web-based, 152
Elementary schools
assessments, standards-based, 50,
  52*f*, 53–56
communication skills activities,
  38*f*
field trips, 187
general education, 38*f*, 50, 52*f*,
  53–56, 74
language arts activities, 99*f*
math skills activities, 38*f*
planning, monitoring, and self-
  evaluation, 97, 100–101, 100*f*,
  101*f*, 102*f*–103*f*, 104, 105*f*,
  106*f*–107*f*
science activities, 34, 54–56
self-determination, 97, 100–101,
  100*f*, 101*f*, 102*f*–103*f*, 104, 105*f*,
  106*f*–107*f*
social studies lesson, 52*f*
standard for accessing information, 34*t*
Employment
relationship to alternate assessments scores, 223, 224*t*, 225
see also Careers; Vocational training
Expectations, importance of high, 74

Family involvement
carryover between school and
  home, 207–210
in ensuring multiple environments, 207–210
examples, 174–176, 182–183
individualized education program
  (IEP) team, 25
in personal futures planning, 194,
  195*f*–197*f*, 197–198
weekly progress form, 209*f*
Field trips, for use in practicing skills
  across multiple environments,
  186–188
Forms
activity sheets, 142*f*, 143*f*
adapting general education lessons, 51*f*, 52*f*, 57*f*, 63*f*
alternate assessment outline, 96*f*,
  98*f*

alternate assessment requirements
  for Kentucky, 84*f*
appendix of, 229–244
book journal/report form, 67*f*,
  108*f*
career choices, 60*f*
classroom questionnaire, 66*f*
clip art for, 73, 116
job shadowing report, 61*f*
journal entry guide, 206*f*
listening/participation skills questionnaire, 66*f*
planning, monitoring, and self-
  evaluation, 70*f*, 96*f*, 98*f*, 99*f*,
  100*f*, 101*f*, 102*f*–103*f*, 105*f*,
  106*f*–107*f*, 111*f*, 142*f*, 143*f*
planning guide for instructional
  unit development, 44*f*–45*f*
weekly progress form, 209*f*
Friendships
development of, 145, 170–174
as educational outcomes,
  169–170, 173–174
examples, 167–169, 172–173,
  174–176
importance of, 169–171
relationship to alternate assessments scores, 223, 224*t*
role of teachers in fostering,
  171–174

General education, *see* Curriculum,
  general education
Goals, in individualized education
  programs (IEPs), 24–27, 26*t*,
  27*t*, 78–79, 124*t*
Goals 2000 (PL 103-227), 2, 29
Grady Profile, The, 150–151, 151*f*

High schools
activities across grade levels to
  meet standards, 34*t*
assessments, standards-based, 62,
  63*f*, 64–65, 66*f*, 67*f*, 68–69, 70*f*,
  71–73
communication skills activities,
  40*f*
general education, 40*f*, 62, 63*f*,
  64–65, 66*f*, 67*f*, 68–69, 70*f*,
  71–73
language arts activities, 64–65,
  66*f*, 67*f*
math skills activities, 40*f*
peer tutoring, 192, 194
planning, monitoring, and self-
  evaluation, 104, 108*f*, 109*f*

High schools—*continued*
  reading activities, 64–65, 66*f*, 67*f*
  science, activities, 68–69, 70*f*,
    71–73 72*f*
  social studies activities, 62, 63*f*, 64
  vocational training, 198–199,
    199*f*, 200*f*–202*f*, 203
  writing activities, 64–65, 66*f*, 67*f*

IASEP, *see* Indiana, Indiana
    Assessment System of
    Educational Proficiencies
IDEA '97, *see* Individuals with
    Disabilities Education Act of
    1997 (PL 105-17)
IEPs, *see* Individualized education pro-
    grams
Inclusion
  general education, 176–182
  postsecondary education,
    198–199, 199*f*, 200*f*–202*f*,
    203–204, 205*f*, 206*f*
  strategies for facilitating, 6–8,
    180–182
  value of, 185–186
Independence, enhancing, 86
Indiana
  Indiana Assessment System of
    Educational Proficiencies
    (IASEP), 154–158, 159*f*,
    160–164, 161*f*, 162*f*, 163*f*
  student performance in multiple
    environments, 185
Individualized education programs
    (IEPs)
  adaptations and accommodations
    in, 23–24, 24*f*
  critical skills, 19–21, 23, 25, 27*t*
  development, 18–27, 19*f*
  ecological model, 20–21
  effects of alternate assessments
    on, 218–221, 220*t*
  emphasis on function, 21–22, 22*f*
  goals, 24–27, 26*t*, 27*t*, 78–79, 124*t*
  Individuals with Disabilities
    Education Act Amendments of
    1997 (IDEA '97) requirements,
    3–5, 6, 8–9, 17–18
  relationship to curriculum and
    student support needs, 24*f*
  standards-based curriculum and,
    18
Individuals with Disabilities Education
    Act of 1997 (IDEA '97; PL 105-
    17) 29–30, 148
  requirements of, 3–5, 6, 8–9,
    17–18, 29–30, 148

State Improvement Plan, 4
Instructional practices and strategies
  adaptations, 81–83, 85–87
  choices, teaching about, 110,
    112–114
  communication skills, 38*f*–41*f*
  community-based instruction, 87,
    90
  culminating performances, 43, 46,
    94, 192
  developing instructional units,
    44*f*–45*f*
  identifying unit organizers, 42–43,
    44*f*–45*f*
  integrating with alternate assess-
    ments, 46–47, 78–83, 87, 88*f*,
    121, 124–126, 124*t*, 125*t*, 126*t*,
    127*t*, 221–222
  journals, 204, 206–207, 206*f*
  keyboarding, 104, 109*f*, 137, 138
  language arts, 56, 57*f*, 58, 64–65,
    66*f*, 67*f*, 99*f*, 125*t*
  math, 38*f*–41*f*, 100–101, 103*f*, 125*t*
  to meet standards across grade
    levels, 33–34, 34*t*
  oral reading, 82–83
  planning guide, 44*f*–45*f*
  reverse planning, 37, 42–43
  science, 34, 43, 54–56, 68–69, 70*f*,
    71–73, 72*f*, 104, 105*f*
  sight-word identification, 80–81,
    187
  social studies, 52*f*, 58, 62, 63*f*, 64,
    80–81
  vocational training, 104, 106*f*–107*f*,
    125*t*, 191–192, 193*f*, 199,
    200*f*–202*f*, 203–204
  writing skills, 64–65, 66*f*, 67*f*,
    104, 105*f*
IntelliKeys alternative keyboards,
    137–141, 138*f*, 140*f*, 141*f*,
    144–146, 144*f*, 145*f*, 146*t*

Job shadowing, 59, 61*f*, 73

Kentucky
  alternate assessment require-
    ments, 84*f*
  documentation issues, 77–78
  eligibility for alternate assess-
    ment, 9–10
  Kentucky Instructional Results
    Information System (KIRIS),
    217
  Kentucky Statewide Alternate
    Assessment Project, 87

social relationships as educational outcomes, 173

student performance in multiple environments, 185

student schedules as alternate assessment, 117–119

TASKS: Teaching All Students in Kentucky Schools, 36–37, 38f–41f

types of alternate assessments, 11

Keyboarding skills, 104, 109f, 114

Keyboards
  Overlay Maker software, 138
  overlays, 137–141, 138f, 140f, 141f, 144–146, 144f, 145f, 146t
  textHELP! software, 139, 141

KIRIS, *see* Kentucky, Kentucky Instructional Results Information System

Language arts activities
  high school, 64–65, 66f, 67f
  middle school, 56, 57f, 58

Learner Profile, 151

Life dimensions
  relationship to alternate assessment scores, 223, 225
  scoring rubric, 224t

Lifelong learning, *see* Postsecondary education

Maryland
  eligibility for alternate assessment, 10
  types of alternate assessments, 11

Math
  activities, 38f–41f, 53–54, 100–101, 103f
  clip art, 116

Middle schools
  American folk culture in curriculum, 58
  assessments, standards-based, 56, 57f, 58–59
  communication skills activities, 39f
  field trips, 187–188
  general education, 39f, 56, 57f, 58–59
  language arts activities, 56, 57f, 58
  math skills activities, 39f
  multiple environments for learning, 187–189, 190f, 191–192
  peer involvement, 188–189, 190f, 191–192

planning, monitoring, and self-evaluation, 104, 108f, 109f

recycling project, 188–189, 190f, 191

standard for accessing information, 34t

vocational training, 191–192, 193f

Modifications, *see* Adaptations

Monitoring performance, 79–80, 82–83, 128t, *see also* Outcomes; Planning, monitoring, and self-evaluation

Multiple environments
  documentation of learning in, 186
  examples, 126t
  family involvement, 207–210
  field trips, 186–188
  personal futures plan, 194, 195f–197f, 197–198
  postsecondary courses, 198–199, 203–204, 206
  state criteria for alternate assessments, 185

Nation at Risk, A, 2

National Commission on Education, 2

National Governors' Association, 2

Objectives, in individualized education programs (IEPs), 24–27, 26t, 27t, 78–79, 124t

On-line resources
  alternative keyboards, 137
  career choices, 73
  clip art, 73, 116
  data security, 164
  job shadowing, 73
  portfolio assessment, 150
  technology, 73

Outcomes
  choice making as, 110
  educators' ratings of importance, 47, 110
  friendships as, 169–170
  performance indicators, 213–215, 214t
  relationship to standards, 11, 31–33
  self-determination as, 93–94
  separate learning outcomes for students in alternate assessment, 215–216, 216t
  social relationships as, 174

Overlay Maker software, 138

Overlays, keyboard, 137–141, 138f, 144–146

Overlays, keyboard—*continued*
  examples, 138*f*, 140*f*, 141*f*, 144*f*,
  145*f*, 146*t*

Paperwork, *see* Documentation of performance
Parents, *see* Family involvement
Peers
  involving in technology use, 140,
    145
  peer evaluation, 189, 190*f*
  peer partners, 188–189, 190*f*,
    191–192
  peer reflections, 114
  supportive roles, 82, 174–180
  tutoring, 192, 194
Performance
  criteria, 213
  indicators, *see* Outcomes
Personal futures planning, 194,
  195*f*–197*f*, 197–198
Person-centered planning, *see* Personal
  futures plan
Picture Communication Symbols, 104,
  107, 115–116, 117
PL 103-227, *see* Goals 2000
PL 105-17, *see* Individuals with Disabilities Education Act Amendments of 1997 (IDEA '97)
Planning, monitoring, and self-evaluation
  activity sheets, 129*f*–130*f*, 142*f*,
    143*f*
  clip art, 116
  elementary school examples, 97,
    100–101, 100*f*, 101*f*, 102*f*–103*f*,
    104, 105*f*, 106*f*–107*f*
  generalized form, 111*f*
  instructional strategies, 95, 96*f*,
    97, 98*f*, 99*f*
  middle/high school examples,
    104, 108*f*, 109*f*
  student schedules, 119, 122*f*–123*f*
  use of technology for, 136–141,
    144–147
Portfolio Assessment Toolkit, 151
Portfolios, 12, 217
  definition of, 148
  electronic, 148–164
  personal futures plan, 194,
    195*f*–197*f*, 197–198
  timetable for, 87, 89*f*
Postsecondary education
  modification of exams, 199,
    200*f*–202*f*
  physical education course,
    203–204, 206

special education course,
  198–199, 199*f*, 200*f*–202*f*, 203,
  204*f*, 205*f*

Reading
  high school, 64–65, 66*f*, 67*f*
  oral skills, 82–83
Reform, education, 2–3, 148
Relationships, *see* Friendships; Peers
Research
  on amount of work for teachers,
    221
  on basing learner outcomes on
    educational standards, 215–216
  on benefits to students, 223–225
  on how schools use alternate
    assessment scores, 217–218
  on instructional practices,
    222–223
  on performance criteria, 213–215
  on relationship between alternate
    and regular assessment scores,
    217–218

Schedules, *see* Daily schedules
Schools Our Children Deserve, The, 30–33
Science
  clip art, 116
  elementary school, 34, 43, 54–56,
    104, 105*f*
  high school, 68–69, 70*f*, 71–73,
    72*f*
Scoring issues
  Indiana Assessment System of
    Educational Proficiencies
    (IASEP) rating rubric, 158*t*
  life dimensions scoring rubric,
    224*t*
  performance criteria, 213–215,
    214*t*
  relationship to postschool out-
    comes, 223, 225
  relationship to teacher time, 77,
    221–222
Self-advocacy, 198
Self-determination, *see also* Choices,
    making
  component skills, 94–95
  definition of, 94
  elementary school examples, 97,
    100–101, 100*f*, 101*f*, 102*f*–103*f*,
    104, 105*f*, 106*f*–107*f*
  enhanced by participation in col-
    lege courses, 199, 203
  as outcome, 93–94, 203
  planning, monitoring, and self-

evaluation, 95, 96f, 97, 98f, 99f
student management of daily
   schedules, 115–119, 118f, 119f,
   120f, 122f–123f, 199, 203
Self-evaluation, see Planning, moni-
   toring, and self-evaluation
Sight-word identification, 80–81, 187
Simultaneous prompting, 80
Social relationships, see Friendships;
   Peers
Social studies, 58, 62, 63f, 64, 80–81
Software
   for creating electronic portfolios,
     150–151, 151f
   Indiana Assessment System of
     Educational Proficiencies
     (IASEP), 154–158, 159f,
     160–164, 161f, 162f, 163f
   for keyboards and overlays, 138,
     139, 141, 150–151, 151f
Special education teachers
   tips for, 180–182
   see also Teachers; Instructional
     practices and strategies
Standards
   critical functions approach, 7–8,
     11, 22f, 31–32, 35, 36f
   defining, 5–6, 30–33
   identifying unit organizers, 42–43,
     44f–45f
   individualized education programs
     (IEPs) and, 7, 18
   integrating with alternate assess-
     ments, 79
   raising, 74
   reform, 2–3
   relationship to outcomes, 11,
     31–33
   skill-based, 37t, 38f–41f
   state and national, 2–3, 4–5,
     29–30
   for students with disabilities,
     33–36, 35f, 36–37, 36f, 38f–41f
   types of, 30
Standards-based assessments, see
   Assessments, standards-based
StickyKeys key-latching setting
   device, 137
Supplementary aids, see Adaptations;
   Assistive technology
Supports, student
   assistive technology, 138, 138f,
     139–141, 140f, 141f, 144f, 145f,
     146f
   family involvement, 174–176,
     182–183, 207–210
   peers, 82, 145, 174–180, 192,
     194

personal futures plan, 194,
   195f–197f, 197–198
relationship to individualized education programs (IEPs), 23–24,
   24f

TASKS: Teaching All Students in Kentucky
   Schools, 36–37, 38f–41f
Teachers
   experiences of, 78–83, 121,
     124–126, 128, 130–131,
     176–180, 207–210
   implications for training, 146,
     147, 162
   importance of communicating
     need for alternate assessment,
     219–221
   role in facilitating friendships,
     171–174
   see also Assessments, alternate;
     Friendships
Technology
   for alternate assessments, 146t
   augmentative and alternative
     communication (AAC) systems,
     113, 222–223
   clip art, 116
   electric wheelchair operation, 62,
     63f, 64
   keyboards and overlays, 137–141,
     138f, 140f, 141f, 144–146, 144f,
     145f, 146t
   on-line resources, 73
   software programs, 138, 139, 141
   staff training, 146, 147, 162
   use of cheek switch, 62, 63f, 64
Tennessee
   alternate assessment require-
     ments, 174
   social relationships as educational
     outcomes, 174
   student performance in multiple
     environments, 185
textHELP! software, 139, 141
Time-delay prompting procedure, 26t
Time for Results, 2
Time management, see Daily schedules
Training, staff
   postsecondary courses, 198–199
   technology, 146, 147, 162

University courses, see Postsecondary
   education

Videotapes, see Electronic portfolios

Vocational training
  college courses as, 199, 200*f*–202*f*,
    203–204
  elementary school, 104, 106*f*–107*f*
  middle school, 191–192, 193*f*
  personal futures plan, 194,
    195*f*–197*f*, 197–198

West Virginia, student performance in
  multiple environments, 185
Writing skills
  elementary school, 104, 105*f*
  high school, 64–65, 66*f*, 67*f*